PREHISTORIC QUARRIES AND LITHIC PRODUCTION

T0381732

PREHISTORIC QUARRIES AND LITHIC PRODUCTION

EDITED BY JONATHON E. ERICSON

Program in Social Ecology, University of California, Irvine

and BARBARA A. PURDY

Department of Anthropology, University of Florida

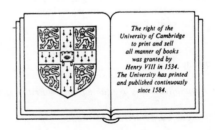

The right of the
University of Cambridge
to print and sell
all manner of books
was granted by
Henry VIII in 1534.
The University has printed
and published continuously
since 1584.

CAMBRIDGE UNIVERSITY PRESS

CAMBRIDGE
LONDON   NEW YORK   NEW ROCHELLE
MELBOURNE   SYDNEY

CAMBRIDGE UNIVERSITY PRESS
Cambridge, New York, Melbourne, Madrid, Cape Town, Singapore, São Paulo, Delhi

Cambridge University Press
The Edinburgh Building, Cambridge CB2 8RU, UK

Published in the United States of America by Cambridge University Press, New York

www.cambridge.org
Information on this title: www.cambridge.org/9780521109239

First published 1984
This digitally printed version 2009

A catalogue record for this publication is available from the British Library

Library of Congress Catalogue Card Number: 83-18822

ISBN 978-0-521-25622-3 hardback
ISBN 978-0-521-10923-9 paperback

CONTENTS

CONTRIBUTORS

Marisa Bolognese, 200 East 16th Street N.Y N.Y.

Robert H. Cobean, Research Reactor Facility, University of Missouri,
    Columbia.

Jonathon E. Ericson, Program in Social Ecology, University of
    California, Irvine.

Frank J. Findlow, Anacapa Research Associates, Los Angeles.

Eric C. Gibson, Department of Anthropology, Peabody Museum,
    Harvard University.

R. Michael Gramly, Buffalo Museum of Science, Buffalo.

Garman Harbottle, Department of Chemistry, Brookhaven National
    Laboratory, Upton, N.Y.

Thomas H. Keifer, Department of Sociology and Anthropology,
    University of Rhode Island, Kingston.

Jerome Kimberlin, Chevron Research, Richmond, California.

Helen Leach, Anthropology Department, University of Otago, Dunedin,
    New Zealand.

Barbara Luedtke, Department of Anthropology, University of
    Massachusetts at Boston.

Barbara A. Purdy, Department of Anthropology, University of Florida,
    Gainesville.

Robert Lee Sappington, Department of Sociology and Anthropology,
    University of Idaho.

Clay A. Singer, Department of Anthropology, California State
    University, Northridge, California.

Michael W. Spence, Department of Anthropology, University of
    Western Ontario, London, Ontario.

Terrance L. Stocker, Department of Anthropology, University of
    Illinois, Urbana.

Robin Torrence, Department of Prehistory and Archaeology, University
    of Sheffield.

Sarah Peabody Turnbaugh, Museum of Primitive Culture, University of Rhode Island, Kingston.

William A. Turnbaugh, Department of Sociology and Anthropology, University of Rhode Island, Kingston.

Dedication:
DON E. CRABTREE

It is impossible to calculate how many times references to Don Crabtree's work have been cited in the archaeological literature of the past 20 years. Citations must number in the thousands, which is pretty good for someone who was not an archaeologist. The observation has been made before that the greatest contributions to a field of study often come from individuals who are not restricted by the rather narrow view that results from indoctrination into a discipline that requires each member to learn and adhere to a certain set of principles.

Most people are aware that Don's studies of lithic techniques have enabled archaeologists to infer behavior about processes of manufacture and uses of chipped-stone implements in ways that had not been explored previously. Don was also interested in quarries and workshops. A very informative but not widely known article about the flint-knapper's raw materials appeared in *Tebiwa* 10, no. 1 (1967). Here the reader gains an insight into the vast information that Don possessed about lithic materials and their properties. He was an excellent lapidarist; in fact, his interest in gemstones probably exceeded and preceded his knowledge about flint materials. His invaluable observations about thermal alteration of silica minerals must have been related to his understanding of the desirable changes that occur in precious and semi-precious stones when they are heated carefully.

Don visited many of the major aboriginal quarries around the world and he was sent raw material from other sources by his many friends. Those of us who have seen Don's 'workshop' in Kimberley, Idaho, can only wonder how archaeologists in the future will interpret his backyard if it is excavated.

Don E. Crabtree died on 16 November 1980. His contributions to archaeology are among the most significant in the twentieth century.

PART ONE

Introduction

Chapter 1

Toward the analysis of lithic production systems
Jonathon E. Ericson

This chapter serves as an introduction to the volume. Its objective is to open discussion on the importance of prehistoric quarries and lithic production in the contexts of procurement, exchange, technology, and social organization.

The concept of lithic production systems is defined and discussed. These systems can be reconstructed by adapting the strategies and techniques developed for exchange systems. The analysis of the quarry, debitage analysis at sites within the study region, the use of production indices and spatial analysis, chemical characterization and chronometric dating of artifacts and debitage will play roles in reconstructing lithic production systems.

The quarry is the most important site and component of these systems. A complete analysis of the quarry will allow the researcher to reconstruct the processes of extraction, selection, knapping, and on-site activity of the average knapper, as well as documenting the reduction sequences, changes in technology and rates of production over time. The quarry remains the logical site to begin the study of a stone-tool-using culture.

It is important to understand the nature of different lithic production systems and the variables which affect their structure and morphology. The paper opens discussion on a number of variables for consideration. It is expected that the regional lithic resource base, the modes of procurement, social distance between knappers and consumers, labor investment, modes of transportation and social organization will be important although not an exclusive list of variables.

Introduction
Among the subjects of a topical approach to archaeology, production—in particular lithic production among stone-tool-

using peoples – requires critical and systematic attention. The results of studying lithic production in a systematic manner will provide new insights into the behaviors of many prehistoric societies.

The primary objectives of this chapter are: to open discussion on the importance of lithic production in the context of procurement exchange, technology, and social organization; to introduce the concept of lithic production system; and to formulate a multidisciplinary strategy integrating a number of techniques presented in this anthology.

Recent research on prehistoric exchange systems has indicated the fundamental importance of understanding lithic production in the context of exchange of obsidian and other lithic materials (Ammerman & Andrefsky 1982; Ericson 1981, 1982; Spence 1982). Although natural unmodified lithic materials do pass through exchange systems, there is a tendency for the material to be modified at one or more points along the system beginning at the source. This process of material modification can be termed lithic production. Production at the quarry and workshops both controls and is controlled by the 'demand' for lithic materials through a series of poorly understood feedback mechanisms (Wright & Zeder 1977). It is critical that we understand these mechanisms in the context of regional exchange. In a diachronic perspective the production of lithic exchange items has been shown to be a sensitive indicator of major changes within regional exchange systems (Frederickson 1969; Ericson 1981; Findlow & Bolognese 1982) and lithic technology (Ammerman & Andrefsky 1982; Ericson 1982; Leach ch. 10; Singer & Ericson 1977). The systemic relationships among technology, production, and exchange need to be more fully investigated.

Despite the long-standing interest in stone-tool production, such research has not culminated in a standardized and systematic approach. Sophisticated advances in lithic technology have been made in the areas of replication and forensic examination of use-wear (Tringham *et al.* 1974; Hayden 1979; Keely 1980) and definition of the stages of lithic reduction (Semenov 1964; Swanson 1975; Hayden 1979; Callahan 1979; Newcomer 1971). However, this important body of information has not been utilized to study lithic production until very recently (Ammerman & Andrefsky 1982; Singer & Ericson 1977). Debitage analysis is critical in this research, yet a review of the literature indicates that very few studies have been directed toward this form of analysis (Brauner 1972; Crabtree 1972; Draper 1982; Flenniken 1978; Flenniken & Stanfill 1980; Osbourne 1965). In fact, it appears that debitage is seldom analyzed and reported. As a consequence, a vital part of the archaeological record has been inadvertently lost.

A quarry site or lithic production workshop would seem the logical place to begin the study of a stone-tool-using culture, as pointed out by Gramly (ch. 2). Yet, a review of the literature indicates that these sites have been neglected relative to other types of sites (cf. Hestor & Heizer 1973). This trend most likely is the result of technical and methodological limitations imposed by a shattered, overlapping, sometimes shallow, nondiagnostic, undatable, unattractive, redundant, and at times voluminous material record. The chapters in this book address many of the methodological problems common to quarries and workshops and demonstrate new strategies for dealing with these sites.

Note on quarries

The following notes are drawn from a lengthy discussion by Purdy (1981b). For the archaeologist who is concerned with all phases of lithic technology, particularly production, the ethnographic documentation is very incomplete. When we consider the wealth of information available on the varieties of human experience, the information on the activities associated with quarries and workshops have to be ranked among the most abysmal. Early explorers apparently took little notice of lithic procurement and production practices. Generally, observations were restricted to village life or observations made along the route of travel. Lithic quarries were infrequently visited. The ethnographic record is far from complete, yet data are available. For example, perhaps the most complete investigation of flintknapping was made of the gunflint industry at Brandon, England (Clarke 1935; and his cited references). Clarke speaks of geographic and geologic availability of the flint, mining techniques, implements employed, selection for quality, historic continuity, and supply and demand. He observed that flintknapping was restricted to a few families among whom intermarriage was 'more than common' (Clarke 1935, 44). He noted that 'knappers die before the age of 40 from consumption caused by inhalation of flint particles' (Clarke 1935, 52).

Observations by Holmes (1894:129–36) and other investigations about quarries pertain to: the procedures involved in quarrying; the quantity of rejected material; and quarry ownership.

Procedures involved in quarrying

Holmes (1919) states that the procedures involved in quarrying were as varied as the geographic and geologic locations. Development of pits, vertical shafts, and horizontal tunneling depend on the outcrop; firesetting, stone, and antler picks, mauls, sledges, and hammerstones were used to break up and remove the stone.

The account of Brandon flintknappers furnishes a valuable description of quarrying procedures. Their metal picks, hammers, spades, and crowbars are probably similar to those used by prehistoric stoneworkers, differing only in the material of which they were made. Some early stoneworkers, however, did not have to dig shafts 10 or more meters deep to reach quality stone, nor did they use exclusively the sophisticated blade technique necessary in the gunflint industry.

Quantity of rejected material

All accounts describing the appearance of quarry areas mention the amount of waste material found there. As many as 1,000 gunflints a day were produced by an expert Brandon knapper. Extrapolating on these figures, it is no wonder that hundreds of thousands of stone tools and inestimable amounts of debitage have accumulated at quarry sites throughout millennia of use. Fowke says that 'probably nine-tenths of the flint carried from the pits . . . was rejected' (Holmes 1919, 178). Bryan states that 'in the study of the great flint quarries one should expect to find large quantities of waste rock' (Bryan 1950, 33). Gould *et al.* (1971) observe that a man can leave behind as many as two hundred waste flakes for each flake he actually chooses and says that this accounts for the tremendous quantities of unused stone which one finds on the surface of aboriginal quarries (Gould *et al.* 1971, 160–1).

However, not all quarry material is rejected debitage. Bryan argues that quarry sites did not exist solely for the production of exportable material. He asserts that many quarries were industrial sites where a variety of articles were made (Bryan 1950, 20–1). Bryan's observation has been substantiated in that a full range of stone implements was found at several Florida quarry sites (Purdy 1981).

Quarry 'access'

Ancient ownership or control of quarries and trading of the raw materials are mentioned by several authors. As previously noted, the practice of mining among the Brandon flintworkers is restricted to a few families (Clarke 1935, 44). In some areas of California, the control of the quarries was 'tribal but related and nearby groups had the right to quarry either freely or on the payment of small gifts. Wars resulted from attempts by distant tribes to use a quarry without payment. On the other hand, the Clear Lake obsidian quarries were neutral ground' (Bryan 1950, 34). The famous red pipestone quarry in Minnesota, according to George Catlin, 'was held and owned in common, and as a neutral group' (Holmes 1919, 262). Flint Ridge, Ohio is thought to have been neutral ground from which the raw material was carried away or traded because it is found at sites throughout a wide area. Gould *et al.* (1971) give no indication of any concept of quarry-site ownership on the part of the Australian aborigines. In fact, they mention that the chipping of stone tools is regarded as an art of little importance. It is of interest, however, that different colors are preferred by certain groups, not because of chipping quality but because of the close totemic ties each man has to the particular region in which he was born and from which he claims totemic descent. 'A man may have a sense of kinship with some of the localities, and he will value the stone material from them as part of his own being. Stone materials thus acquired are not sacred in any strict sense but are nevertheless valued highly enough to be transported over long distances by the owners' (Gould *et al.* 1971, 160–3). Again, a different level of analysis is needed 'to understand how materials are found occurring on sites many miles from the localities where they were quarried or collected' (Gould *et al.* 1971, 160–3).

Ethnographic data supports the concept of nonprivate ownership of property among hunting-gathering groups. A clue to quarry rights comes from the Senator Edwards site in Florida, where at least eight different varieties of Preceramic Archaic stemmed projectile points were recovered (Purdy 1975). Since some of the varieties exist in a single time period, it is possible to deduce that autonomous but related groups had access to the same raw material, i.e., neutral ground. It is not likely, however, that ownership rights changed much when a higher socioeconomic level was reached about 2,000 years ago in Florida. There was no production of large ceremonial blades like those associated with cultures in other parts of North America (California, Tennessee, Meso America, Ohio Valley), which necessitated specialized crafts and, possibly, central control of quarries.

Archaeologists must devise a methodological framework to reconstruct lithic production activities; this anthology is the logical first step (Purdy 1975).

Analysis of lithic production systems

A lithic production system can be defined for purposes of discussion as the total of synchronous activities and locations involved in the utilization and modification of a single source-specific lithic material for stone-tool manufacture and use in a larger social system (Ericson 1982). Production is seen as a process of material modification with intent to form a particular object. During the course of the many stages of production of the material, debitage will be created at the sites of production, which will be indicative of the stages of production (Crabtree 1972). Debitage analysis is a basic technique used in the reconstruction of a lithic production system. Spatial analysis, temporal control, and perhaps chemical characterization (Harbottle 1982) of the debitage have to be incorporated into the research strategy (cf. Sappington ch. 3). For purposes of analysis we must concentrate on the dominant patterns for any given region.

In the context of this volume, the reconstruction of lithic production systems is fully justified from a phenomenological point of view. The structure of a lithic production system will reveal a great deal about the investment of human energy involved in production and decision-making, having economic import. The nature and internal organization of these systems are important to further our understanding of production and resource utilization in the context of procurement, exchange, technology, and social organization.

Reconstruction of a lithic production system can be achieved by adopting the techniques used in reconstructing exchange systems. Production indices are calculated and used like an exchange index to reconstruct a synchronous lithic production system in space (Ericson 1982). A number of different indices based on data from archaeological sites have been formulated as presented in table 1.1. Each index has a

Table 1.1 *Site and material-specific indices for lithic production analysis.*

	Variable (numerator)	Normalizer (denominator)	Units of analysis	Relevance
Exchange index	single source	total material in chipped-stone-tool-category	pieces or wt. ratio %	after Renfrew, Dixon, & Cann 1968
Debitage index	debitage*	total tools and debitage	pieces or wt. or size ratio %	general production index *excluding retouch/sharpening flakes
Cortex index	primary and secondary decortication flakes	total debitage[†]	pieces ratio %	indicative of the import of raw materials on site [†]excluding retouch/sharpening flakes
Core index	spent cores	total cores and tools	pieces ratio %	important index if cores are transported, and a medium of exchange
Biface index	Biface thinning flakes	total debitage	pieces ratio %	biface production

particular function in reconstructing the amount and location of different stages of production of a specific lithic material. The Debitage Index is the most generalized index. The Cortex Index is indicative of the extent of exportation of raw materials in the system. The Core Index is important if prepared cores are the medium of exchange. The Biface Index is indicative of biface manufacture. Other indices can be created ad hoc to serve as indicators of different stages of lithic production. The spatial patterns of these indices describe components of a lithic production system.

It is expected that the morphology and internal structure of these systems will vary a great deal. Some types of systems are immediately apparent. In some cases, all stages of production will be restricted to a particular zone; this is termed terminal production. More frequently, reduction is taken to a particular stage in one area and then completed in other areas of the system where the final production is completed at or near the site of consumption and use; this is termed sequential production. Production can also be quite irregular and dispersed throughout a region; this is termed irregular production. The zone of production can also vary. Some production systems will be centered and restricted to the source, a quarry-based lithic production system. Other systems will extend out into the local area surrounding the source, a local lithic production system. These differences are probably related to quarry ownership and the supply of labor involved in production. Production will frequently occur throughout the entire region, a regional lithic production system. The types of production form a continuum, from terminal to sequential to irregular. Each require different energy budgets and varying numbers of producers. The sites of production can occur at the quarry, within the local area, or within the region. Some of the possible systems are presented in table 1.2.

The quarry and its workshops are perhaps the most important components of a lithic production system. Most of the chapters in this book demonstrate the importance of the quarry in understanding prehistoric lithic production. A number of important activities and behavior patterns can be studied directly on the quarry site.

The processes of extraction and selection are really dependent on the geological setting of the resource (Holmes 1919). Often the source is a surface deposit which requires only sorting and testing of cobbles and blocks (Sappington ch. 3; Singer ch. 4; Torrence ch. 5; Gibson ch. 13). In some settings, the extraction process is subsurface (Stocker and Cobean ch. 8) and in hard rock (Gramly ch. 2; Turnbaugh *et al.* ch. 12).

The process of knapping and the stages of the reduction technology can be reconstructed. Singer (ch. 4) uses a reconstruction technique to reconstruct the reduction technology on two quarry workshops in California. Leach (ch. 10) focuses on reduction sequences at a blade-making quarry site in New Zealand in order to understand adze manufacture. She notes that adze manufacture requires the same technological steps used to produce blades. She uses a three-dimensional jigsaw to determine the actual details of manufacture at the quarry. Although this reconstruction technique has been used in the past, Leach demonstrates its potential in reconstructing actual steps of the lithic reduction. She reconstructs the actual patterns of behaviour on the quarry that can be ascribed to chipping, including some motor habits, numbers of people involved, location on the site, and so on. Leach has been able to show the actual *event* of production, using the three-dimensional recovery with the jigsaw technique. This is an important methodological advance in quarry-site analysis: indeed, to be able to 'see' the individual knapper and his comrades at work.

Table 1.2 *Stages, zones of production, and products.*

Zone of production	Stages of production		
	Terminal	Sequential	Irregular
Quarry	final product produced here, then conveyed to region	partially completed products to region	some production at quarry
Local	final products produced here, then conveyed to region	partially completed products to region	final and incomplete natural materials are supplied from quarry
Regional	n/a	production completed at or near site of consumption and use	natural material supplied from quarry and local production zone

The changes in lithic technology on the quarry workshop can also be studied. Singer and Ericson (1977), studying the Bodie Hills quarry in eastern California, have been able to link changes in production rates with changes in reduction technology. These changes in production and technology also occur simultaneously at other quarry workshops in central and eastern California (Ericson 1981, 1982). Leach observes a transfer of technology from one tool form to another in her New Zealand study.

The rate of production can be determined with quarry workshop data. Luedtke (ch. 6) uses ethnographic data to evaluate the lithic production rate of lithic materials at Flint Ridge, Ohio. She observes common patterns in the amount of material used at a given point in time, and concludes that flint procurement was a rather casual, mundane, and low-labor-intensive activity. She formulates a lithic-demand equation using as a model the observations of Gould and other researchers.

Torrence (ch. 5) examines the Melos quarry in the Mediterranean. She comes to terms with production rates of regional exchange during the time period 12,000–3,000 B.P. The obsidian was distributed over the whole of the Aegean peninsula and the Greek islands. Torrence observes a low-intensity production rate in keeping with Luedtke (ch. 6) and Singer and Ericson (1977).

The analysis of the quarry and its workshops provides primary data for determining extraction technology, raw material selection processes, knapping behavior, reduction technology, material products, production rates, changes in technology, and the dynamic stability of production, exchange, and technology over time.

Discussion

The morphology and structure of lithic production systems will vary, depending on a number of underlying factors. The structure of the regional lithic resource base, the modes of procurement, social distance between producers and consumers, labor investment, the modes of transport, and social organization are among the important factors to consider – not an exclusive list by any means.

The regional lithic resource base

An important step in understanding procurement and production is to understand the regional lithic resource base. Generally, researchers are only interested in the dominant lithics, particularly those traveling long distances as exchange items. For a stone-tool-using society it is important to understand the structure of the lithic resource base. Preliminary work by Wright (1974) indicated the need to consider alternative lithic materials in reconstructing prehistoric exchange systems. The location of and distance to alternative lithic resources tend to affect the morphological characteristics of obsidian exchange systems (Ericson 1977, 1981). Reconstruction of the regional lithic resource base will allow the researcher to account for this type of interaction and other processes.

Such a reconstruction can be achieved through a series of steps. Archaeological museum collections can provide sufficient samples to assemble a list of rocks and to tabulate their frequency of occurrence in the archaeological record. Subsequently, a geologist can assemble a list of potential locations of different rock types using geological maps, and literature on the regional geology. Then, petrographic analysis of selected artifacts and samples from geological museum collections can be compared to identify specific sources. For certain rocks, it will be necessary to characterize chemically different sources. Once a preliminary picture of the resource base is constructed, the sources should be verified in the field, surveyed, and sampled. It should be mentioned that this suggested procedure is time-consuming and not always conclusive. However, a lithic resource base map which locates quarries and the frequency or range of occurrence of specific resources in the archaeological record provides important baseline data for comparison and interpretation of regional procurement and production strategies.

The continuation of this line of research opens up some interesting possibilities. Findlow and Bolognese (ch. 7) illustrate the usefulness of reconstructing the regional resource base to understand the decision-making and economics of lithic procurement and production strategies. They locate the regional sources and quantify the frequency of use of a number of different lithic materials in the Animas Valley of the American southwest. They test a model of observed frequency and elevation-corrected distance (cf. Ericson & Goldstein 1980) for optimality of use. The principle of optimality appears to be operating on decisions to procure lithic materials on a regional scale. This is an important finding; their methodology should be applied to other study regions.

Future studies of optimality should also include variables related to technology and function. For example, different materials often appear in different categories of function and tool typology. This is particularly the case in regions where there is a great diversity of rock type. Since the physical properties of rocks are quite variable, these properties most likely play an important role in the processes of selectivity and function. Although the importance of physical properties on selection of stone-tool material has been discussed (Goodman 1944; Ericson & Singer 1977), these relationships have not been adequately demonstrated. Future optimality studies will be even more fruitful in understanding decision-making of prehistoric stone-tool-using peoples if a full range of variables is included. We do not yet have a fundamental understanding of processes of selection of lithic resources.

Procurement strategies

Lithic production systems will vary in structure depending on the procurement strategies used to acquire the material. These, in turn, appear to be linked to territoriality within a region (Gibson 1981; Bettinger 1982). For example, direct access and regional exchanges are different procurement strategies which tend to result in different lithic production systems (cf. Alden 1982). Direct acquisition of a resource by the people of a region can be termed regional direct access if members acquire the raw material at its source. The production, transportation, and consumption of the material are related to the activities of a knapper and his group. Within a region there will be many individuals who visit the source to obtain raw material. Production often will be completed at the source/quarry in order to reduce transport of waste flakes. Since there is little to regulate the actual behavior of a great number of individuals involved in production, it is expected that the resultant lithic production systems will be quite irregular and heterogeneous in internal organization in terms of reduction technology and products (but cf. Gibson ch. 13). Even so there will be discernible patterns within a particular range of variability for a particular time period and socio-economic level. On the other hand, lithic production systems linked to regional exchange are expected to have greater regularity due to certain regularities in production of specific items. In regional exchange the resource can be procured as a product from local producers through a network of trade partners or other forms of exchange.

In a quarry-based or local lithic production system, the number of producers is small compared to the number of individuals involved in transportation/distribution, final production, and consumption. As a consequence, redundancy and a degree of regularity are built into these geographically restricted production systems. A sequential production strategy will often be employed to produce utilitarian exchange items, whereas there is a tendency for luxury exchange items to be completed at the quarry or in the local region (Ericson 1981).

The archaeological criteria which distinguish these two types of lithic procurement strategies are not clearly defined. In direct access, the falloff tends to be rapid (Bettinger 1982) and possibly linear with distance (Findlow & Bolognese 1982). These procurement systems tend to be smaller in size (Ericson 1981). These criteria clearly have limited utility. Data derived from the analysis of quarries and workshops in this book may shed light on the problem.

Gramly (ch. 2) infers on several lines of evidence that the people who used the Mount Jasper rhyolite source used direct access to obtain their rock. He noticed that spent tools from regionally diverse sources were frequently discarded at the quarry or workshop. He also observed multiple technological components over the history of the workshop. Purdy (1975; ch. 11) verifies this pattern in that diverse and overlapping lithic traditions are observed at the Florida chert quarries and workshops. Sappington (ch. 3) suggests that obsidian was acquired by direct access during the seasonal mobilization of people to fish salmon along the Snake River. Most of the lithic production here occurred away from the obsidian sources in the surrounding region.

Social distance and production

Social distance may play an important role in influencing lithic production. If the knapper is related to or in contact with the intended tool-users, he can respond directly to the needs of the consumer. In such cases, the knapper may tend to produce finished items from the raw material. However, as the social distance increases between the knapper and intended tool-user, he may tend to produce less specific forms or use a mixed strategy of finished items and blanks. The cross-cultural occurrence of blanks and preforms as exchange items can be interpreted to demonstrate the operation of this principle — i.e., these products represent the response of a knapper to the anonymous consumer. As pointed out by Spence (1982), trade partners are notoriously slow to respond to changes in the needs of the 'consumers' within the exchange systems (Harding 1967; Rappaport 1968). If social distance within a lithic production system governs the amount of production of particular items and the completeness of production, this relationship opens up some interesting possibilities for interpretation. For example, it would follow that the final stages of lithic production will become more extensive in space as the social distance is increased between knapper and consumer. The production of esoteric items for luxury use in simple societies and mass-produced tools for anonymous consumers in complex societies (Spence, Kimberlin & Harbottle ch. 9) are special cases.

Labor investment

The labor investment will play a role in the structure of a lithic production system. In direct access the labor requirements are ad hoc and occasional, depending on the needs of the groups using the source. Gould *et al.* (1971) present a good example of this case. However with many knappers and groups visiting the source, the carrying capacity of the catchment of the quarry may become a limiting factor. It is not surprising to learn of compensatory rules and customs to avoid these ecological impacts. For example, round-trip fasting was practiced by the Wintun groups in California when traveling to obsidian sources (Dubois 1935). As a region grows in population, however, population may be an autocatalytic factor which promotes and is promoted by the development of regional exchange systems. Sedentism, which changes people—land relationships, requires increased scheduling and dependability of resources. Sedentism, population growth, and a growing dependency of the population on regional resources as well as the establishment of territoriality within the region favor the growth of a regional exchange system. An immediate advantage in the change of procurement strategy is reduction in travel. Regional exchange is far more cost effective than direct access in regard to regional travel costs (Ericson 1981; Alden 1982).

There are problems in switching procurement strategies with regard to labor investment even if the processes of change are slow and gradual. The people of the source begin to have new roles as suppliers, and eventually as producers in order for the system to develop and continue. If the requirements of a region are small, the impact on the local people is most likely negligible. However, if the source has utilitarian function to the region as a whole, the labor investment will have to be underwritten by increased specialization and support of the specialists. This support will have ramifications on the subsistence economy of the population and on the lithic production system. I have argued for such a case in California where the lithic production systems change as a response to technology and resource function in prehistoric California societies (Ericson 1982).

The labor investment will play a role in the structure of lithic production systems, whether there are many producers scattered throughout a region as in direct access, or whether the producers are concentrated at the quarry or local area near the quarry, as in production for exchange. The changes and fluctuation in lithic production systems may reflect responses to changes in internal organization of labor supply and the consumer demands in the region (cf. Wright & Zeder 1977).

Modes of transportation

Notwithstanding the above arguments, we do not yet understand the mechanisms of production by others and reasons why it occurs in primitive societies. The act of production at least sets values, reduces transport weight, or both. The production of finished items minimizes transportation of waste yet fixes forms. Gould *et al.* (1971) mention that nearly 200 flakes are produced for each flake retained; Newcomer (1971) reports that debitage forms 92 per cent of the product weight. Most likely there is a balance struck between production and transportation costs. The production system is thus tied to transportation. As transport costs are reduced, say with the introduction of water transport or domesticated animal transport, raw materials or products tend to be transported longer distances. Ammerman and Andrefsky (1982) studied the effects of water transport on obsidian production in Calabria, Italy. They observe that the obsidian is further reduced when it arrives on land, at the juncture between the water and land transportation systems. Production for exchange or consumption in direct access is considered to be a waste reduction process to reduce transport cost. It will be interesting to learn whether the principle of optimality is adhered to in the relationship between production and transportation in addition to resource selectivity (Findlow & Bolognese ch. 7).

Social organization

Several patterns of lithic production systems appear to emerge relative to social organization and socioeconomic complexity. Generally, lithic production becomes more organized in structure, increases in size, volume, and efficiency in response to larger and more complex stone-tool-using populations (cf. Torrence ch. 5).

In simple societies direct access, ad hoc production by the occasional knapper and, at times, the creation of a no-man's land around the quarry appear to be recurrent patterns in many region for many millennia. Among tribal and more sedentary people, direct access is not particularly abandoned since it is highly interactive to meet the demands of the consumers. If for any reason that access to a quarry is restricted to the people of a region, this change can lead to conflict and sets up the pre-conditions for stimulating production for exchange. It is possible that both forms of procurement operate simultaneously for long periods of time. However, as patterns of territoriality become fixed and land tenure is proscribed, it is suspected that direct access procurement is abandoned or limited to the people of the local region. The above changes produce fundamental changes in the structure and morphology of lithic production systems. We will need many more case studies to fully understand all of these interrelationships.

In complex societies, the form and degree of regional administration will determine the system. Even within the political domains of a centralized administration, it is possible that the production systems involving secondary sources of similar material are not affected. It will be interesting to know more about the effects of administration on production systems and if there exists a cross-cultural development sequence related to levels of social organization.

Spence (1982) was able to trace the influence of the Teotihuacán administration on the lithic craft specialists through time. He notes that 'although the Teotihuacan administration eventually played a larger role in the industry, particularly in the regional sector, the well-developed social identities of the craft groups and their history of self-sufficiency protected them from being absorbed or replaced by the state.'

More often the primary producers lose their self-sufficiency and identity when supported by other members of their society. Often there will be many divisions of labor involved in extracting and exporting the raw material, knapping the stone, and transporting the product. Frequently raw materials will travel to centers of production, often highly populated areas. This pattern of displaced off-quarry production appears to be a recurrent trend and most likely is cost effective.

Spence, Kimberlin and Harbottle (ch. 9) examine the movement of Sierra de las Navajas obsidian through the Teotihuacán state system. They use neutron activation analysis to differentiate intrasource areas. This demonstration is an important methodological finding in its own right. They are able to define a prehistoric warehouse that stored material from specific points in the quarry, which were then produced into items, and distributed within Teotihuacán. Although specific quarry areas can be defined chemically within this source, the Teotihuacán obsidian warehouse indicates that the materials from the different quarries were stored and removed in a random manner. Earlier, specific flows of this source were used by specific groups or regions. The obsidian moved along kinship lines and/or lines of political affiliation.

Another aspect of social organization and lithic production is the stability of the systems and patterns of procurement. We might expect that production systems are going to fluctuate a great deal in time. As a result, diachronic rates of production will be indicators of other changes in the region, as argued by Wright and Zeder (1977). Preliminary evidence from California suggests that the production of lithic materials, observed at the lithic quarries, is regular and quite conservative over many millennia (Ericson 1981, 1982). In contrast, Findlow and Bolognese (1982) have indicated that there are extreme fluctuations in lithic procurement strategies in the American southwest. The sensitivity of production systems to other systemic variables makes the study of lithic production important for prehistoric research.

Conclusions

When we consider the wealth of information on the varieties of human experience, our information on the activities at quarries and workshops ranks among the most abysmal. This trend can be traced to existing technological and methodological limitations. The chapters of this book demonstrate the value of studying lithic production of quarries and workshops. If we are to advance our understanding of regional patterns of procurement, exchange, and technology, we must know what events have occurred at the quarries. This is fundamental information vital to our understanding of stone-tool-using cultures. The concept of a lithic production system is introduced to provide a construct for systemic analysis. The quarry and its nearby workshops are the most important components of such a system.

This chapter suggests that there are tremendous advantages of extending the study of production to the entire region using procedures developed for studying regional exchange. If we look at production on a regional scale, we can begin to understand more about the investment of human energy involved in production and decision-making, having economic import. The nature and variability among different systems will further our understanding of production and resource utilization relative to other variables. It is expected that the structure and morphology of a given lithic production system will be controlled in part by a number of complex, interacting variables. The structure of the regional lithic resource base, the mode of procurement, social distance between knappers and consumers, labor investment, modes of transport, and social organization, as well as technology, and other variables, are expected to affect the development and maintenance of any given system.

Finally, we must begin to focus our attention on the quarry, the workshops, and other sites of production if we are to understand production in the contexts of exchange and technology in the years to come.

References

Alden, J. R. 1982. Marketplace exchange as indirect distribution: an Iranian example. In J. E. Ericson & T. K. Earle, eds., *Contexts of prehistoric exchange.* New York: Academic Press, 83–101.

Ammerman, A. J. & Andrefsky, W., Jr. 1982. Reduction sequences and the exchange of obsidian in Neolithic Calabria. In J. E. Ericson & T. K. Earle, eds., *Contexts of prehistoric exchange.* New York: Academic Press, 149–72.

Bettinger, R. L. 1982. Aboriginal exchange and territoriality in Owens Valley, California. In J. E. Ericson & T. K. Earle, eds., *Contexts of prehistoric exchange.* New York: Academic Press.

Brauner, D. R. 1972. Space, time, and debitage: a study of lithic debris, Chagvon Bay, Alaska. Master's thesis, Department of Anthropology, Washington State University.

Bryan, K. 1950. *Flint quarries—the sources of tools and, at the same time, the factories of the American Indian.* Harvard University, Peabody Museum Papers XVII (3), Cambridge, Mass.

Callahan, E. 1979. The basics of biface knapping in the eastern fluted point tradition: a manual for flintknappers and lithic analysts. *Archaeology of Eastern North America* 7 (1): 1–180, Washington, D.C.

Clarke, R. 1935. The flint-knapping industry at Brandon. *Antiquity* 9: 38–56.

Crabtree, D. E. 1972. An introduction to flintworking. Occasional Papers, Idaho State University Museum 28.

Draper, J. A. 1982. An analysis of lithic tools and debitage from 35CSI: a prehistoric site on the southern Oregon coast. *Tebiwa* 19:47–65.

Dubois, C. 1935. Wintun Ethnography. *University of California Publications in American Archaeology and Ethnology* 28 (5): 279–403.

Ericson, J. E. 1977. Egalitarian exchange systems in California: a preliminary view. In T. K. Earle & J. E. Ericson, eds., *Exchange systems in prehistory,* New York: Academic Press, 109–26.

Ericson, J. E. 1981. *Exchange and production systems in California prehistory.* British Archaeological Reports, International series S 110.

Ericson, J. E. 1982. Production for obsidian exchange in California. In J. E. Ericson & T. K. Earle, eds., *Contexts of prehistoric exchange.* New York: Academic Press, 129–48.

Ericson, J. E. & Goldstein, R. 1980. Workspace: a new approach to the analysis of energy expenditure within site catchments. In F. J. Findlow & J. E. Ericson, eds., *Catchment analysis: essays in human resource space,* Anthropology UCLA 10 (1–2): 21–30.

Ericson, J. E. & Singer, C. A. 1977. Hypotheses of lithic selection and use, CARD manuscript file, Peabody Museum, Harvard University.

Findlow, F. J. & Bolognese, M. 1982. Regional modeling of obsidian procurement in the American southwest. In J. E. Ericson & T. K. Earle, eds., *Contexts of prehistoric exchange.* New York: Academic Press, 53–81.

Flenniken, J. J. 1978. Further technological analysis of the lithic artifacts from the Miller Site 45FR5. *Washington Archaeological Research Center* 72: 81–132.

Flenniken, J. J. & Stanfill, A. 1980. A preliminary technological examination of 20 archaeological sites located during the cultural resource survey of the Whitehorse Ranch. *Public Land Exchange Contract Abstracts and CRM Archaeology* 1 (1): 23–30.

Frederickson, D. A. 1969. Technological change, population movement, environmental adaptation, and the emergence of trade: inferences on culture change suggested by midden constituent analysis. *UCLA Archaeological Survey, Annual Report* 11: 105–25.

Goodman, M. E. 1944. The physical properties of stone tool materials. *American Antiquity* 4: 415–33.

Gould, R. A., Koster, D. A. & Sontz, A. H. L. 1971. The lithic assemblage of the Western Desert aborigines of Australia. *American Antiquity* 36: 149–69.

Harbottle, G. 1982. Chemical characterization in archaeology. In J. E. Ericson & T. K. Earle, eds., *Contexts of prehistoric exchange.* New York: Academic Press, 13–51.

Harding, T. G. 1967. *Voyagers of the Vitiaz Straits: a study of a New Guinea trade system.* Seattle: University of Washington Press.

Hayden, B., ed., 1979. *Lithic use-wear analysis.* New York: Academic Press.

Hestor, T. R. & Heizer, R. F. 1973. *Bibliography of archaeology I: experiments, lithic technology and petrography.* Addison-Wesley Module in Anthropology 19:1–56.

Holmes, W. H. 1894. Natural history of flaked stone implements, Memoirs of the International Congress of Anthropology 120–39.

Holmes, W. H. 1919. *Handbook of aboriginal American antiquities.* New York: Burt Franklin Reprints.

Keely, L. H. 1980. *Experimental determination of stone tool uses: a microwear analysis.* Chicago: University of Chicago Press.

Newcomer, M. H. 1971. Some quantitive experiments in handaxe manufacture. *World Archaeology* 3:85–94.

Osbourne, D. 1965. Chipping remains as an indication of cultural change at Wetherhill Mesa, Contributions of the Wetherill Mesa Archaeological Project. *Memoirs of the Society for American Archaeology* 19:30–44.

Purdy, B. A. 1975. The Senator Edwards chipped stone workshop site (8-MR-122), Marion County, Florida: a preliminary report of investigations. *The Florida Anthropologist* 28:178–89.

Purdy, B. A. 1981a. An investigation into the use of chert outcrops by prehistoric Floridians. *Florida Anthropologist* 34 (2):90–108.

Purdy, B. A. 1981b. *Florida's prehistoric stone technology.* Gainesville: University Presses of Florida.

Rappaport, R. A. 1968. *Pigs for the ancestors.* New Haven: Yale University Press.

Semenov, S. A. 1964. *Prehistoric technology.* London: Cory, Adams & Mackay.

Singer, C. A. & Ericson, J. E. 1977. Quarry analysis at Bodie Hills, Mono County, California: a case study. In T. K. Earle & J. E. Ericson, eds., *Exchange systems in prehistory.* New York: Academic Press, 171–88.

Spence, M. W. 1982. The social context of production and exchange. In J. E. Ericson & T. K. Earle, eds., *Contexts of prehistoric exchange.* New York: Academic Press, 173–97.

Swanson, E., ed., 1975. *Lithic technology – making and using stone tools.* The Hague: Mouton Publishers.

Tringham, R., Cooper, G., Odell, G., Voytek, B. & Whitman, A. 1974. Experimentation in the formation of edge damage: a new approach to lithic analysis. *Journal of Field Archaeology* 1: 171–96.

Wright, G. A. 1974. *Archaeology and trade.* Addison-Wesley Module in Anthropology 49:1–48. Reading, MA.

Wright, H., & Zeder, M. 1977. The simulation of a linear exchange system under equilibrium conditions. In T. K. Earle & J. E. Ericson, eds., *Exchange systems in prehistory.* New York: Academic Press, 233–54.

PART TWO

Procurement, production, and exchange

Chapter 2

Mount Jasper: a direct-access lithic source area in the White Mountains of New Hampshire
R. M. Gramly

Archaeological excavations at Mount Jasper, a rhyolite source in northern New England, reveal that it was exploited at a slow rate over 7,000 years. Although stone from the mountain was transported over a broad region, its movement was in the hands of miners rather than traders or other intermediaries. An unexpected benefit of the work at Mount Jasper was the discovery that workshops may yield three classes of artifacts. One of these classes, exhausted tools of exotic stones, holds valuable information about subsistence activities, the range of seasonal movements, and general culture history. Archaeologists can no longer afford to overlook this rich source of data in their studies of stone-tool-using groups.

The object of this discussion is to present the fruits of archaeological research at a small-scale lithic source area located in the White Mountains of New Hampshire, a region that was as thinly populated in prehistory as it is today. Mount Jasper is an example of a lithic resource that was consumed at a slow rate over a long period. The stone that was quarried there for flaked tools was not transported very far from the site. As we shall argue, the most economical explanation for the distribution of Mount Jasper stone is that users satisfied only personal needs. Since there is no evidence of exchange networks at any period in the region, there was no surplus production. The appearance of Mount Jasper stone at distant habitation sites reflects actual movements of quarrymen in pursuit of game, fish, and other necessities of life.

Excavations since 1976 at Mount Jasper have laid bare prehistoric industry spanning 7,000 years. The stone sought by ancient toolmakers is a glassy, flow-banded rhyolite with good flaking properties (Gramly & Cox 1976). Outcrops of the best grade of stone occur at the top of sheer cliffs. The relative inaccessibility of the stone and its inconspicuous occurrence delayed exploitation until the close of the sixth millennium B.C. or roughly 4,000 years after man's entry into northern New England (Gramly & Rutledge 1981).

By any standard Mount Jasper was a small-scale lithic source area. Only 100 m³ of rhyolite were won from the workings, a volume equivalent to 275,000 kg or a scant 39 kg of stone per year over the presumed life-span of the quarry (7,000 years). Such a low rate of usage would be expected if Mount Jasper were visited but once or twice a year by small hunting parties in need of fresh tools. The movement of Mount Jasper rhyolite appears to have been confined to a system of lakes and streams stretching northeastward of the site (fig. 2.1). This region is heavily forested and experiences severe winter weather. Archaeological sites are numerous, but small.

With so little stone being extracted and processed at Mount Jasper each year, it is evident that toolmaking specialists did not reside there. Ancient workshops have not yielded hearths, postholes, or any other traces of lengthy stays. Not even one potsherd was unearthed on a large Ceramic Period workshop.

Considering the harsh climate of the northern New England interior and the low productivity of plants and animals useful to man, population density must always have been low in the region. Traditional aboriginal horticulture was impossible due to a short frost-free season. In a territory with few attractions for prehistoric man, save for a network of navigable waterways and large game animals such as the moose, only minor workings at lithic sources would be anticipated.

Had northern New England been more heavily settled, the demand for Mount Jasper rhyolite might have spurred development of an exchange system. Sizable supplies of similar-quality stone are unknown nearer than 125 km in any direction. Mount Jasper supplied ancient tool-users with a scarce good, but consumers had no choice but to fend for themselves when a need for fresh raw material arose.

The mine, quarry pits, and workshops

The ancient workings at Mount Jasper (figs. 2.2, 2.3) have been known since 1859 when they were discovered accidentally by a farmer. The mountain was visited by natural historians and archaeologists several times after this discovery, but no excavations were attempted until 1976. The main attraction was an adit, 10 m deep, with a pillar left standing to support the roof (fig. 2.4). Although to some visitors the adit appears to be a natural cavity, excavations in 1976 and 1979 laid bare fresh surfaces showing hammer marks and many greenstone hammers discarded by prehistoric miners. There can be no doubt that most of the volume of the cavity, roughly 63 m³, is artificial. True mines at sources of flakable stone are rare, and in eastern North America the adit at Mount Jasper may be unique.

Along the strike of the rhyolite dike where the adit is located are smaller, open-face workings or quarries. A conservative estimate of the volume of rhyolite dug away from these exposures is 30 to 40 m³. Some of the open pits are perched precariously high on cliff faces and access is difficult and dangerous.

At the crest of the mountain, where footing is sure and the rhyolite easily accessible, is the oldest workshop at Mount Jasper. This 'Hill Workshop' straddles a badly weathered section of the dike. The quality of the stone there is rather poor, and quarrying and reduction generated a large amount of waste. Gradually, as the supply of rock suited to tool production was exhausted, quarrying extended down the cliff face. Approximately 30 m below the top of the mountain a good grade of stone was found, and mining in the adit began. The pillar that was allowed to stand was a wise precaution against moderately strong earth tremors that trouble the region from time to time (Barosh 1979).

The most recent workshops, all dating to the Ceramic Period (500 B.C. or more recent), are located at the base of the mountain on well-drained ground fronting on the Dead River (fig. 2.5). Additional workshops may have existed on gravelly knolls nearby, but ballast quarrying in recent years has disturbed these features of the Dead River Valley.

It is not immediately obvious why ancient miners of the Ceramic Period chose to process rhyolite below the mountain and not at the crest where most of the outcrops and the earliest workshops are found. Considering the directions from which miners approached Mount Jasper yields a possible explanation. In the earliest period of exploitation,

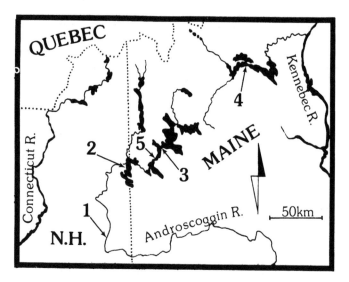

Fig. 2.1. Map of New England showing study area. Numbered localities are archaeological sites where tools of Mount Jasper rhyolite have been unearthed.
1, Mount Jasper, Berlin; 2, Molls Rock, Lake Umbagog; 3, Upper Dam, Upper Richardson Lake; 4, Unnamed site, Flagstaff Lake; 5, The Narrows, Richardson Lakes.

Fig. 2.2. Mount Jasper. The circled star is the location of the ancient mine with quarries extending along the cliff face to either side. *Hw,* Archaic Period Hill Workshop; *Drw,* Ceramic Period Dead River Workshop. In the far distance rise hills of the White Mountain National Park.

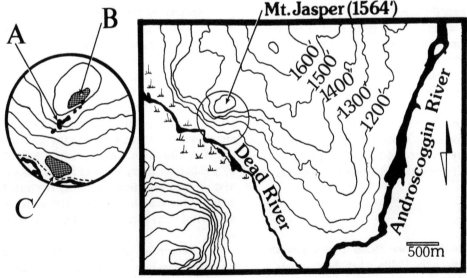

Fig. 2.3. Topographic map of Mount Jasper and vicinity, Berlin, Coos County, N. H. The positions of the ancient mine (A) and quarries at the edge of an upland plateau are shown. The shaded areas (detail, B, C) are prehistoric workshops.

Fig. 2.4. Entrance to the prehistoric mine (adit), Mount Jasper. *P*, pillar supporting roof; *C*, country rock (a metatuff or gneiss); *R*, rhyolite.

that is, from Middle Archaic times onward (5000–500 B.C.), bark canoes and other lightweight watercraft did not exist. Hunters would have shunned rapid rivers such as the Androscoggin which flows near the site. They would have traveled instead on foot across uplands. Being at the edge of an extensive upland plateau stretching northward for many kilometers, Mount Jasper was easily reached by land from the north. In a later era when birchbark canoes were used extensively, access to the mountain would have been easiest by water, in which case workshops below the mountain would have been logical places for fashioning implements. Workshops on and below the mountain possess no special advantages apart from the direction of access. All are amply provided with water, and none has any evidence whatsoever of prolonged occupation or activities besides toolmaking.

Excavations

Most of the fill in the adit was found to be slopewash that had accumulated since the 1940s, when the mine was ransacked by amateur excavators in search of impressive relics. Judging by a pocket of ancient fill they overlooked, they

seem to have found none. The Indian miners had left behind little else but heavily battered greenstone hammers weighing several kilograms apiece and rhyolite chunks that were too small to be used for toolmaking. Soil conditions in the adit were unfavorable for preservation of organics, and no wooden, antler, or bone mining tools have ever been reported.

On the limited evidence it cannot be established how the rhyolite was extracted. Hammering alone could not have freed the rock as it adheres tenaciously to the gneiss (metatuffs) surrounding the dike, and further, striking platforms would have been quickly rounded. Wedges or gads must have been employed to force open joints and attack the rhyolite mass. Some of the heavy-duty scrapers unearthed at the workshops might have been used to make gads and other mining tools such as shovels, indispensible aids for exposing the dike and raking away piles of tailings left by other miners.

Since further work in the mine would have been fruitless, our attention shifted to the workshops. Our modest goals were to obtain samples of debitage and imperfect specimens illustrating stages in the manufacture of bifaces. We harbored a faint hope of encountering culturally diagnostic artifacts. Soils at all workshops were thin, and the depth of accumulated flaking debris appeared too small for cultural stratigraphy to be present. As expected, our excavations (figs. 2.6, 2.7) produced abundant flakes, hammerstones, cores, and imperfect bifaces, numbering several thousand specimens per square meter in some places. We were totally unprepared, however, for the recovery of finished implements of delicate manufacture. Many of these tools were heavily worn and had been resharpened. In addition, we were surprised to observe that the workshop at the base of Mount Jasper along the Dead River yielded finished tools made of a wide variety of raw materials, representing lithic sources at considerable distances from Mount Jasper. These finds, which one would normally expect at habitation sites, were novel, and a search through the literature for comparable assemblages went unrewarded.

Spurred by these unprecedented finds, a decision was made to devote as much energy to excavating the Mount Jasper workshops as might be given to any prehistoric habitation site in the region. The stupendous quantity of debitage presented problems, as delicate tools of exotic stones could easily be overlooked among the thousands of flakes in each sieveful of dirt. Ultimately it was decided that for ease of sorting all sievings, often amounting to 10 to 15 kg per square meter, should be transported to the laboratory for washing and close inspection. This precaution paid off handsomely by yielding small fragments of fragile flake tools that would have escaped detection otherwise. The distributions of fragments of the same tools were useful evidence for deriving the number of visits ancient stone knappers made to the workshops.

After sorting, tools and debitage were tallied and weighed for each excavation unit. These figures were transferred to working field maps of the workshop excavations, and there emerged distributional patterns that were highly revealing

Fig. 2.5. View of excavations underway at the Ceramic Period Dead River Workshop. The aspen logs outline previously excavated areas. Two weeks were spent clearing the site of a dense growth of saplings and field of boulders.

of prehistoric activities. Density maps also helped guide the direction of excavations and ensured that rewarding areas were not overlooked. For the workshop along the Dead River it was observed that flake concentrations coincided with high densities of delicate finished tools of foreign raw materials. Hammerstones and heavy-duty scrapers appeared to cluster separately from flakes and finer tools.

Table 2.1 *Tally of Class I artifacts at the Mount Jasper workshops.*

	Number	Weight	N/W
Dead River Workshop			
Alpha-1	83,330	262.98 kg	318/kg
Alpha-2	24,070	83.59 kg	287/kg
Beta	60,557	153.95 kg	393/kg
	(also 3 large chunks weighing a total of 11.81 kg)		
Hill Workshop			
Main excavation	19,673	103.28 kg	190/kg
Testpit (see fig. 2.7)	6,020	12.12 kg	497/kg

One-meter and two-meter squares were adopted as units of excavation. The choice was dictated by bouldery ground and the presence of many tree stumps, which had to be uprooted in nearly every square. It was not possible to pinpoint the location of every tool due to the difficulties of excavation and the masking presence of thousands of dirty flakes. Smaller excavation units, such as 50-cm-square blocks, were employed as conditions permitted. Smaller units afforded better control in plotting finds, especially in sections where worked stone had to be removed *en masse* for sieving and sorting.

Table 2.2 *Tally of Class II artifacts at the Mount Jasper workshops.*

	Alpha-1	Alpha-2	Beta	Hill Workshop[a]
Hammerstones	14	2	5	17
Large scrapers	25	11	11	13[b]
Flaked adzes	0	0	2	0

[a]Objects from the testpit are not included.
[b]Some of these scrapers might have been transported from the workshop on an earlier occasion and belong in Class III. Most are badly weathered.

Table 2.3 *Tally of Class III artifacts at the Mount Jasper workshops (whole tool counts).*

	Alpha-1	Alpha-2	Beta	Hill Workshop[a]
Projectile points	5	11	13	5
Perforators	5	10	2	0
Bifaces (knives)	7	7	2	0
Endscrapers	5	8	4	1
Hollow scrapers	4	27	8	1
Sidescrapers and irregular scrapers	9	2	1	3
Utilized flakes	7	25	3	8[b]
Pièces esquillées	0	1	0	0
Gravers	0	2	0	2
Totals	42	93	33	20
Tool fragments	27	34	15	2

[a]Objects from the testpit are not included.
[b]Other utilized flakes in Mount Jasper rhyolite may have been overlooked due to the weathered condition of the stone.

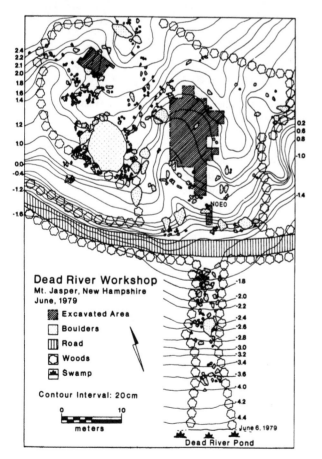

Fig. 2.6. Contour map of the Ceramic Period Dead River Workshop at Mount Jasper showing excavations from 1976 to 1979. Construction of the trackway along the edge of the terrace destroyed thick deposits of lithic debris.

The Dead River workshop

Two concentrations of debitage (termed loci) were observed. One of these, Locus Alpha, was subsequently resolved into Alpha-1 and Alpha-2 (fig. 2.8). Although these loci were only a few meters apart on relatively level ground, the other major concentration, Locus Beta, was separated by uneven, stony soils and a dense thicket of aspen from the others. The intervening 15 to 20 meters was virtually barren of finished tools in exotic raw materials.

Among the thousands of flakes in each locus were small-to medium-sized hammerstones, rejected projectile point preforms (fig. 2.9), heavy-duty scrapers of Mount Jasper rhyolite (fig. 2.10), and last, a variety of complete but heavily worn and polished tools of exotic stones (fig. 2.11). For ease of analysis, artifacts were relegated to three classes. Class I (table 2.1) encompassed all debitage and preforms. Included were heavy blocks of rhyolite that had been brought to the workshop with considerable effort but abandoned nonetheless after only partial reduction. Class II (table 2.2) was composed of hammerstones, large scrapers, and a few flaked adzes. The lack of signs of heavy usage on the scrapers, plus the fact that they are unknown on habitation sites elsewhere in the northern New England interior, indicate that they were intended for service at the workshops only. Class II tools would have been used to reduce rhyolite blocks and to create gads, shovels, and rakes, without which mining would have been arduous. Class III (table 2.3) featured a wide range of abraded and heavily reworked tools. Many items, especially projectile points, exhibited old breakage, which, although minor, may have loosened them in their hafts. A brief stay at Mount Jasper could hardly have produced such extensive wear and damage. One concludes that these tools reflect activities performed off the workshop. The implications of this observation are discussed elsewhere (Gramly 1980).

Class III tools provided ironclad evidence of the antiquity of the Dead River Workshop. Their form and finish place them squarely within the Late Ceramic Period (Sanger 1979) or the last few centuries before European contact (sixteenth century). Most of the sites with tools resembling those from Mount Jasper have been reported from coastal Maine and the Maritimes. Undoubtedly interior sites with identical cultural remains await discovery, and in this light it is interesting to note that a suite of projectile points closely matching the series from Mount Jasper has been illustrated for a site on the upper St John River in northwestern New Brunswick (Clarke 1970). The St John, rather then the Androscoggin, may have been the route followed by hunters of the northern interior moving to and from the Atlantic coast. This hypothesis is borne out by the presumed origins of the raw materials of Class III artifacts. Most stones are linked to lithic sources in the northern counties of Maine and as far afield as Passamaquoddy Bay on the Maine–New Brunswick border. This immense region is drained by the St John River and other smaller river systems.

At Locus Beta, Classes II and III were clearly segregated

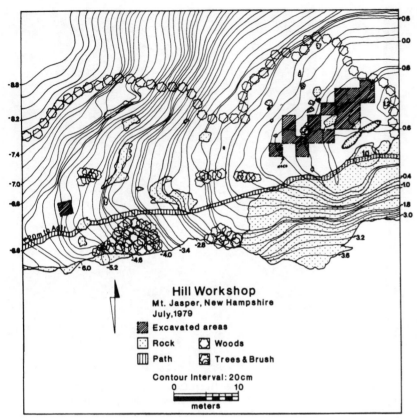

Fig. 2.7. Contour map of the Archaic Period Hill Workshop at Mount Jasper showing archaeological excavations in 1979. A continuous blanket of rhyolite debitage extends from the main excavations to the test pit, 35 m to the west.

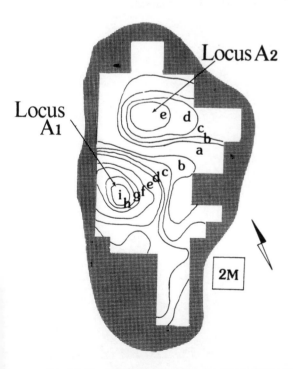

Fig. 2.8. Density contours of Class I artifacts delineating Loci Alpha-1 and Alpha-2, Dead River Workshop, Mount Jasper. Number of artifacts per sq. m; a, fewer than 250; b, 250–499; c, 500–999; d, 1,000–1,499; e, 1,500–2,499; f, 2,500–4,999; g, 5,000–9,999; h, 10,000–14,999; i, 15,000 or more.

(fig. 2.12). A similar situation was observed for Loci Alpha-1 and Alpha-2 although it is difficult to portray artifact positioning on a small-scale map. Two dense clusters of Class II artifacts were noted for Alpha-1 and a less obvious clustering was detected at Alpha-2 (fig. 2.13). In view of the extraordinary amount of debitage present at Locus Alpha-1 in association

Fig. 2.9. Class I artifacts, specifically a series of preforms illustrating stages in the production of corner-notched projectile points (Ceramic Period), from the Dead River Workshop, Mount Jasper.

Fig. 2.10. *Top row,* Class II artifacts, specifically large scrapers manufactured of Mount Jasper rhyolite, from the Ceramic Period Dead River Workshop. *Bottom row,* large flaked and notched axe of Mount Jasper rhyolite, which was unearthed at the Molls Rock site, Lake Umbagog, N.H.

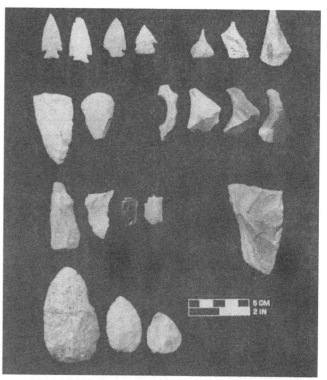

Fig. 2.11. Class III artifacts from the Ceramic Period Dead River Workshop. *First row,* corner-notched projectile points and perforators; *second row,* trianguloid endscrapers and hollow scrapers (exhausted sidescrapers); *third row,* utilized flakes and an irregular scraper; *fourth row,* bifacial knives. All raw materials are chert, quartzite, and quartz crystal.

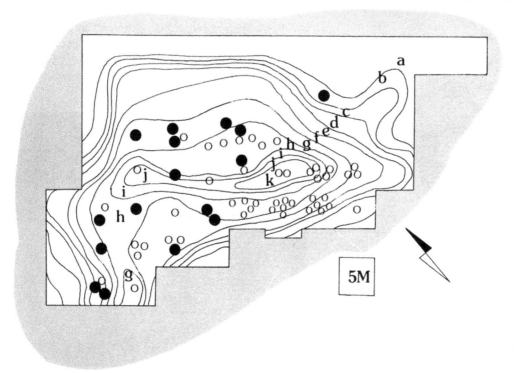

Fig. 2.12. Contour map of Class I artifact densities and locations of Class II and III artifacts, Locus Beta, Dead River Workshop, Mount Jasper. Number of artifacts per sq. m: a, fewer than 200; b, 200–399; c, 400–799; d, 800–1,199; e, 1,200–1,999; f, 2,000–3,900; g, 4,000–7,999; h, 8,000–11,999; i, 12,000–15,999; j, 16,000–19,999; k, 20,000 or more.

The open circles are Class III tools and the filled circles are Class II tools.

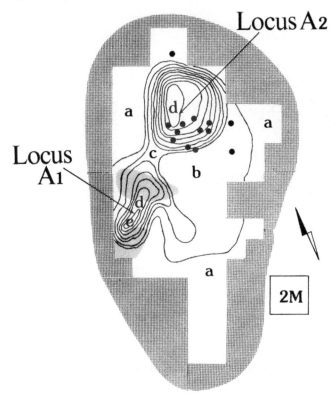

Fig. 2.13. Density contours of Class III tools which help delineate Loci Alpha-1 and Alpha-2, Dead River Workshop, Mount Jasper. The shaded areas overlapping the contours of Locus Alpha-1 are concentrations of Class II tools with a density exceeding 3 tools/m². For Locus Alpha-2 occurrences of individual Class II objects per sq. m are plotted: a, fewer than 4 fragmentary or entire Class III tools; b, 4–7 fragmentary of entire Class III tools; c, 8–11 fragmentary or entire Class III tools; d, 36–43 fragmentary or entire Class III tools; e, 44 or more fragmentary or entire Class III tools.

Values for other contours may be interpolated directly.

with two Class II clusters, two episodes of flaking may be represented. Alternatively, Alpha-1 may be the leavings of a large party of miners who processed more stone and manufactured more mining implements than workers at Loci Alpha-2 and Beta.

Although Alpha-1 and Alpha-2 differ in their totals of Class I artifacts, the number of objects per unit weight (kilogram) are nearly equivalent. At Locus Beta, on the other hand, Class I artifacts are smaller in size, with each rhyolite flake weighing a trifle less than an 'average' flake at the other loci. This difference is explained by referring to a breakdown of Class III tool types. As I have argued elsewhere (Gramly 1980), relatively more projectile points were manufactured at Locus Beta than at the Alpha loci. The heavy production of bifaces at Beta yielded a proportionately greater number of small trimming flakes than at Alpha-1 and Alpha-2 where flake tools were more common. Flake tools, on the whole can be shaped with fewer removals than projectile points, and in some cases they are usable freshly struck from the core without further preparation.

The differing end products of tool manufacture at the loci tell us that parties of miners, previous to their arrival at Mount Jasper, had performed different tasks. The miners at Beta had completed many hunts and their weapons had suffered much damage. The other parties had hunted less and perhaps had devoted a greater share of their time (and tool use) to other subsistence activities such as fishing. Interestingly, the only marked difference in tool-type frequencies between Alpha-1 and Alpha-2 lies with the percentages of sidescrapers and hollow scrapers. Since sidescrapers ultimately become hollow scrapers through hard usage and constant resharpening resulting in concave working edges, one concludes, that the toolkits of miners as well as the tasks they performed before coming to Mount Jasper were similar. One party, however, was in greater need of a fresh toolkit, having perhaps just traveled in regions poorly supplied with flakable stones.

The season of the year when miners visited Mount Jasper may account for differences among Class III assemblages. The timing of visitations can certainly be related to a seasonal round, but as there have been all too few archaeological excavations at prehistoric sites in the northern interior, what the round may have been is open to question.

The Hill Workshop

A tough mat of blueberries and shrubs covers the crest of Mount Jasper and its prehistoric workshop, making it difficult to discover concentrations of debitage by test-holing. Large excavations were made only in lightly vegetated areas but, as luck would have it, it was there where an ancient trench in the rhyolite dike was found. Parallel to the dike a thick deposit of debitage and waste stone was unearthed and mixed among these materials were Class I, II and III artifacts (fig. 2.14).

All the procedures that were applied to investigating the Ceramic Period Dead River Workshop were used at the top of the mountain. Certain problems arose, however, due to the greater antiquity of the Hill Workshop. First, discriminating between true toolmaking flakes and tabular chunks of low-grade rhyolite chiseled out and discarded by the quarrymen was not an easy task. All the rhyolite was heavily weathered and had a soft, chalky surface. Bulbs of percussion were difficult to detect where weathering was far advanced. Second, as there were fewer exotic stones used by the Archaic Period toolmakers (fig. 2.15), it became a challenge to sort scrapers, for example, into Classes II and III. Sorting became less burdensome, however, after it was noted that small scrapers, no matter how badly weathered, still retained traces of polish developed by heavy use. On this ground these tools were relegated to Class III rather than Class II. Third, recognizing hammerstones was difficult because natural cobbles, which had been attacked by ground acids, often showed dimpled surfaces typical of a well-battered hammerstone. Confronted with greenstone cobbles that might or might not be tools, a conservative approach was adopted and they were discarded.

At the Hill Workshop there is no recognizable pattern of

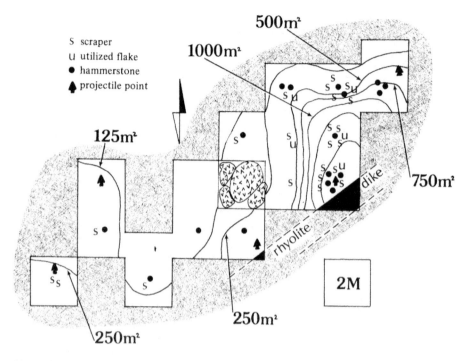

Fig. 2.14. Contour map of Class I artifact densities and locations of individual Class II and III tools for the Hill Workshop, Mount Jasper. Contours ranging from 250 to 1,500 artifacts/m² are shown.

Fig. 2.15. Artifacts unearthed at the Archaic Period Hill Workshop, Mount Jasper. *Top row,* projectile points of Middle–Late Archaic age; *middle row,* utilized flakes and perforator; *bottom row* (left) scrapers and (right) Middle Archaic projectile point of Mount Jasper rhyolite found at the Molls Rock site, Lake Umbagog, N.H. Both foreign raw materials (quartzite, quartz, chert, and rhyolite porphyry) and the Mount Jasper stone were used for these tools.

artifact distribution as was noted for Alpha-1, Alpha-2, and Beta below the mountain. The densest occurrence of tools does indeed overlap the thickest accumulations of flakes, but the ratio of Class I artifacts to Classes II and III is everywhere the same. This fact and the knowledge that flake weights (numbers per kilogram) are equivalent in all squares confirm the unpatterned character of the Hill Workshop. Concentrations of flakes did not accumulate in a single episode of toolmaking but rather grew in size after every visit. At the Dead River Workshop, on the other hand, thick deposits of flakes yielded different sorts of artifacts than did thin deposits. The patterning of the Dead River loci suggests that thousands of artifacts were laid down at once, while at the Hill Workshop repeated small operations are so well mixed that discrete events cannot be recognized.

One gains the impression from the distribution of artifacts on the Hill Workshop that quarrymen of the Archaic Period processed a great deal less rhyolite at each visit to Mount Jasper than did Ceramic Period toolmakers. They may have visited the mountain more often, however. Traveling on foot and lacking the means to transport surpluses, Archaic hunters had to return periodically to replenish their toolkits. With their canoes, Ceramic Period hunters were not tied down to a few lithic sources. They could range widely and remain away from quarries for longer periods. On the other hand, by staying on the hunt for extended periods more stone had to be extracted for toolmaking when they camped at a lithic workshop. Their entire toolkit, and not just a few elements of it, needed replacing.

General considerations

It is evident from the archaeological excavations at Mount Jasper that lithic sources may yield a good deal more information than just technical data about tool production and raw-material procurement. In fact, one might argue that the logical place to begin an investigation of a stone-tool-using culture is at lithic sources. By estimating the volume of stone extracted by mining and quarrying for various sources, an impression of the magnitude of prehistoric industry at a single locality is obtained. Going a step further and dating a mining operation and then dividing its time span by the quantity of rock removed, a measure is provided of human activity in a given region. The prehistoric demand for a raw material derived by calculations should indicate to the archaeologist what role, if any, it played in exchange networks. In lightly populated regions such as interior northern New England during the Archaic and Ceramic Periods access to supplies of flakable stones was direct, and finished tools of Mount Jasper rhyolite were transported in the hands of the same individuals who dug it from the earth.

We have attempted to demonstrate that mining operations and tool production may vary from period to period and, within a single cultural period, from visit to visit. All depends upon the transportation available to miners and perhaps the season when a source was exploited. Outside of our study area other factors, of course, might account for variation among loci at workshops.

Arguments about the changing record of exploitation of a source hinge upon analyses of artifact classes at workshops. Interassemblage comparisons demand sizable samples for patterns to become evident. Techniques for eliciting the maximum amount of information from workshop assemblages are in their infancy. Only more spadework will define our ability to interpret the record buried at lithic sources, and our rewards will be commensurate with the effort expended.

Acknowledgments

Support for continuing archaeological research at Mount Jasper has been provided by L. T. Clay, the National Geographic Society, the New Hampshire Charitable Fund, the University of Massachusetts at Boston, *Earthwatch* of Belmont, Mass., and the Maine Historic Preservation Commission. The generous contributions of these individuals and institutions are gratefully acknowledged.

This chapter is based in large measure upon an article published in *Man in the Northeast,* Franklin Pierce College, Ridge, New Hampshire (Gramly 1980). The editorial assistance of H. Sargent and E. Sargent was most helpful. Omissions and shortcomings, however, are only those of the author.

References

Barosh, P. J. 1979. *Earthquake zonation in the northeastern United States.* Preprint 3602. Boston: American Society of Civil Engineers.

Clarke, G. F. 1970. *Someone before us.* Fredericton, N.B.: Brunswick Press.

Gramly, R. M. 1980. Raw materials source areas and 'curated' tools assemblages. *American Antiquity* 45 (4): 823–33.

Gramly, R. M. & Cox, S. L. 1976. A prehistoric quarry-workshop at Mt Jasper, Berlin, New Hampshire. *Man in the Northeast* 11:71–4.

Gramly, R. M. & Rutledge, K. 1981. A new Palaeo-Indian site in the state of Maine. *American Antiquity* 46 (2):354–60.

Sanger, D., ed., 1979. *Discovering Maine's archaeological heritage.* Augusta: Maine Historic Preservation Commission.

Chapter 3

**Procurement without quarry production:
examples from southwestern Idaho**
R. L. Sappington

Obsidian was the lithic material preferred by the aboriginal inhabitants of southwestern Idaho but archaeologists and ethnographers have reported that this material was obtained in Yellowstone National Park and central Oregon. Evidence for tool production in the vicinities of the two local sources is minimal, superficially indicating little procurement of these materials. However, X-ray fluorescence analysis of regional sources and archaeological collections demonstrates that, in fact, both sources were exploited over a period of 10,000 years. This study indicates that lithic-tool production occurred primarily at the consumer sites rather than at the source areas.

Introduction

Obsidian commonly occurs in parts of northwestern North America and this material was widely used by regional aboriginal groups. Archaeologists have been investigating the significance of outstanding quarries such as Obsidian Cliff since 1879 (Holmes 1919, 214). Obsidian artifacts are abundant in archaeological sites in southwestern Idaho but the raw material for these items has long been assumed to have been imported from the well-known sources in Yellowstone National Park and/or central Oregon (Gruhn 1961, 50). The local obsidian resources were either ignored or dismissed as occurring 'only in small pieces unacceptable for tool making' (Davis 1972, 42). Ethnographic reports reinforced the case against procurement at the southwestern Idaho sources. The Shoshoni in west central Idaho 'must' have obtained their obsidian 'from no other place' than Glass Buttes in central Oregon (Liljeblad 1957, 88). Similarly, the Nez Percé centered

in north central Idaho reportedly acquired their obsidian in northeastern Oregon and possibly in Yellowstone Park (Spinden 1908, 184).

A series of rhyolitic extrusions determined by K-Ar dating to have occurred over 9 million years ago formed obsidian in two areas in southwestern Idaho (Bennett 1976, 8). In the vicinity of Timber Butte (fig. 3.1) nodules are present on the butte itself and as float material along Squaw Creek Valley across an area of approximately 16 km^2. While obsidian is common in gravel deposits, individual nodules are relatively small. The largest specimen recovered to date weighs 435 g and has a maximum diameter of 8 cm. Production evidence is scarce and consists of scattered decortication flakes, debitage, and tool fragments associated with the gravel deposits. Concentrations of manufacturing debris such as large biface fragments commonly found at quarry sites are absent.

Obsidian also occurs in the Owyhee Mountains (fig. 3.1) in gravel deposits intermittently across an area of approximately 1,500 km^2. The largest specimen recovered to date weighs 276 g and has a maximum diameter of 7.3 cm, although larger nodules may be found occasionally (J. P. Green 1979, pers. comm.). Production evidence is minimal, consisting of scattered decortication flakes, debitage, and tool fragments associated with gravel deposits. No major quarry or workshop sites have been discovered despite over 50 years of archaeological investigation of the area.

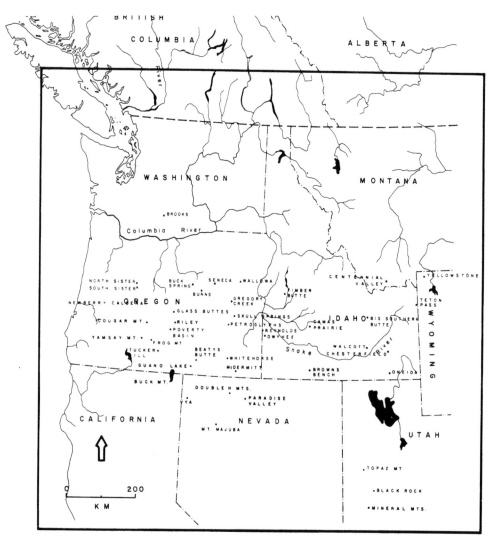

Fig. 3.1. Location for the sources characterized in Idaho and adjacent states.

Elsewhere across the region much greater amounts of obsidian are concentrated in smaller areas and individual nodules are much greater in size. For example, at Glass Buttes in central Oregon (fig. 3.1) a 'mountain of obsidian' covers over 80 km² (Alt & Hyndmann 1978, 186–9). Tremendous amounts of debitage and tool fragments cover the area and experimental knappers have produced a biface over 1 m long from a boulder that originally weighed over 545 kg (D. E. Crabtree 1978, personal communication). Compared with Glass Buttes, the small nodules and the limited presence of production debris at the southwestern Idaho sources indicate that these sources were minimally important and apparently confirm the archaeological and ethnographic reports.

The ethnographic record

Aboriginally, southwestern Idaho was populated by numerous Northern Shoshoni and Northern Paiute groups who moved across the region to obtain a variety of seasonally abundant resources, especially anadromous fish and roots

(Murphy & Murphy 1960, 316; Steward 1938, 172). The temporary abundance of these staples supported brief population concentrations at favored locations and attracted visitors from central and southeastern Idaho, eastern Oregon, northern Nevada, and the Columbia Plateau to the northwest (Blyth 1938, 404; Chaffee 1931, 1; Harris 1940, 39; Liljeblad 1972, 19; Spinden 1908, 175). Social interaction between members of these diverse parties was intense and trade was an important activity. Various commodities were reportedly exchanged, including deer hides, camas roots, horses, flint knives, and obsidian arrowpoints (Liljeblad 1972, 19; Steward 1941, 336, 347).

There is a consensus in the ethnographic record that the people who resided in and visited southwestern Idaho preferred obsidian for the fabrication of flaked lithic tools and they obtained it in two ways (Kelly 1932, 141; Liljeblad 1957, 37; Spinden 1908, 184). The Northern Paiute from eastern Oregon introduced obsidian projectile points specifically for exchange purposes (Liljeblad 1972, 19). Among the parties who obtained these points were visitors from southeastern Idaho who

```
D629334979 16.5.39.      300SECS
ID CENTR   INT-BG      BG       2

         1
FE   6480      486      2140
RB  13480      254       177
SR  14320       18       194
Y   15120      122       191
ZR  15840      165       187
NB  16600      227       203
SN  25400       26       311
BA  32120      196      1186
LA  33480     -111      1694
CE  34720      -15      2168
```

Fig. 3.2. Sample printout for an artifact from Lydle Gulch correlated with the Timber Butte source. From left to right, the columns list the ten elements employed for the analysis, their code numbers for the computer, the intensity for the elements corrected for the background noise, and the background noise. Correction of the background noise results in a negative number for elements absent from the sample. This sample lacks barium and cerium, and is fairly low in strontium and tin.

valued this obsidian over that available in their home territory (Liljeblad 1957, 88). In contrast, the Nez Percé procured obsidian directly at the sources. Despite a variety of locally abundant alternatives, obsidian was 'most prized' and 'parties were sent to collect it'. An intriguing aspect of their procurement activity is that 'no evidence that the implements were roughly shaped at the quarries could be obtained' (Spinden 1908, 184). If obsidian was collected without modification at the sources, even well-used areas would exhibit little evidence of having served as quarries.

The single description of aboriginal knapping techniques indicates an orientation toward obtaining usable flakes rather than biface production. The Northern Shoshoni 'made knives by breaking pieces of obsidian' and 'selecting suitable sharp-edged fragments often of irregular shape . . . a piece an inch or two long was not rejected as long as it could cut' (Lowie 1909, 174). This strategy would be well suited for the reduction of the small nodules found in southwestern Idaho.

While the ethnographic evidence pertaining to aboriginal obsidian procurement and tool production is admittedly limited, it is possible to assume that some regional groups might have obtained raw material at the southwestern Idaho sources without leaving production evidence. The lack of such evidence at the Timber Butte and Owyhee sources might therefore reflect a deliberate procurement strategy rather than a lack of use as the record indicates. To determine the significance of these sources it is therefore necessary to examine collections from potential consumer sites.

Chemical characterization as an approach to the problem

Obsidian was the most frequent lithic material recovered at the Lydle Gulch site on the Boise River in southwestern Idaho. It accounted for over 62 per cent of over 9,300 items, although knappable basalt and cryptocrystalline silica are locally available and the nearest obsidian source is 65 km

distant (Sappington 1981a). The demonstrable selection for 'exotic' obsidian in favor of the much more accessible alternatives precipitated the development of a project to locate the sources for these artifacts that developed into a regional study (Sappington 1981b).

Each obsidian flow represents a unique geological event and therefore possesses a distinct chemical composition. Consequently, it is possible to employ trace-element data to differentiate sources and to correlate artifacts with their areas of origin. Since the late 1960s archaeologists across western North America have successfully applied the geochemical technique of X-ray fluorescence spectrometry toward those ends (Ericson 1981; Ericson, Hagan & Chesterman 1976; Jack 1976; Jack & Carmichael 1969; Jackson 1974; Nelson, D'Auria & Bennett 1975; Nelson & Holmes 1979). The X-ray fluorescence system employed here consists of a Tractor Northern NS-880 instrument, a Nuclear Semiconductor 512 amplifier, a silicon (lithium-drifted) detector with a New England Nuclear americium-241 100 millicurie source and a dysprosium secondary target, a PDP 11/05 computer and a Decwriter II printer. Analysis is performed for a 300-second counting period in free air and the intensities of ten trace elements are determined for each sample (fig. 3.2).

These data are submitted to the Statistical Package for the Social Sciences (SPSS) DISCRIMINANT subprogram (Nie *et al.* 1975). Discriminant analysis is a multivariable statistical technique designed to examine similarities and differences between predetermined groups of cases. The MAHAL stepwise method was selected because it ranks the discriminating ability of the variables (elements) and maximizes the differences between the two closest groups. After determining the reliability of all pairs of source groups by F statistics, individual samples are examined to test the validity of their membership in the assigned groups. Artifacts are analyzed as ungrouped cases and delegated to their two most likely source groups according to their discriminant scores. Because the program is designed so that all ungrouped cases must be assigned to source groups, artifacts originating at sources not included in the analysis may be incorrectly placed into a source. Therefore, those items correlated to a source group having a probability outside the range of one standard deviation, or less than 0.68, are regarded as being unknown.

The results of these analyses vary across the region according to the location of the sites and the various neighboring sources, since it is impossible to compare all artifacts with all sources characterized across western North America. Results are excellent for projects in central Idaho. For example, over 99 per cent of 128 artifacts from sites in the area of the South Fork of the Salmon River were assigned to their sources with acceptable results (Arnold 1981). Elsewhere the results are much less rewarding; only 59 per cent of 283 artifacts from sites along the Buckley–Summer Lake Transmission Line in central Oregon were accepted (Sappington & Toepel 1981). The correlation of virtually all samples from central and southwestern Idaho indicates that the sources

Table 3.1. *The occurrence of Timber Butte obsidian at archaeological sites.*

	no. in sample	% Timber Butte obsidian	distance and direction from Timber Butte source (km)	no. cores in sample	% cores from Timber Butte source	no. Timber Butte flakes in sample	% Timber Butte flakes with cortex	age of site	references
South Fork of Payette River survey	7	100.0	20 E	0	0	0	0	ca. 4000 B.P. to historic	Moore & Ames 1979
Lydle Gulch	779	79.9	60 S	39	79.5	297	25.6	1170 ± 90 B.P. (WSU 2061) 790 ± 100 B.P. (WSU 2062)	Sappington 1981
Givens Hot Springs	24	66.7	80 SW	0	0	11	36.3	4620 ± 270 B.P. (Tx 3656) to late prehistoric	Green 1980
10-OE-1847	1	100.0	100 SW	0	0	0	0	unknown	Moe, Eckerle & Knudson 1980
Warm Lake	62	98.3	80 NE	nr	nr	nr	nr	ca. 4000–300 B.P.	Boreson 1979; Sappington 1979
Middle Fork of Salmon River survey	242	88.9	90-180 ENE	3	66.7	169	14.2	ca. 6000 B.P. to historic	Knudson et al. 1982 Sappington 1982
Reynolds Creek survey	191	21.9	100 SW	11	9.0	11	31.4	ca. 9000 B.P. to historic	Moe 1981
Redfish Overhang	16	12.5	100 E	0	0	0	0	10,100 ± 300 B.P. (WSU 1396) 9860 ± 300 B.P. (WSU 1395)	Gallagher, Sappington & Wylie 1979 Sargeant 1973
South Fork of Salmon River and Payette National Forest sites	128	90.6	110 N	6	50.0	70	35.7	ca. 3000 B.P. to late prehistoric	Arnold 1981
Triangle Lake	1	100.0	140 NW	1	100.0	0	0	unknown	none

Site	N	%	Direction	n	%	n	%	Age	References
Lower Salmon Falls	69	1.4	170 SE	0	0	1	0	unknown	Moe, Eckerle & Knudson 1980; Moe, Sappington & Eckerle 1980
ID-4	3	100.0	190 N	0	0	2	50.0		none
Dirty Shame Rockshelter	132	3.0	200 SW	0	0	0	0	Zones V-III, 7900-5900 B.P.	Aikens, Cole & Stuckenrath 1977
Stockhoff	21	4.7	200 NW	0	0	0	0	unknown	Womack 1977
Brown's Bench	16	18.7	220 SE	1	100.0	0	0	ca. 2000 B.P. to 870 B.P.	Barnes 1964; Bowers & Savage 1962; Green n.d.
East Kamiah	2	100.0	240 N	0	0	1	100.0	1380 ± 100 B.P. (WSU 2199)	Waldbauer, Knudson & Dechert 1981
Deer Creek Cave	28	10.7	260 SE	0	0	0	0	ca. 1350 B.P. to historic	Green n.d.; Shutler & Shutler 1963
Aurora Joint Venture Project sites	23	8.7	260 SW	0	0	0	0	ca. 2000 B.P. to 870 B.P.	Minor 1980; Sappington 1980b
Hatwai	29	48.2	270 N	1	100.0	0	0	9850 ± 870 B.P. (Tx 3158) to 150 ± 70 B.P. (Tx 3158)	Ames, Green, Pfortner 1981
Lenore	21	61.9	270 N	0	0	0	0	ca. 7000 B.P. to late prehistoric	Toups 1969; Ames & Green 1979
Spalding	8	75.0	270 N	0	0	6	0	ca. 2500 to late prehistoric	none
Dworshak Reservoir	28	92.0	275 N	1	100.0	14	7.1	ca. 6000 B.P. to late prehistoric	Corliss & Gallagher 1972; Mattson et al. 1983
Graybeal	13	13.0	350 E	0	0	2	0	140 ± 180 B.P. (GaK 8536)	Flint & Sappington 1982
Fort Sherman	4	25.0	400 N	0	0	1	0	unknown	none
Kettle Falls	206	27.7	480 NW	6	16.7	41	19.5	5000 B.P. to historic	Chance, Chance & Fagan 1977; Sappington 1980c

Note: nr = not recorded

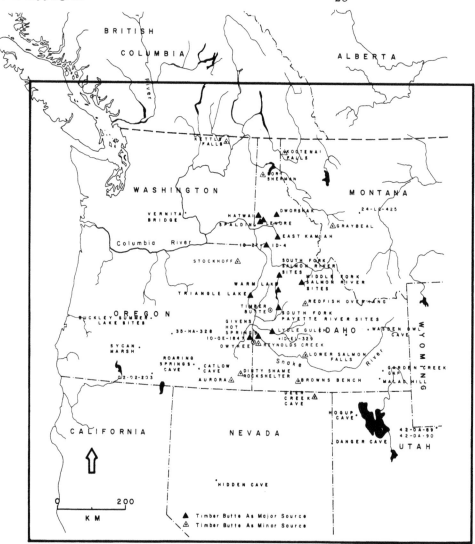

Fig. 3.3. Location of all sites where Timber Butte obsidian has been identified. Sites where Timber Butte obsidian occurs as the most frequent source are indicated by a solid triangle, while sites where Timber Butte obsidian appears less frequently than other sources are indicated by an open triangle. Sites where Timber Butte obsidian have not been identified are indicated by the dots.

employed for the manufacture of obsidian tools in this area have been located. Conversely, sources for many tools recovered in central Oregon remain to be located.

The spatial occurrence of Timber Butte and Owyhee obsidian

Timber Butte obsidian has been identified at numerous archaeological sites across the Northern Great Basin–Southern Columbia Plateau region (fig. 3.3, table 3.1). This obsidian predominates in collections across central Idaho where it accounts for up to 91 per cent of some samples. Farther north at its most distant identification point at Kettle Falls in northeastern Washington, 480 km from the source, Timber Butte comprises nearly 28 per cent of the sample. To the south, Timber Butte obsidian exhibits a much more rapid falloff with increasing distance. While it accounts for 80 per cent of the Lydle Gulch sample, it diminishes to 22 per cent at the Reynolds Creek sites, and represents only 3 per cent at

Dirty Shame Rockshelter 200 km southwest of its area of occurrence.

Owyhee obsidian is secondary to material from other sources at all sites where it has been identified (fig. 3.4, table 3.2). Its greatest frequency is among the Reynolds Creek sites in close proximity to the source area; even there it represents less than 18 per cent of the sample. Owyhee obsidian represents only 13 per cent of the Lydle Gulch collection and it is altogether absent at sites located further north and east. Owyhee obsidian accounts for less than 7 per cent of the Dirty Shame Rockshelter sample 90 km southwest of the source; it is virtually absent at other sites further to the west and south.

The temporal distribution of Timber Butte and Owyhee obsidian

Many sites where Timber Butte obsidian occurs have been radiocarbon-dated so it is possible to delineate its

Table 3.2. *The occurrence of Owyhee obsidian at archaeological sites.*

	no. in sample	% Owyhee obsidian	distance and direction from Owyhee source (km)	no. cores in sample	% cores from Owyhee source	no. Owyhee flakes in sample	% Owyhee flakes with cortex	age of site	references
Reynolds Creek survey	191	17.8	40 N	11	45.4	21	76.1	c. 9000 B.P. to historic	Moe 1981
Givens Hot Springs	24	4.1	50 NW	0	0	1	0	4620 ± 270 B.P. (Tx 3656) 4060 ± 100 B.P. (Tx 3655)	Green 1980
Lydle Gulch	779	13.2	65 NE	39	15.4	66	45.4	1170 ± 90 B.P. (WSU 2061) 790 ± 100 B.P. (WSU 2062)	Sappington 1981a
10-EL-329	1	100.0	70 E	0	0	0	0	c. 850 B.P. to historic	Moe, Eckerle & Knudson 1980
Dirty Shame Rockshelter	132	6.8	90 SW	0	0	0	0	9500–400 B.P.	Aikens, Cole & Stuckenrath 1977; Hanes 1980; Sappington 1980a
Brown's Bench	16	6.2	160 SE	1	100.0	0	0	c. 4000 B.P. to historic	Barnes 1964; Bowers & Savage 1962; Green n.d.
Deer Creek Cave	28	7.1	200 SE	0	0	0	0	c. 4000–870 B.P.	Green n.d.; Shutler & Shutler 1963

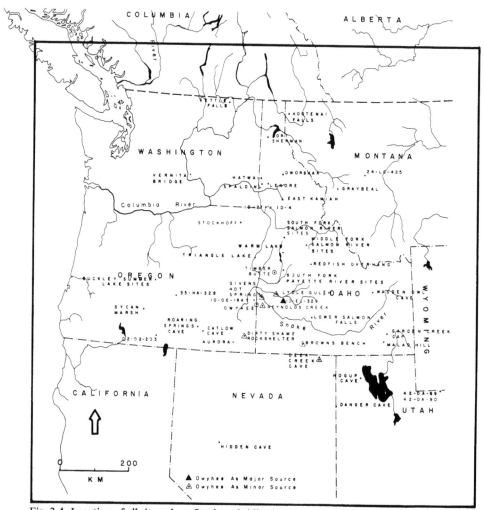

Fig. 3.4. Location of all sites where Owyhee obsidian has been identified. Sites where Owyhee obsidian occurs as the most frequent source are indicated by a solid triangle, while sites where Owyhee obsidian appears less frequently than other sources are indicated by an open triangle. Sites where Owyhee obsidian has not been identified are indicated by the dots.

temporal distribution with considerable confidence. Its earliest known appearance is in the Windust Phase component at Redfish Overhang where it was associated with determinations of 10,100 ± 300 B.P. (WSU 1396) and 9860 ± 300 B.P. (WSU 1395) (Gallagher, Sappington & Wylie 1979; Sargeant 1973, 62–3). Another Windust Phase projectile point at the Hatwai site was associated with a comparable determination of 9850 ± 870 B.P. (Tx 3158) (Ames, Green & Pfortner 1981, table 2). Elsewhere a typologically contemporaneous Folsom point was recovered along Reynolds Creek (Moe 1981). Timber Butte obsidian is present somewhat later at 7900–5900 B.P. at Dirty Shame Rockshelter (Aikens, Cole & Stuckenrath 1977, 8; Hanes & Sappington n.d.). At Givens Hot Springs Timber Butte artifacts were associated with a house pit dated 4620 ± 270 B.P. (Tx 3656) to 4060 ± 100 B.P. (Tx 3655) (Green 1980). More recent determinations of 1170 ± 90 B.P. (WSU 2061) to 790 ± 100 B.P. (WSU 2062) at Lydle Gulch and 1380 ± 100 B.P. (WSU 2199) (Sappington 1981a, table 5; Waldbauer, Knudson & Dechert 1981, 38) document its use across the region at that time. Finally, two very late determinations of 150 ± 70 B.P. (Tx 3090) at the Hatwai site and

140 ± 180 B.P. (GaK 8536) at the Graybeal site indicate that Timber Butte obsidian was used into the historic period (Ames, Green & Pfortner 1981, table 2; Flint & Sappington 1982).

The relatively more limited distribution of Owyhee obsidian at archaeological sites coincides with an association with fewer radiocarbon determinations, but its temporal span is comparable to that indicated for Timber Butte obsidian. Owyhee obsidian is present in all but one of the occupation zones at Dirty Shame Rockshelter encompassing the radio-carbon-dated sequence between 9500–400 B.P. (Aikens, Cole & Stuckenrath 1977, 8; Hanes & Sappington n.d.). At Givens Hot Springs an Owyhee item was recovered from a house pit associated with determinations of 4620 ± 270 B.P. (Tx 3656) and 4060 ± 100 B.P. (Tx 3655) (Green 1980). At Lydle Gulch Owyhee obsidian appeared prior to 1170 ± 90 B.P. (WSU 2061) and after 790 ± 100 B.P. (WSU 2062) (Sappington 1981a, table 5). Two projectile points from Deer Creek Cave assigned to the Humboldt and Elko series dated typologically 4000–870 B.P. (Green n.d.; Heizer & Hester 1978, 155–7, 159–60). Finally, a Desert side-notched series projectile point from 10-OE-329 dated typologically 850 B.P. to the historic period (Heizer & Hester 1978, 163–5; Moe, Eckerle & Knudson 1980, 76).

The production evidence for Timber Butte and Owyhee obsidian

While sources such as Bodie Hills in east central California, where a 'solid pavement' of worked and unworked obsidian occurs over an area of 8 km² have been reported (Singer & Ericson 1977), very little research has been conducted at sources where the material occurs as small scattered nodules. One exception is at the Whitehorse source in southeastern Oregon (fig. 3.1) where on-site analysis indicated that different reduction strategies were employed depending on the size of the nodules and the desired end products. These include one system designed to fabricate tools from small nodules by bipolar percussion similar to that described by Lowie for the Northern Shoshoni (Flenniken & Stanfill 1979, 15, 43). Knapping evidence associated with gravel deposits included decortication flakes, chunks, and split cobbles with some decortication flakes due to 'testing' the quality of the nodule. Satisfactory material was often removed to other sites.

The removal of cortex from nodules is commonly considered one of the first steps in lithic-tool production (Bucy 1971, 92; Muto 1971, 48; Muto 1976, 31; Womack 1977, 27). The presence of cortex on debitage is therefore indicative of the initial stages in knapping. Decortication flakes are common at quarry sites but they rapidly become scarce farther afield. For example, at sites in south-central Oregon where flakes and bifacial blanks obtained at the nearby Yamsay Mountain source (fig. 3.1) were reduced, cortex appeared on only some 2 to 5 per cent of the debitage because virtually all cortex had been removed where the flake or blank was collected (Flenniken, Warburton & Gilreath 1980, 9).

Examination of Timber Butte flakes indicates that in samples that include ten or more items, cortex is present on some 20 to 36 per cent (table 3.1). The percentage of flakes retaining cortex falls off with increasing distance. For example, at Givens Hot Springs 80 km southwest of Timber Butte cortex is present on over 36 per cent of the Timber Butte flakes; in comparison, at Kettle Falls 480 km northwest of the source, cortex appears on only 19 per cent of the Timber Butte flakes. Timber Butte cores are seldom recovered, as would be expected if the material was valued and used sparingly. However, they have been recovered at sites as distant from their point of origin as Kettle Falls and Brown's Bench. Timber Butte provided nearly 80 per cent of the obsidian cores at Lydle Gulch and it was likewise the most common source for obsidian cores recovered at other sites across central Idaho. Timber Butte cores are generally found at sites where this obsidian predominates; where other sources are most frequent, cores as an artifact class are usually absent, suggesting that the obsidian introduced to those sites from other sources was relatively more modified prior to arriving at those places.

Examination of items correlated to the Owyhee source indicates a similar pattern. At sites along Reynolds Creek in close proximity to the source, cortex was present on over 76 per cent of all Owyhee flakes, while farther away at Lydle Gulch cortex was present on 45 per cent of the Owyhee items (table 3.1). Owyhee cores have been infrequently recovered but this was the most prevalent source for cores at sites along Reynolds Creek (Moe 1981). Owyhee cores are second to those from Timber Butte at Lydle Gulch, but the largest obsidian item found there was a virtually unmodified nodule from which only a single 'testing' flake had been removed (Sappington 1981a, 147).

Conclusions

The reported sources for obsidian artifacts in southwestern Idaho were in Yellowstone National Park and central Oregon. Although several Oregon sources are in fact represented at Lydle Gulch, taken together they include just over 4 per cent of the total collection (Sappington 1981a, table 20). While Oregon obsidian accounts for 7 per cent of items from the Payette National Forest sites (Arnold 1981), these sources are insignificant at sites farther east. Similarly, Yellowstone-area obsidian represents 7 per cent of the Middle Fork collection (Sappington 1982) but it rarely occurs at sites farther west. Consequently, the reports indicating that the people of southwestern Idaho were dependent on nonlocal sources are not substantiated by the source identifications.

On-site investigation of the Timber Butte and Owyhee sources does not indicate that these materials were used to any considerable extent and certainly not on an interregional scale for some 10,000 years. However, the natural occurrence of the material as small nodules scattered over broad areas limits procurement options considerably. Biface production is an extremely wasteful use of raw material; replication experiments have demonstrated that as much as 92 per cent of the original nodule is discarded (Newcomer 1971, 90). Where material is abundant and occurs in nodules up to 20 cm in diameter such as at Bodie Hills (Singer & Ericson 1977, 174) biface production is possible and, in fact, is desirable in order to remove the relatively useless cortex prior to transportation. However, where material is scarce such as in southwestern Idaho, a production strategy oriented toward conservation of the raw material is a much more expedient approach.

Examination of the frequency falloff of Timber Butte and Owyhee obsidian in various directions indicates that simple distance was not the variable controlling aboriginal use of these materials. Rather, the location of the next neighboring source determines which sources appear at the archaeological sites. Timber Butte obsidian predominates at sites across central Idaho quite simply because it is the most accessible source. Elsewhere, such as toward the Oregon sources, Timber Butte obsidian disappears from archaeological contexts almost immediately. The Owyhee source is completely circumscribed by alternate sources, which accounts for its limited presence at archaeological sites. Despite a long period of use, this material is infrequent in archaeological collections and has yet to be identified at any site over 200 km from the source. While extra-areal visitors to southwestern Idaho brought in obsidian, they seldom took the local material back if they were returning to an area with alternate sources. Timber Butte and Owyhee obsidian were only popular in areas where they were the most accessible sources.

This procurement model is apparently not an isolated case. Investigation of nearly 700 obsidian artifacts from 20 sites in Chaco Canyon, New Mexico, has led to the identification of over a dozen sources in use there (Sappington & Cameron 1981). Several procurement strategies were in effect simultaneously depending on the occurrence of the various obsidians. Red Hill obsidian occurs as small scattered nodules and Chaco Canyon artifacts correlated to that source include small unmodified or tested nodules with cortex present on nearly half of over 100 items. Jemez obsidian is available in much greater concentrations of much larger nodules and Chaco Canyon artifacts correlated to that source are mostly tools with cortex present on only 15 per cent of over 400 items.

Anahim obsidian in central British Columbia also occurs in circumstances similar to those in southwestern Idaho. Despite the small size of the nodules and the absence of major quarry sites, Anahim obsidian has been identified at sites across southern British Columbia spanning a period of 9,000 years (Apland 1979; Nelson, D'Auria & Bennett 1975). Unworked nodules were transported away from the source area to conserve raw material for future use and retention of the cortex was suggested as providing an advantage in handling material during transportation (Apland 1979, 34–5).

All evidence concerning aboriginal procurement of the obsidian sources in southwestern Idaho, including the archaeological and ethnographic literature as well as on-site examinations, indicated that the Timber Butte and Owyhee sources were inconsequential within the aboriginal economy. However, application of X-ray fluorescence to this problem demonstrates that, on the contrary, these sources were of considerable significance on a regional scale for 10,000 years. The procurement strategy was not discernible due to the natural characteristics of the raw material but by examining the potential consumer sites it was possible to determine that tool production often occurred at considerable distances from the source areas. This manner of lithic-quarry production was extremely well adapted to the resource and provided the optimal means of exploiting these limited materials.

Acknowledgments

This project was supported by grants to the author from the Idaho State Historical Society and the Idaho Bureau of Mines and Geology. T. Green and M. Wells of the Historical Society and C. Knowles of the Bureau were especially helpful throughout the development of the program. D. Chance, R. Knudson, F. Leonhardy, and R. Sprague edited various versions of this chapter and provided much needed advice.

W. Eckerle and J. Moe drafted the maps, D. Forster took care of the statistics, M. Arnold assisted with the artifact descriptions, and dozens of other people provided the samples and information that this project required. Special thanks go to C. Carley who spent most vacations during the past four years collecting rocks and provided the encouragement necessary for the completion of this project.

References

Aikens, C. M., Cole, D. L. & R. Stuckenrath. 1977. Excavations at Dirty Shame Rockshelter, southeastern Oregon. *Tebiwa* 4. Pocatello, Idaho.

Alt, D. D. & Hyndmann, D. W. 1978. *Roadside geology of Oregon.* Missoula, Mont.: Mountain Press.

Ames, K. M., Green, J. P. & Pfortner, M. 1981. Hatwai (10 NP 143), interim report. *Boise State University Archaeological Reports* 9. Boise, Idaho.

Apland, B. 1979. Reconnaissance survey in the Rainbow Mountains region of west-central British Columbia. In B. O. Simonsen, ed., *The Annual Report for the year 1976; activities of the Provincial Archaeologist Office of British Columbia and selected research reports.* Victoria, B.C.

Arnold, M. 1981. Field report of the prehistoric archaeology of Long Valley, Idaho. Paper presented at the 34th Annual Northwest Anthropological Conference, Portland, Oreg.

Barnes, P. L. 1964. The archaeology of the Dean site: Twin Falls County, Idaho. *Washington State University Laboratory of Anthropology Report of Investigations* 25. Pullman.

Bennett, E. H. 1976. Reconnaissance geology and geochemistry of the South Mountain–Juniper Mountain Region, Owyhee County, Idaho. *Idaho Bureau of Mines and Geology Pamphlet* 166. Moscow.

Blyth, B. 1938. Northern Paiute bands in Oregon. *American Anthropologist* 40:402–5.

Boreson, K. 1979. Archaeological test excavations at 10-VY-165, South Fork Salmon River satellite facility, Valley County, Idaho. *University of Idaho Anthropological Research Manuscript Series* 57. Moscow.

Bowers, A. W. & Savage, C. N. 1962. Primitive man on Brown's Bench: his environment and his record. *Idaho Bureau of Mines and Geology Information Circular* 14. Moscow.

Bucy, D. R. 1971. A technological analysis of a basalt quarry in western Idaho. Master's thesis, Idaho State University, Pocatello.

Chaffee, E. B. 1931. Early history of the Boise region, 1811–1864. Master's thesis, University of California, Berkeley.

Chance, D. H., Chance, J. V. & Fagan, J. L. 1977. Kettle Falls: 1972 salvage excavations in Lake Roosevelt. *University of Idaho Anthropological Research Manuscript Series* 31. Moscow.

Corliss, D. W. & J. G. Gallagher. 1972. Final report 1970–1971 archaeological survey of the Dworshak Reservoir. Report on file, Pacific Regional Office, National Park Service, Seattle.

Davis, L. B. 1972. The prehistoric use of obsidian on the northwestern Plains. Doctoral dissertation, University of Calgary.

Ericson J. E. 1981. California obsidian: dating, exchange, and production. *British Archaeological Reports, International Series.*

Ericson, J. E., Hagan, & Chesterman, C. W. 1976. Prehistoric obsidian in California II: geologic and geographic aspects. In R. E. Taylor, ed., *Advances in obsidian glass studies.*, 218–39. Park Ridge, N.J.: Noyes Press.

Flenniken, J. J. & Stanfill, A. L. 1979. A preliminary technological examination of 20 archaeological sites located during the cultural resource survey of the Whitehorse Ranch public land exchange. Report of the Washington State University Laboratory of

Lithic Technology to the Bureau of Land Management, Vale District. Pullman.

Flenniken, J. J., Warburton, M. & Gilreath, A. 1980. A preliminary lithic technological examination of 20 archaeological sites in the Sycan Archaeological District, Oregon. *Report of the Washington State University Laboratory of Lithic Technology to the Fremont National Forest.* Pullman.

Flint, P. R. & Sappington, R. L. 1982. Geological sources of archaeological obsidian in the Flint Creek Valley area, Northern Rocky Mountain Region. *Archaeology in Montana* 23 (1): 19–26.

Gallagher, J. G., Sappington, R. L. & Wylie, H. G. 1979. Further analyses of the Redfish Overhang Haskett material cache. Paper presented at the 32nd Annual Northwest Anthropological Conference, Eugene, Oreg.

Green, J. P. n.d. Prehistoric land use patterns as indicated by focal lithic resources in the northeastern Great Basin. Ms. in preparation.

Green, T. J. 1980. Excavations at Givens Hot Springs 1979–1980. Paper presented at the 17th Great Basin Anthropological Conference, Salt Lake City.

Gruhn, R. 1961. The archaeology of Wilson Butte Cave, south-central Idaho. *Occasional Papers of the Idaho State College Museum* 6. Pocatello, Idaho.

Hanes, R. C. 1980. Lithic technology of Dirty Shame Rockshelter, in the Owyhee Uplands on the northeastern edge of the Great Basin. Doctoral dissertation, University of Oregon, Eugene.

Hanes, R. C. & Sappington, R. L. n.d. X-ray fluorescence analysis of obsidian artifacts from Dirty Shame Rockshelter. Ms. in preparation.

Harris, J. S. 1940. The White Knife Shoshoni of Nevada. In Ralph Linton, ed., *Acculturation in seven American Indian tribes.* New York: D. Appleton-Century.

Heizer, R. F. & T. R. Hester, 1978. Great Basin, In R. E. Taylor & C. W. Meighan, eds., *Chronologies in new world archaeology* New York: Academic Press.

Holmes, W. H. 1919. Handbook of aboriginal American antiquities, part I, *Bureau of American Ethnology* Bulletin 60, Washington, D.C.

Jack, R. N. 1976. Prehistoric obsidian in California I: geochemical aspects. In R. E. Taylor, ed., *Advances in obsidian glass studies*: 183–217. Park Ridge, N.J.: Noyes Press.

Jack, R. N. & Carmichael, I. S. E. 1969. The Chemical 'fingerprinting' of acid volcanic rocks. *California Division of Mines and Geology Special Report* 100:17–32.

Jackson, T. L. 1974. The economics of obsidian in central California prehistory: applications of X-ray fluorescence spectrography in archaeology. Master's thesis, San Francisco State University.

Kelly, I. T. 1932. Ethnography of the Surprise Valley Paiute. *University of California Publications in American Archaeology and Ethnology* 31 (3): 67–210.

Knudson, R., Stapp, D. T., Hackenberger, S.; Lipe, W. D. & Rossillon, M. P. 1982 A cultural resource reconnaissance in the Middle Fork Salmon River Basin, Idaho, 1978. *University of Idaho Anthropological Research Manuscript Series* 67. Moscow.

Liljeblad, S. 1957. Indian peoples in Idaho. Unpublished Ms., Idaho State University, Pocatello.

1972. *The Idaho Indians in transition, 1905–1960.* A special publication of the Idaho State University Museum, Pocatello.

Lowie, R. H. 1909. The Northern Shoshone. *Anthropological Papers of the American Museum of Natural History* 2 (2): 165–306.

Luedtke, B. E. 1979. The identification of sources of chert artifacts. *American Antiquity* 44 (2): 744–57.

Mattson, D. M., Knudson, R., Sappington, R. L. & Pfleiffer, M. A. 1983. Cultural resource investigations of the Dworshak Reservoir Project, North Fork Clearwater River, Northern Idaho. *University of Idaho Anthropological Research Manuscript Series* 74.

Minor, R. 1980. A survey for cultural resources for the Aurora Joint Venture Project, southern Malheur County, Oregon. Report to VTN Consolidated, Inc., Oregon State Museum of Anthropology, University of Oregon, Eugene.

Moe, J. M. 1981. Prehistoric settlement of Reynolds Creek Watershed, Owyhee County, Idaho. Paper presented at the 34th Annual Northwest Anthropological Conference, Portland, Oreg.

Moe, J. M., Eckerle, W. P. & Knudson, R., with an appendix by D. D. Gillette. 1980. Southwestern Idaho transmission line heritage resources survey, 1979. *University of Idaho Anthropological Research Manuscript Series* 58. Moscow.

Moe, J. M., Sappington, R. L. & Eckerle, W. P. 1980. Prehistoric occupation at Lower Salmon Falls. Paper presented at the 33rd Annual Northwest Anthropological Conference, Bellingham, Wash.

Moore, J. & Ames, K. M. 1979. Archaeological inventory of the South Fork of the Payette River, Boise County, Idaho. *Boise State University Archaeological Reports* 6, Boise.

Murphy, R. F. & Murphy, Y. 1960. Shoshone-Bannock subsistence and society. *Anthropological Records* 16 (7): 293–338.

Muto, G. R. 1971. A technological analysis of the early stages in the manufacture of lithic artifacts. Master's thesis, Idaho State University, Pocatello.

1976. The Cascade technique: an examination of a Levallois-like reduction system in early Snake River prehistory. Doctoral dissertation, Washington State University, Pullman.

Nelson, D. E., D'Auria, J. M. & Bennett, R. B. 1975. Characterization of Pacific Northwest Coast obsidian by X-ray fluorescence analysis. *Archaeometry* 17 (1):85–97.

Nelson, F. W. & Holmes, R. D. 1979. Trace element analysis of obsidian sources and artifacts from western Utah. Utah State Historical Society Division of State History. *Antiquities Section Selected Papers* 15, Salt Lake City.

Newcomer, M. H. 1971. Some quantitative experiments in handaxe manufacture. *World Archaeology* 3 (1): 85–94.

Nie, N. H., Hull, C. H., Jenkins, J. G., Steinbrenner, K. & Bent, D. H. 1975. *SPSS: statistical package for the social sciences,* 2nd ed. New York; McGraw-Hill.

Sappington, R. L. 1979. X-ray fluorescence analysis of obsidian flakes from 10-VY-165. Appendix A in Archaeological test excavations at 10-VY-165, South Fork Salmon River Satellite Facility, Valley County, Idaho. *University of Idaho Anthropological Research Manuscript Series* 57, Moscow.

1980a. Trace element characterization of obsidian and vitrophyre artifacts from Dirty Shame Rockshelter and correlations with geological sources. Appendix B in Lithic technology of Dirty Shame Rockshelter, in the Owyhee Uplands on the northeastern edge of the Great Basin, by R. C. Hanes. Doctoral dissertation, University of Oregon.

1980b. X-ray fluorescence analysis of obsidian artifacts from the Aurora Joint Venture Project, southern Malheur County, Oregon. Appendix A in Rick Minor, *A survey for cultural resources for the Aurora Joint Venture Project, southern Malheur County, Oregon.* Report to VTN Consolidated, Inc., Oregon State Museum of Anthropology, University of Oregon.

1980c. Obsidian trade and exchange at Kettle Falls, 7,000 B.C. to the 19th century. Paper presented at the 33rd Annual Northwest Anthropological Conference, Bellingham Wash.

1981a. The archaeology of the Lydle Gulch site (10-AA-72): prehistoric occupation in the Boise River Canyon, southwestern Idaho. *University of Idaho Anthropological Research Manuscript Series* 66. Moscow.

1981b. A progress report on the obsidian and vitrophyre sourcing project. *Idaho Archaeologist* 4 (4): 4–17.

1981c. *X-ray fluorescence analysis of artifacts from the Stockhoff and Marshmeadow sites, Union County, Oregon.* Report to Western Cultural Resource Consultants, Inc., Boulder, Colo.

1982. Obsidian procurement along the Middle Fork of the Salmon River in central Idaho. Appendix G in A cultural resource reconnaissance in the Middle Fork Salmon River Basin, Idaho, 1978. *University of Idaho Anthropological Research Manuscript Series* 67. Moscow.

Sappington, R. L. & Cameron, C. M. 1981. Obsidian procurement at Chaco Canyon, northwestern New Mexico, A.D. 500–1200. Paper presented at the 46th Annual Meeting of the Society for American Archaeology, San Diego.

Sappington, R. L. & Toepel, K. A. 1981. X-ray fluorescence analysis of obsidian samples. Appendix D in K. A. Topics and S. D. Beckham, Survey and testing of cultural resources along the proposed Bonneville Power Administration's Buckley–Summer Lake Transmission Line Corridor, Central Oregon. *Eastern Washington University Reports in Archaeology and History* 100-5, Cheney.

Sargeant, K. 1973. The Haskett tradition: a view from Redfish Overhang. Master's thesis, Idaho State University, Pocatello.

Shutler, M. E. & Shutler, R., Jr. 1963. Deer Creek Cave. *Nevada State Museum Anthropological Papers* 11. Carson City.

Singer, C. A. & Ericson, J. E. 1977. Quarry analysis at Bodie Hills, Mono County, California: a case study. In T. K. Earle & J. E. Ericson, eds., *Exchange systems in prehistory*: 171–88. New York: Academic Press.

Spinden, H. J. 1908. The Nez Percé Indians. *Memoirs of the American Anthropological Association* 2.

Steward, J. H. 1938. Basin-plateau aboriginal sociopolitical groups. *Bureau of American Ethnology Bulletin* 120, Washington, D.C.

1941. Nevada Shoshoni. Cultural element distributions XIII. *Anthropological Records* 4 (2).

Toups, P. A. 1969. The early prehistory of the Clearwater Valley, north-central Idaho. Doctoral dissertation, Tulane University, New Orleans.

Waldbauer, R. C., Knudson, R. & Dechert, T. 1981. The East Kamiah site, Clearwater River Valley, as known from test excavations. *University of Idaho Anthropological Research Manuscript Series* 64, Moscow.

Womack, B. R. 1977. An archaeological investigation and technological analysis of the Stockhoff basalt quarry. Master's thesis, Washington State University, Pullman.

Chapter 4

The 63-kilometer fit
C. A. Singer

A number of simple geoarchaeological techniques were used to study the distribution of prehistoric populations and to reconstruct behavior patterns at sites in the Colorado Desert region of southern California. Samples from two quarry-workshop sites, RIV-1814 and RIV-1819, at opposite ends of Chuckwalla Valley, were systematically collected and micromapped, and knapping technology was reconstructed. Distribution patterns for the artifact forms and materials from these quarry workshops were determined by examining samples from other sites within and adjacent to Chuckwalla Valley. Hypotheses regarding the long duration of site utilization and late prehistoric/protohistoric occupation by Numic peoples were verified. Artifact production analysis, including refitting of flakes and cores, proved highly successful. One set of flakes from RIV-1819 near the Colorado River was refitted with a core from an occupation site 63 kilometers away, at the opposite end of the valley. Prehistoric quarry workshop sites are viewed as an underexplored resource with great potential for yielding important data on technology and population demography.

Introduction

Prehistoric quarry workshops were an important early focal point in American archaeology (e.g., Holmes 1919) and such sites are once again beginning to attract the attention of archaeologists concerned with the reconstruction of extinct cultural systems. Today's trend toward technological, functional, and behavioral lithic analyses is well grounded in past research (e.g., Holmes 1894) but owes much of its current foundation to the pioneering work of scholars such as S. A. Semenov (1964) in the U.S.S.R., F. Bordes and others in France, and Don Crabtree and his many students in the U.S. But, for the most part, quarry workshops remain understudied, probably because of the variety of problems they seem to present. The areal extent and vast quantity of artifacts can be the most overwhelming aspects of a quarry-workshop site — debitage usually covers thousands of square meters, sometimes square kilometers, and frequencies in the hundreds of thousands or millions of artifacts are ordinarily present (Singer & Ericson 1977). Therefore, most scholars have attempted to describe finished tools and other unique pieces at these sites, primarily for dating purposes, products manufactured, worked materials, and sometimes the manufacturing or lithic-reduction technique(s) represented. Viewed in the broader perspective, prehistoric stone-quarry-workshop sites are not adequately represented in the archaeological literature (cf. Brézillon 1971; Hester & Heizer 1973; Schmider 1973; Swanson 1975; Moeller & Reid 1977; Wright 1977; Johnson 1978). This is especially true in California, even though these sources are often well known and documented (Heizer & Treganza 1944; Ericson 1981). The focus of this study, therefore, is directed at two points: first, to show the feasibility of tracing the movements of prehistoric populations by examining the distribution of stone materials from specific sources or quarry-workshop sites, and second, to demonstrate the utility of a pair of complementary techniques for observing and reconstructing extinct behaviors or patterns, that is, micromapping and reconstruction of

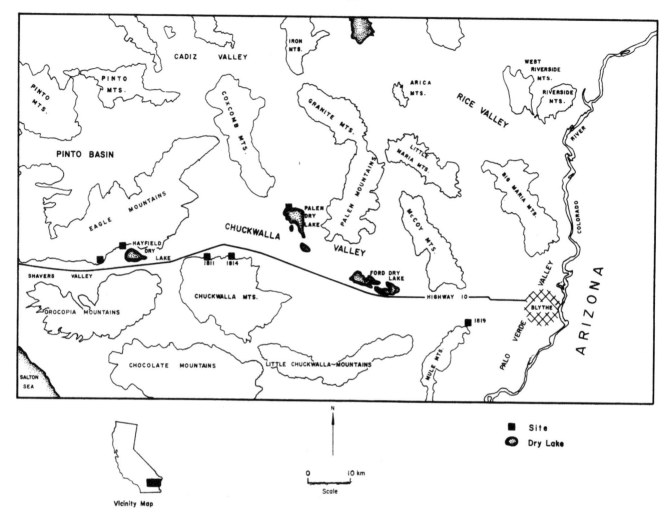

Fig. 4.1. Chuckwalla Valley and vicinity, Riverside County, California.

artifacts from quarry workshops and other sites (Leroi-Gourhan & Brézillon 1972; Singer 1975; Schild 1976). The study area is located in the desert region of southeastern California, in and around the Chuckwalla Valley in eastern Riverside County (fig. 4.1). Situated in the southwestern corner of the greater Colorado Desert, Chuckwalla Valley drains eastward into the Colorado River near Blythe. The natural and cultural resources of the region have been described in several recent publications (King & Casabier, 1976; Davis, Brown, & Nichols 1980; Warren *et al.* 1981). A number of dry lake beds (Palen, Ford, and Hayfield) mark the floor of the valley, which is flanked on all sides by punctuated ranges of steep, rugged mountains. To the east are the terraces of the Colorado River, to the South is the Imperial Valley and Salton Sea, to the west is the Coachella Valley, and to the north the Pinto Basin.

Within this region are several hundred recorded prehistoric site localities, including about a dozen stone-quarry workshops situated either on a Colorado River terrace, or within one of the flanking mountain ranges. The two quarry workshop sites described here, RIV-1819 and RIV-1814, are located on the terrace south of Blythe, and at the foot of the Chuckwalla Mountains in the south-central portion of the Valley, respectively. Site RIV-1814 consists of a number of discreet localities on and around a small granite hill about 2 km north of the base of the Chuckwalla Mountains (fig. 4.2). Site RIV-1819 is located 56 km east-southeast of RIV-1814 near the base of the Mule Mountains, on the Palo Verde Mesa, several km west of the Colorado River. Much of the archaeological data on the area were collected during the first half of this century by M. J. Rogers (n.d., 1939, 1966); most data remain unpublished or have limited circulation (Carrico, Quillen & Gallegos 1982).

Ethnology

While much is known about the general history and prehistory of the region, almost nothing specific is known about the Chuckwalla Valley, the materials which occur there, nor the people who inhabited the specific areas in question. Populations in this region appear to have been extremely mobile, particularly in the late prehistoric and early historic periods.

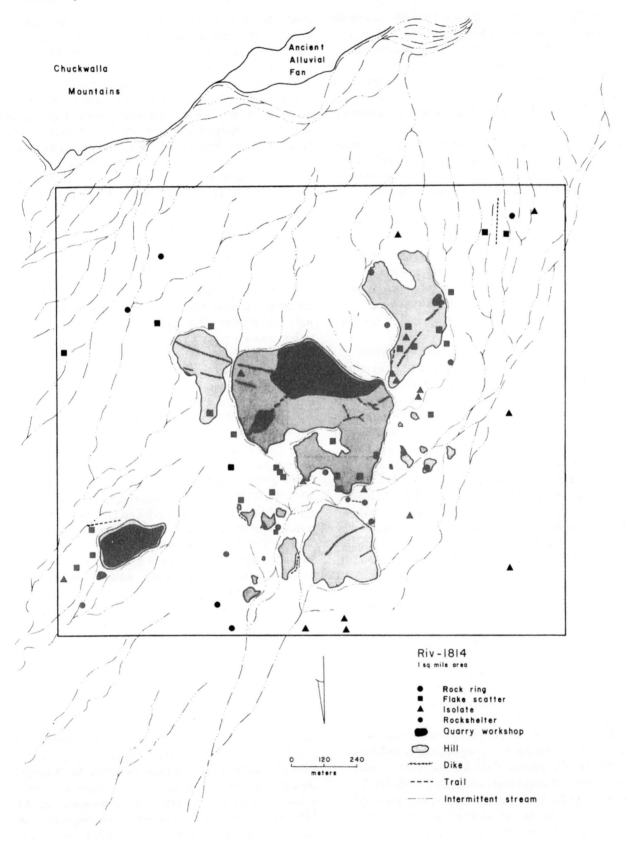

Fig. 4.2. Site RIV-1814, the District, with quarry-workshop areas and associated site locations and features.

Native Cahuilla and Chemehuevi Indians still occupy the area and maintain ownership of some traditional lands and knowledge. Some of their knowledge has been shared and made available to anthropologists. Of particular interest here are the works of Powell (Fowler & Fowler 1971), Rogers (n.d., 1939, 1966), Strong (1929), Bean (1972), Bean *et al.* (1972, 1974, 1978), Laird (1976), and ethnographers of neighboring groups.

Contemporary and recent Native American settlements that can be documented in the region are Chemehuevi towns along the Colorado River near RIV-1819, Cahuilla towns in nearby Coachella Valley, a Desert Cahuilla hamlet at Cottonwood Spring (RIV-937), and a Serrano village at Twenty-nine Palms. RIV-1819 falls squarely within the territory of the Chemehuevi (a southern Numic or Piute subgroup). Even though the Chemehuevi claimed no land south of the Maria Mountains (Laird 1976, 8), RIV-1819 was apparently within their territory. At least four groups occupied, at one time or another, the territory around RIV-1819: the Chemehuevi, Mojave, Halchidoma, Cahuilla, and the Quechan (Ortiz 1979, ix).

RIV-1814 and the main body of Chuckwalla Valley are not clearly delineated on existing maps of tribal or ethnic territories (cf. Strong 1929; Kroeber 1953; Fowler & Fowler 1971; Bean 1972; Laird 1976; Roth 1977; Bean & Vane 1978; Warren *et al.* 1981). However, RIV-1814 lies close to the west end of Chuckwalla Valley near the boundary of three cultural groups: Cahuilla, Serrano, and Chemehuevi. Bean and Vane (1978, 5—20) present a strong case for Chemehuevi expansion westward into Serrano territory, possibly before A.D. 1000. If true, Desert Chemehuevi (*Tiiraniwiwi*, Laird 1976, 8) most likely occupied RIV-1814 and the entire Chuckwalla Valley. According to Schroeder (1979), the entire Chuckwalla Valley was occupied by Hakataya pottery-making people beginning some time around A.D. 500, and continuing on to the present day.

At the present time, there is no evidence that suggests Cahuilla groups moved into the area following the desiccation of Lake Cahuilla (Wilke & Lawton 1975), nor is there any information linking Chuckwalla Valley with either the Pinto Basin to the north, or the Corn Spring area within the Chuckwalla Mountains to the south. These east-west-trending Valleys may well have been relatively closed exploitation zones. a hypothesis that can be investigated by examining the distribution of unique lithic materials.

Alternatively, Chuckwalla Valley could easily have served as an east—west trade route or corridor to and from the Pacific. The Chemehuevi, Cahuilla, and Diegueño were involved in the well-established exchange network which existed between the Santa Barbara Channel region and the Colorado River—Arizona southwest region (Sample 1950; Davis 1961; Bean & Vane 1978; King 1981).

The entire desert area, including Chuckwalla Valley, is crisscrossed by ancient trails. Trails run along both sides of the valley connecting villages, springs, and other important places. Some run north—south parallel to the Colorado River, while others run east—west connecting the river and the Pacific Coast (Johnson & Johnson 1957; Davis 1961).

Because of its orientation and location, the Chuckwalla Valley and its resources may have been neutral territory unclaimed by neighboring groups. This type of territorial arrangement may be also demonstrable archaeologically and may have considerable antiquity here in California and elsewhere. Bean and Vane (1978, 5-1 to 5-7) discuss the nature and extent of the 'Pacific Ocean —Great Plains Trade Routes' within the southern California region. They provide a list of twenty-nine commodities involved in this exchange system which could have passed through the Chemehuevi Valley on the established trail network.

Stone Age peoples of southern California undoubtedly had sophisticated and detailed knowledge of stones and lithic resources within their territory, but because stone tools were quickly abandoned after contact, and traditional territorial rights and boundaries changed, much of this knowledge has been lost. Knowledge of a general nature and specific information on ceramic materials (clays and tempers) survived longer, probably because ceramic technology persisted longer than tool manufacture. Since most ethnographers were geologically naive, mineralogical information was often overlooked, ignored, and lost. Nevertheless, there is some information on use of resources and minerals for the area (Hohenthal 1950; Laird 1976; Levi 1978).

Powell recorded only 15 Western Numic terms for rocks and minerals and even fewer among central and southern Numic groups (Fowler & Fowler 1971, 131, 143—4, 156, 164, 174, 249, 253). Among the Diegueño, Hohenthal (1950) recorded 17 different terms, and Levi (1978) has recently reviewed the use of crystals among southern California Yumans. For the Chemehuevi, Laird (1976, 87—9) has recorded about 20 terms and a number of songs, myths, and tales which contain information about stones and stone artifacts. Chemehuevi knowledge of geology and lithic resources was quite extensive and precise, based on information that has survived (Laird 1976, 86—9). Schroeder (1979, 100, 102, 105) states that the Hakataya were 'rock oriented people' who used 'percussion hand mullers' (angular, abrading hammerstones), made 'plainware ceramics with temper containing mica', and maintained an extensive network of trails throughout their heartland.

Of particular importance for the interpretation of the archaeological data is the information on the ownership and distribution of specific resources. Resources tended to be owned by unilineal corporate groups among the Chemehuevi, the Cahuilla, and the Diegueño (lineages, clans, sibs, and sometimes moieties). Therefore, sites in the study area, like RIV-1814 and RIV-1819, were most likely 'owned' by one particular group at any given time. The small RIV-1819 site may have been the property of a single lineage or village unit, but RIV-1814 could have served the needs of a far larger group and was probably utilized by several families or lineages comprising a single corporate entity. Certain distinctive stone materials, such as different grades of felsite, basalt, milky and clear quartz, and various colored cherts and chalcedony, could have been used to indicate territorial boundaries. As a result, they may not have been distributed beyond the limits of a specific territory. Unique materials, like the 'candy-cane' quartzite and the felsites in this study, present some fascinating possibilities for tracing the movement of people and materials across desert valleys and mountain ranges.

Archaeology

The Chuckwalla Valley falls within Rogers's 'Central Aspect,' even though Riverside County is not delineated on his published map (1966, 151). It is clear that the region has been occupied for at least the past 10,000 years by a succession of populations identified by Rogers (1939) as the Playa/San Dieguito, Pinto/Gypsum, Amargosa, Yuman, and Shoshonean Culture Complexes. While the span of occupation has more than tripled since Rogers's first estimates, the cultural sequence has changed little (Davis, Brown & Nichols 1980, 125; Warren *et al.* 1981, 47). What has changed in recent years is the popular conception of native California political and economic organization (Bean & King 1974), coupled with a renewed appreciation of and for traditional knowledge and oral literature (i.e. ethnoarchaeology).

In order to determine the general prehistoric settlement pattern(s) in this region, copies of official state site location maps and Site Record Forms for all recorded archaeological sites were examined along with site data abstracted by M. A. Brown, Malki Museum, Banning. At the close of 1980, more than 200 separate prehistoric sites had been recorded on the eight maps studied: Pinto Basin, Coxcomb Mountains, Palen Mountains, Midland, McCoy Spring, Sidewinder Well, Chuckwalla Mountains, Hayfield, and a portion of Chuckwalla Springs, USGS 15-minute topographic quadrangles.

Sites appear to cluster around springs, wells, and other obvious and important features or resources. Site types include villages with cemeteries, other occupation sites with and without pottery, large and small concentrations of sherds and stone artifacts, rock-art sites (petroglyphs and pictographs), rock shelters with perishable items, rock rings and stone circles, intaglios, and cleared areas, along with a vast network of trails and trail segments, markers, and shrines.

A number of quarry-workshop sites other than RIV-1814 and RIV-1819 were also noted. Many gravel sources are recorded near the Colorado River in the Palo Verde Mesa area, and other outcrop or block quarry workshops are known in the Eagle Mountain and Coxcomb Mountain areas. Three probable village locations were also noted, at Palen Dry Lake, Granite Well, and Hayfield Canyon, all in the central or western part of Chuckwalla Valley. Another distinctive group of sites is clustered around the base of the Mule Mountains near RIV-1819. The cluster of sites which surrounds the RIV-1814 quarry-workshop hill does not appear to represent a village location, but rather an extensive array of temporary habitation and special activity sites (fig. 4.2).

Determining precisely when the quarry workshops were used is a most difficult matter, primarily due to the lack of datable organic material and diagnostic artifact forms such as projectile points, ceramics, or beads. Three criteria can be used, with due caution, to estimate the relative ages of the materials at these sites: (1) degree of weathering (patination at RIV-1814 and sandblasting at RIV-1819); (2) artifact size, and to a lesser degree location; and (3) association with dated materials from other sites in the immediate vicinity (e.g., ceramics, organics, or biface forms). Using these criteria it appears that RIV-1814, and probably RIV-1819 as well, has been used periodically since the beginning of the Holocene. This estimate is consistent with the models and chronologies proposed by Rogers (1939, 1966), Davis, Brown & Nichols (1980), Warren (1966) and others. These data are also supportive of Rogers's notion that Chuckwalla Valley was occupied, abandoned, and reoccupied by a succession of ethnic groups.

Artifacts from various sites in Chuckwalla Valley show a progression of forms and styles, as do the sites themselves. The region may have been densely settled during Playa/San Dieguito times, but only sporadically visited or inhabited during Pinto/ Gypsum times, and then reoccupied by later Yuman and Shoshonean peoples (Chemehuevi and Cahuilla). The region was certainly involved in the coastal-interior exchange system during the Late Horizon of California prehistory (*c.* A.D. 500–1769), and probably earlier. Rogers (n.d.) made special note of a 'channel islands steatite tube' at the Hayfield Canyon site (San Diego Museum of Man site number C-55), probably a Chumash Phase M-5 tube bead from *c.* A.D. 800 or earlier (King 1981, 224–36).

Obvious difficulties notwithstanding, a fairly precise chronology for the Chuckwalla Valley seems entirely possible, considering the number of recorded sites and the demonstrated presence of organic debris and abundant ceramics. Rogers's unpublished notes and existing collections provide an ample data base. For example, a thermoluminescent dating curve can probably be generated using ceramic samples collected by Rogers from the Chuckwalla, Coachella, and Imperial Valleys, and the Palo Verde Mesa. Furthermore, within the past several years new information has been developed on the origin and age-dating of desert varnish (Dorn 1981), sourcing of stone materials (Earle & Ericson 1977; Ericson 1981; Dodge, Millard & Elsheimer 1982), sandblasting as a chronological indicator (Borden 1971), and the dating of weathered basaltic and andesitic rocks (Colman & Pierce 1981; Colman 1982). All of these techniques could be combined to establish a chronology.

Sites and materials

The workshops at RIV-1814 and RIV-1819 appear to have functioned solely as lithic extraction and reduction sites,

Table 4.1. *Volume estimates for workshop areas on RIV-1814 Hill.*

Sample areas	Est. total workshop area	Total cores and anvils observed	Total worked pieces observed	Total flakes
SW area (4 loci)	50 + m²	4 test blocks 1 discoidal core 1 polyhedral core	1 core/hammer	65 +
SC area (25 loci)	3,875 + m²	500 + block cores 6 + polyhedral cores 1 + discoidal core 70 + block anvils	3 biface preforms 17 core/hammers 18 core/hammers 1 large denticulate 1 flake scraper	38,000 +
SE area (13 loci)	2,700 + m²	70 + block cores 6 + block anvils	1 core/hammer 5 core/scrapers 4 biface preforms	5,000 +

centers for the acquisition and manufacture of stone cores, flakes, blades, and assorted tools and 'blanks'.

Both sites appear to consist of a sequence of distinct, sometimes isolated but sometimes overlapping, workshops or knapping loci. Since there are far too many of these workshop loci to have been simultaneously occupied, particularly at RIV-1814, chronological differences can be assumed, and such phenomena lend themselves well to diachronic analysis (Singer & Ericson 1977). The sites were relatively undisturbed and lacked subsurface components, conditions which allow for selective sampling and behavioral reconstruction. The basic sampling strategy for these sites consisted of a surface reconnaissance of each site, followed by formulation of a sampling design and set of data collection procedures. These procedures included topographic mapping of the sites, extensive black-and-white and color-slide photography, characterization of workshop areas and artifact materials, and intensive microsampling (mapping and collecting) of selected areas. The analytical strategy called for the interpretation of patterning and distributions observed with the aid of both macro- and micromaps, precise identification of the stone materials and artifact forms at each site, and preliminary evaluation of the production modes at various localities.

Initial investigations were directed at determining the overall size and configuration of the deposits; intensive micromapping and sampling followed.

RIV-1814

The area designated RIV-1814 is an 810-acre parcel which encompasses a block and tabular felsite source with a concentration of workshop areas which cover the greater part of the west and south slopes of a granite hill (fig. 4.2). The hill is bisected by narrow, parallel dikes of intrusive material, herein designated felsite, which breaks into angular blocks and

cascades down the south slopes as angular chunks and tabular clasts. Dikes are generally several meters thick, but the detached blocks and chunks seldom exceed a meter in diameter. Three distinct grades of felsite were distinguished: (1) light to medium gray, fine grained, sometimes with small, dark phenocrysts; (2) dark gray to greenish, glassy; and (3) banded dark and light gray, glassy material. The last two materials are uncommon in the central and western portions of the site where grainy gray rocks predominate.

Several other lithic materials are available at RIV-1814. Milky-white quartz and blocks of ferruginous crystalline quartz occur, as well as small plagioclase crystals and a wide variety of altered and unaltered granites. Other quarry-workshop sites near RIV-1814, at the southern end of the Coxcomb Mountains and Hayfield Canyon, for example, have yielded similar felsite materials. However, each suite of materials seems to be unique and distinct. Each outcrop or area of outcrops seems to yield a rather restricted set of rocks which share a particular set of characteristics such as color, phenocrysts, and texture. Rogers (n.d.) also noted this distinction which is evident in the collections at the San Diego Museum of Man and the University of California, Los Angeles.

Workshop debris at RIV-1814 covers about 50,000 square meters on the main granite hill. At least 25 separate workshop areas can be detected, ranging in size from about 4 m², probably a single knapper's work space, to about 1,000 m². The larger areas contain dozens, and in some cases hundreds, of overlapping individual work areas. Data collected during the survey of the outcrop and slope areas yielded the estimates of production and debris listed in table 4.1. These estimates are as much as 50 to 100 per cent too low, based upon subsequent data derived from the analysis of three 3-by-3 meter collection units.

Samples from three separate areas at RIV-1814 were

systematically sampled, analyzed, and compared. Every artifact within the sample units was collected and micro-mapped, washed and cataloged. Refitting of flakes and reconstitution of cores was then undertaken. A total of 587 pieces was analyzed from a total sample area of 27 m². The items recovered from each sample unit are described in Table 4.2.

The technology manifested at RIV-1814 is relatively simple and straightforward. Blocks or tabular chunks were first tested by striking off an edge or corner, and if deemed appropriate the piece was further reduced by direct, hard hammer percussion. No indirect or pressure flaking was detected at the RIV-1814 workshops. Most, if not all, of the cores, preforms, tools, blades, and flakes studied appear to have been produced using hammers and anvil stones of like material (i.e. felsite); indeed, battered cores (angular hammer-stones) and block anvils occur with regularity in the workshop areas. Macroflakes and macroblades (for future use as cores and core tools), polyhedral and shaped platform cores (hemi-spherical, pyramidal, keeled, and tortoise forms for the pro-duction of regular flakes and blades), core tools of similar form (cores used as choppers, scrapers, and planning tools),

Table 4.2. *Artifacts recovered from Test Units at RIV-1814.*

Unit 1 — Moderately large material with cores up to 20 kg. Primarily grainy to glassy gray material with light to heavy weathering.

   14 cores
   1 flake scraper
   1 macroflake scraper
   1 angular core-hammer
   18 blades
   230 flakes of all sizes
      (9 reconstitutions totaling 28 pieces)

Unit 2 — Medium-size material. Primarily grainy to glassy gray material with light to heavy weathering.

   11 cores
   4 biface preforms
   9 blades
   186 flakes of all sizes
      (11 reconstitutions totaling 42 pieces)

Unit 3 — Smaller material, no cores or blocks over 500 g. Glassy gray and greenish material with little weathering.

   12 cores
   2 possible tools (core chopper and cutting tool)
   2 biface preforms
   7 blades
   80 flakes
      (6 reconstitutions totaling 19 pieces)

and small to moderate size biface preforms were regularly produced at the workshops. Hardwood or antler billets may have been used in biface preform and tool production.

Figures 4.3 and 4.4 show the distribution of flakes, cores, and other artifacts in two sampled areas at RIV-1814, including pieces which were reconstituted or refitted. Each of the three area samples from RIV-1814 show clear and measurable quantitative and qualitative differences. For example, there are marked differences in the distribution of the various felsite materials and the artifacts made from them.

The patina or desert varnish on some materials from RIV-1814 ranges from a glossy black, through shades of reddish brown, to a tan or beige on very old, unmodified pieces, and from a dull, dusty graying to a deep reddish brown on flakes, cores, and other artifacts. Discoloration is always heaviest on the underside of artifacts found *in situ*; however, deterioration can be detected on the upper surfaces, particu-larly on older(?) pieces. Using the patination as a guide, the oldest and heaviest concentrations of debris seem to occur nearest the dike outcrops, and the optimum degree of weathering seems to correlate with the largest artifacts. In the south-central area, the material in Unit 1 seems to be the oldest, closely followed by that from Unit 2 in the south-eastern area. Thus, the oldest workshop areas at the site may be nearest the crest of this hill, followed by materials on the western and southern slopes. The youngest areas, that is the last places exploited for felsite, may be the southeastern slopes in the vicinity of Unit 3. It is important to note that examples showing varying degrees of weathering, including light, moderate, and profound discoloration, were found in all sampled areas.

Although several unmodified quartz and granite pebbles were found in workshop areas at RIV-1814, they probably were carried to the site. Absolutely no exotic or imported stones or tools of any type were found in the quarry-workshop areas. These few pieces appear to have been carried up from the desert floor just below the workshop areas. The quartz which occurs on the RIV-1814 hill was apparently not utilized for chipped-stone tools or hammers, although worked pieces of quartz were found on the desert floor near the workshop areas. Aside from their lithic resources, the quarry-workshop areas are somewhat marginal in terms of other available materials, although the surrounding desert is a diverse and relatively rich resource zone with many plants and animals.

Occupation seems to have been in areas close to the actual quarry workshops but on the desert floor, or in nearby hills and canyons. Intensive reconnaissance of the desert floor around the RIV-1814 quarry-workshop hill showed that this zone was the focal point for a range of activities throughout the occupational history of the valley. Some of these satellite sites have already been destroyed by natural agencies, and many others have been damaged or destroyed by modern 'off-road' activities. A very similar situation seems to exist in the vicinity of RIV-1819.

RIV-1819

The area designated RIV-1819 is a gravel quarry workshop of rather minor proportions in contrast to RIV-1814. RIV-1819 yielded artifacts and natural gravels of variously colored cherts (red, yellow, brown, black, mottled), chalcedony, quartzites, black glassy basalt, a few kinds of durable metavolcanics, and an occasional piece of fossilized wood. Materials occur on and below the surface of eroded ancient terrace segments along the Colorado River. They are cemented in a hard limestone matrix a few centimeters below the surface.

The spectrum of materials here is bewildering. Rogers assumed that the suites of materials from each of the many small segments along the river were indistinguishable. However, his hypothesis remains untested and unproven.

RIV-1819 consists of three separated terrace segments, only one of which was sampled. Here, an area of approximately 5,000 m² was carefully mapped and collected, with eight areas micromapped and excavated. Twenty-one workshop areas

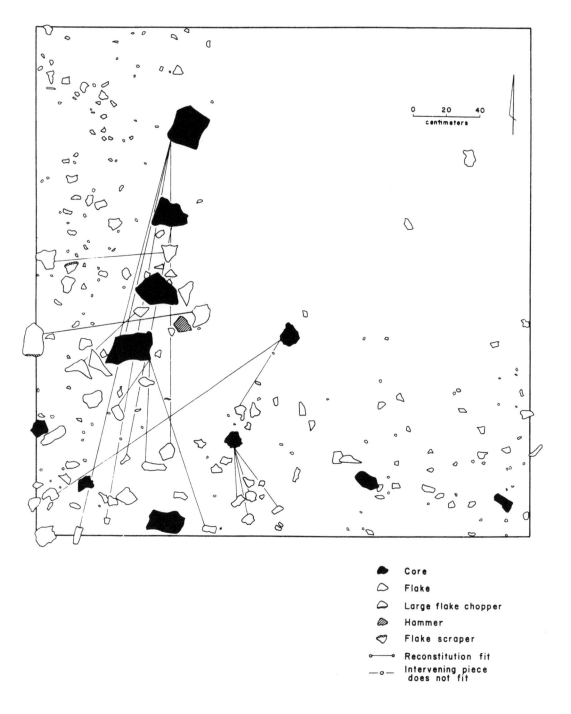

Core
Flake
Large flake chopper
Hammer
Flake scraper
Reconstitution fit
Intervening piece does not fit

Fig. 4.3. Core production in the south central area; Test Unit 1, RIV-1814 quarry-workshop hill.

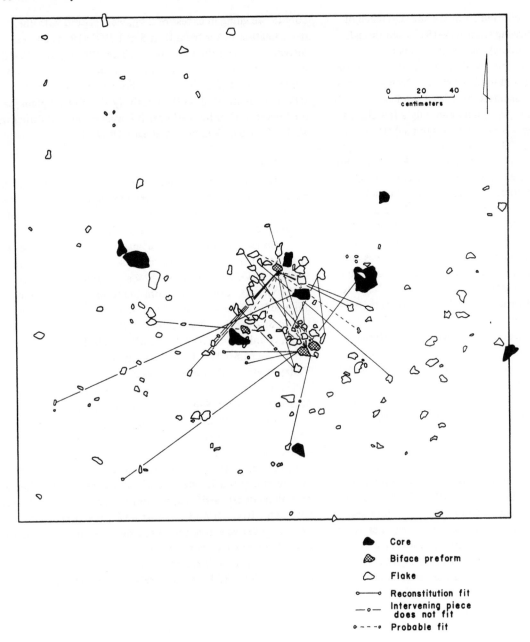

Core

Biface preform

Flake

Reconstitution fit

Intervening piece
does not fit

Probable fit

Fig. 4.4. Biface preform production in the southeastern area; Test Unit 2, RIV-1814 quarry-workshop hill.

were collected, and 380 artifacts recovered and analyzed (listed in table 4.3). Of these, only six pieces were identifiable tools: two quartzite spherical hammers, three flake scrapers (two quartzite, one felsite), and a quartzite flake denticulate. The microsampled and collected areas produced a total of 25 reconstitutions of 142 pieces, which is 37 per cent of all the artifacts recovered in the sample. Cores and flakes of chert, quartzite, and chalcedony appear to have been the primary materials removed from RIV-1819.

Reduction technology at RIV-1819 is not dissimilar from that at RIV-1814 in spite of the gross differences in site structure and lithic materials. Ends or edges of small cobbles and pebbles were obliquely struck (with another pebble) to

expose the unweathered interior of the stone. Usually, the decortication flake was discarded and the core removed for use elsewhere, but in some instances additional core preparation or shaping was done. Occasionally, cores were immediately reduced to flakes and blades, but only a few flakes or blades were carried away, while the rest was ignored. Only two spherical quartzite flaking hammers were recovered at RIV-1819 along with a single quartzite anvil fragment. Here, too, only direct percussion with hard hammers was evident, while tool production and retouch are virtually absent.

Finished tools are rare at RIV-1819, as they are at RIV-1814. Cores, flakes, and occasional blades appear to have been the products removed from the site. Evidence of biface manufacture is missing from RIV-1819 even though projectile points were probably one of the items made from RIV-1819 flakes and blades. Projectile points and tools seem to have been made and used elsewhere. Occupation and use of the resources here seems to have been brief and sporadic. No evidence of habitation was found and only a few sherds were recovered from the workshop areas sampled (Carrico, Quillen & Gallegos 1982, 99–106).

A large proportion of the artifacts from RIV-1819 shows some weathering, and a small number are extremely eroded from sandblasting. Discoloration is not present, but some degree of surface erosion from sandblasting is detectable on practically every piece. The most weathered and eroded pieces are large decortication flakes ('teshua flakes'), most of which have no matching core or kindred flakes. Smaller flakes and cores seldom show equivalent degrees of surface erosion, but all have matted or dulled surfaces. It is therefore difficult to sort chronologically the various materials and artifacts (flakes and cores) from RIV-1819.

Unlike the quarry workshops at RIV-1814, internal variability is not outstanding at RIV-1819, yet certain things about the site and its materials are evident. After sampling the naturally occurring gravels, and then comparing them with the artifacts, it was noticed that most of the natural unmodified stones remaining at the site were small pebbles averaging just over 50 g in weight. On the other hand, the abundance of large decortication flakes recovered clearly indicates that many cores larger than 50 g were removed from the site. One example is a core made from an unusual cobble of pink and white 'candy-cane' quartzite found at RIV-1811. It seems that this cobble was originally found and tested for quality and soundness at RIV-1819, where three flakes were struck from one end of the rock and discarded, and the core carried westward to a small site near Granite Wells, RIV-1811. The source of the quartzite is certain since the nearly complete

cobble, weighing in excess of 2 kg, was refitted with the decortication flakes from Unit 5 at RIV-1819. The linear distance between the two sites is 63 km (39 miles). RIV-1811 is a small habitation site containing felsite tools and flakes derived from RIV-1814 located about 5 km to the east. RIV-1811 is situated on the relatively flat alluvial plain just northwest of Granite Well near the western end of Chuckwalla Valley (Carrico, Quillen & Gallegos 1982, 81–3).

Discussion

It is important to discuss the spatial distribution of stone materials from both of the quarry workshops which can be traced some distance from their sources, and the nature of the behavior of the stone knappers at both locations.

Collections submitted for material and chronological analysis for this study came from a series of controlled samples made at RIV-1814 and RIV-1819 and a number of other sites in the vicinity. Collections from the following sites were analyzed: the Baker Site (SBR-350; Glennon 1974), the Calico Site (SBR-1500A; Singer 1979), Palen Dry Lake (RIV-201), Granite Well (RIV-1811, RIV-1820, RIV-1823), and from 22 separate localities along the south side of Chuckwalla Valley (Carrico, Quillen & Gallegos 1982). In addition, collections from more than 100 sites were examined at the Museum of Man in San Diego (Rogers collections).

Stones from the Pinto Basin area do not appear prominently in the Chuckwalla Valley (Campbell & Campbell 1935). Collections from sites along the northern edge of Palen Dry Lake (Rogers's site C-82, and Koloseike's Areas A and B) contain abundant basalt, cherts, chalcedony, felsite, rhyolite, and crystalline quartz artifacts, but only a few pieces which may have come from RIV-1814. Most felsite materials appear to have been derived from sources in the Coxcomb Mountains, Eagle Mountains, or northerly sources. River gravel cherts and chalcedonies are well represented, particularly at RIV-201 (Rogers's site C-82A, and Koloseike's Area A), a large village

Table 4.3. *Artifacts and materials of RIV-1819.*

Sample Units	Quartzite cores	Quartzite flakes	Chert cores	Chert flakes	Basalt cores	Basalt flakes	Chalcedony cores	Chalcedony flakes	Other cores	Other flakes	Totals
Misc. surface	8	4	15	24	–	–	2	1	–	–	54
1	–	5	3	22	1	55	–	1	–	3	90
2	–	2	5	25	–	1	1	1	–	–	35
3	–	2	5	33	–	–	–	2	–	–	42
4	8	2	13	54	–	3	–	5	1	–	86
5	1	10	–	4	1	–	–	3	–	–	19
6	2	4	2	11	–	–	–	–	–	–	19
7	–	–	5	19	–	–	–	4	–	–	28
8	–	4	1	2	–	–	–	–	–	–	7
Totals	19	33	49	194	2	59	3	17	1	3	380

site with a cremation area, ceramics, milling equipment, and many small projectile points. Black basalt bifaces and flakes characterize a second collection, from Koloseike's Area B (possibly RIV-187), which may correspond to the 'Amargosa I settlement' collected by Rogers (site C-82). Rogers's Palen Lake site sample contains a variety of bifaces and tools of different materials, including some felsites similar to RIV-1814 materials. Several quarry-workshop sites have been recorded about 10 km west of RIV-201 on a hill near Victory Pass (RIV-1140, 1141, 1142). The Palen Lake felsites may come from these sources.

According to Rogers (n.d.), the Hayfield Canyon area has 'considerable flaking about, and the entire mesa is a quarry' (site C-55). No felsite from RIV-1814 was noted here or at Lost Palms Canyon farther west.

Only three sites in the RIV-1814 area sample yielded artifacts made from stones other than local felsites. Felsite artifacts occur with greatest frequency at the 70+ loci within the 810-acre sampled block surrounding the RIV-1814 hill, that is, the RIV-1814 District (Carrico, Quillen & Gallegos 1982, fig. 7-25). The site loci recorded within this area include five other quarry-workshop localities, two rock shelters (one with ceramics and a midden deposit), 15 locations with one or more rock rings, four locations with one or more cleared circles or areas, 8 separate trail segments, 18 locations of isolated flakes or tools, and 45 locations with stone artifacts, nearly all felsite (fig. 4.2).

At least 20 of the sites in the RIV-1814 district sample appear to be habitation loci, while others are small work and activity areas associated with particular resources such as trees or other plants. Tools and other artifacts from the 810-acre area sample were not collected or carefully analyzed by the surveyors, but records indicate that the majority of pieces appear to be flakes and cores; the few tools identified seem to be knives and scrapers. All of the tools recovered from the workshop areas at RIV-1814, with the exception of the hammerstones, are heavy-duty woodworking implements, choppers and scrapers, quite possibly for manufacturing digging or prying sticks and shafts of various kinds. Absolutely no habitation debris was associated with these tools, nor were any clear signs of habitation found anywhere on the hills where the quarry workshops occur (Carrico, Quillen & Gallegos 1982, 141–56).

To date, none of the felsites from RIV-1814 has been identified in collections from outside Chuckwalla Valley. Artifacts produced at the RIV-1814 quarry workshops appear, so far, to have a very limited distribution. Identical felsite materials have been identified in collections from Palen Dry Lake, but occur in major proportions at Granite Well and at sites along the south side of Chuckwalla Valley, from the eastern margins of Ford Dry Lake to a point just south of Hayfield Dry Lake, a distance of about 70 km.

Nearly the opposite may be said of the materials from RIV-1819. Pebble cores and other artifacts made of cherts, quartzites, and chalcedonies, undoubtedly from RIV-1819

and other similar sources along the river, are found all over the valley. Terrace gravel artifacts found as far west as Granite Well, RIV-1811, firmly link this area with a specific site on the Palo Verde Mesa, RIV-1819, and the inhabitants of the Colorado River. The 63 km distance between the refitted artifacts from RIV-1819 and RIV-1811 argues against Rogers's (n.d.) contention that Colorado River Yumans never occupied the west end of Chuckwalla Valley, and supports the Chemehuevi expansion hypothesis (Bean & Vane 1978). Characterization of the felsites and other unique stones which occur in this region will undoubtedly be a key element in our future attempts to understand the dynamics of prehistoric populations.

On a smaller scale, the actions of individual knappers can easily be detected and measured at both RIV-1819 and RIV-1814. One chert pebble core from Unit 4 at RIV-1819 was matched with 25 accompanying flakes, while in another 2-by-2 m test area, Unit 1, one reconstitution matched a basalt core 14 flakes and 39 tiny chips and spalls (shatter).

The larger test units at RIV-1814 (3-by-3 m) show more detail. Unit 1 (fig. 4.3) revealed two core production and reduction stages and several tools, while Unit 2 (fig. 4.4) illustrated the production of biface preforms. The massive block cores and macroflakes seen on the west side of Unit 1 (fig. 4.3) contrast sharply with the prepared platform, pyramidal cores, and flakes in the southern part of the unit. The concentration of biface preforms and debitage flakes in the center of Unit 2 (fig. 4.4) is interesting for several reasons. This unit shows clearly the bidirectional distribution of removals from the two sets of biface preforms, and the exact size of the knapping area used by two knappers working simultaneously, or a single knapper who shifted his orientation 180 degrees. The cores here are smaller and flatter than those in Unit 1 and were probably preform rejects. Biface production appears to distribute debitage in an arc of 120 degrees or more, quite unlike the distributions seen in Unit 1 where core production occurred.

The artifact distribution in Unit 1 (fig. 4.3) reflects the energetics of both block-on-block and hard-hammer, direct percussion core production, along with a secondary activity, tool production and use. The large flake scraper and even larger chopper are assumed to be woodworking implements, although their actual function is unknown. Furthermore, since the RIV-1814 hill is solid granite and devoid of trees, wood from the valley floor must have been transported to the workshop areas. It is suggested that the chopper and scraper were used for the production and maintenance of levers (pry bars) or digging sticks, and batons utilized in the workshop areas. The four flakes removed from the platform core in the south-central part of Unit 1 (fig. 4.3) may have been removed with a wood baton.

A complete picture of core production can be reconstructed from fig. 4.3. First, a large core hammer was used to split two large flakes into four pieces and modify one into a large chopper. The chopper was used to make a lever to move a large block into a favorable position for splitting. A somewhat smaller block, possibly the one closest to the hammerstone, was hurled, splitting the larger block into two manageable pieces. These pieces were further reduced with the angular hammer, which may also have been used to make the flake scraper. The chopper and scraper were then used to fashion a shaft, possibly of desert hardwood, and once sufficiently shaped, the conical platform core was further modified with the baton. Interestingly, the debitage arc here (15 to 60 degrees) is far smaller than for biface production represented in Unit 2 (fig. 4.4), although the distances traveled by flakes may be greater.

Both production areas sampled share one feature in common, a cleared or artifact-free zone adjacent to the knapping area. But because these zones have no artifacts and manifest no features, they may be purely natural phenomena, open spaces between workshop areas. While additional archaeological samples from quarry workshops are needed, these data may be compared with existing data from habitation sites and experimental (replicative) studies.

Summarizing and concluding remarks

We have attempted to show how geoarchaeological research in an isolated desert valley in California can reveal information about the movement and resource utilization of prehistoric populations by tracing the distribution of specific rock types. We have also tried to demonstrate the application of combining the techniques of micromapping and artifact reconstitution which serve to identify and reassemble extinct behavior patterns.

Long-term occupation and utilization has been demonstrated for both areas and the potential for further work in the region is excellent. One technological trend is clear — stone tools and other artifacts became smaller as time passed (cf. Ericson 1982). This general trend has been noted at other quarry workshops (Singer & Ericson 1977) and may be due, in part, to the depletion of raw materials at the sources. It is also clear what kinds of objects were manufactured and carried away from these sites, as well as their final destinations. Further analyses may eventually yield information on the size and structure of social units in the remote past.

Quarry-workshop sites are viewed as ideal laboratories for the study of lithic reduction technology, as well as ideal locations for reconstructing the actual behavior of stone knappers. Between 10 and 40 per cent of all the artifacts recovered from the two sites sampled could be reconstituted, and the use of the microsampling and micromapping techniques made the refitting of specimens relatively simple. Selective sampling of other specific loci could have led to even higher reconstitution frequencies.

Quarry-workshop analysis should be no more difficult than the analysis of any other accumulation of rocks. Examples of most artifact forms are already stored in museums, and a virtually complete guide to the analysis of bifaces, preforms, production errors, and debitage is now

available (Callahan 1979). Excellent and precise research schemes and techniques are available which make it possible to study and analyze quarry-workshop sites in a systematic and culturally meaningful fashion.

Finally, in light of the constant changes in our perceptions of the nature of archaeological research, it seems fruitful periodically to re-examine works such as Holmes (1894, 1919), Bryan (1950), White (1963), Binford and Binford (1966), Movius *et al.* (1968), Wilmsen (1967), Geier (1973), Bucy (1974), Swanson (1975), Wright (1977), and Hayden (1979), and then re-evaluate our own ideas about ancient quarry workshops.

Acknowledgments

Many people contributed to this study, but the following persons I wish to thank again: R. Kaldenberg and J. Reed of the Bureau of Land Management, Riverside, California; D. Quillen of Westec Services, San Diego; Ken Hedges of the San Diego Museum of Man; A. L. Christensen of the University of California, Los Angeles, Museum of Cultural History; B. Biggs and W. Schumaker, who assisted with the cartography; and T. Caruso and J. Knaack, who typed the manuscript. J. E. Ericson edited the final version of the manuscript.

References

Bean, L. J. 1972. *Mukat's people: the Cahuilla Indians of Southern California.* Berkeley: University of California Press.

Bean, L. J. & King, T. F. 1974. *'ANTAP – California Indian political and economic organization.* Ramona, Calif.: Ballena Press.

Bean, L. J. & Vane, S. B. eds., 1978. *Persistence and power – a study of native American peoples in the Sonoran Desert and the Devers–Palo Verde high voltage transmission line.* Report prepared for Southern California Edison Company by Cultural Systems Research, Inc., Menlo Park.

Binford, L. R. & Binford, S. R. 1966. A preliminary analysis of functional variability in the Mousterian of Levallois facies. *American Anthropologist* 68 (2), part 2: 238–95.

Borden, F. W. 1971. *The use of surface erosion observations to determine chronological sequence in artifacts from a Mojave Desert site.* Archaeological Survey Association of Southern California, paper no. 7.

Brézillon, M. N. 1971. *La dénomination des objets de pierre taillée.* Supplement 4, *Gallia Préhistoire.* Paris: C. N. R. S.

Bryan, K. 1950. *Flint quarries – the sources of tools and, at the same time, the factories of the American Indian.* Peabody Museum Papers XVII (3), Harvard University, Cambridge, Mass.

Bucy, D. R. 1974. A technological analysis of a basalt quarry in western Idaho. *Tebiwa* 16 (2): 1–45. Pocatello.

Callahan, E. 1979. The basics of biface knapping in the eastern fluted point tradition: a manual for flintknappers and lithic analysts. *Archaeology of Eastern North America* 7 (1): 1–180, Washington, Conn.

Campbell, E. W. C. & Campbell, W. H. 1935. *The Pinto Basin Site.* Southwest Museum Papers 9, Los Angeles.

Carrico, R. L., Quillen, D. K. & Gallegos, D. R. 1982. *Cultural resource inventory and national register assessment of the southern California Edison Palo Verde to Devers transmission line corridor (California portion).* Report prepared for the U.S. Department of the Interior, Bureau of Land Management, by Westec Services, San Diego.

Colman, S. M. 1982. *Chemical weathering of basalts and andesites:*

evidence from weathering rinds. Geological Survey Professional Paper 1246, U.S. Department of the Interior, Washington, D.C.

Colman, S. M. & Pierce, K. L. 1981. *Weathering rinds on andesitic and basaltic stones as a Quaternary age indicator, Western United States.* Geological Survey Professional Paper 1210, U.S. Department of the Interior, Washington, D.C.

Davis, E. L. Brown, K. H. & Nichols, J; 1980. *Evaluation of early human activities and remains in the California desert.* Report prepared for U.S. Department of the Interior, Bureau of Land Management, by Great Basin Foundation, San Diego.

Davis, J. T. 1961. *Trade routes and economic exchange among the Indians of California.* Reports of the Archaeological Survey 54. University of California, Berkeley.

Dodge, F. C. W., Millard, H. T., Jr. & Elsheimer, H. N. 1982. *Compositional variations and abundances of selected elements in granitoid rocks and constituent minerals, central Sierra Nevada batholith, California.* Geological Survey Professional Paper 1248, U.S. Department of the Interior, Washington, D.C.

Dorn, R. I. & Oberlander, T. M. 1981. Microbial origin of desert varnish. *Science* 213:1245–7.

Earle, T. K. & Ericson, J. E. 1977. *Exchange systems in prehistory.* New York: Academic Press.

Ericson, J. E. 1981. *Exchange and production systems in California prehistory.* BAR International Series 110, Oxford.

1982. Production for obsidian exchange in California. In *Contexts of prehistoric exchange.* New York: Academic Press, 129–48.

Fowler, D. D. & Fowler, C. S. eds. 1971. *Anthropology of the Numa: John Wesley Powell's manuscripts on the Numic peoples of western North America, 1868–1880.* Contributions to Anthropology 14, Smithsonian Institution, Washington, D.C.

Geier, C. R. 1973. The flake association in archaeological interpretation. *The Missouri Archaeologist* 35 (3–4): 1–36, Columbia.

Glennon, W. S. 1974. The Baker site (SBr-54). *Pacific Coast Archaeological Society Quarterly* 10 (2): 17–34, Costa Mesa, Calif.

Hayden, B. ed. 1979. *Lithic use-wear analysis.* New York: Academic Press.

Heizer, R. F. & Treganza, A. E. 1944. Mines and quarries of the Indians of California. *California Journal of Mines and Geology*, Report XL of the State Mineralogist, pp. 291–359, Sacramento, Calif.

Hester, T. R. & Heizer, R. F. 1973. *Bibliography of archaeology I: experiments, lithic technology and petrography.* Addison-Wesley Module in Anthropology 29:1–56.

Hohenthal, W. D., Jr. 1950. Southern Diegueño use of knowledge of lithic materials. *Kroeber Anthropological Papers* 2, Berkeley, Calif.

Holmes, W. H. 1894. Natural history of flaked stone implements. *Memoirs of the International Congress of Anthropology:* 120–39, Chicago.

1919. *Handbook of aboriginal American antiquities.* New York: Burt Franklin Reprints.

Johnson, F. J. & Johnson, P. H; 1957. An Indian trail complex of the central Colorado Desert: a preliminary survey. *Reports of the Archaeological Survey* 37:22–34, University of California, Berkeley.

Johnson, L. L. 1978. A history of flint-knapping experimentation, 1838–1976. *Current Anthropology* 19 (2): 337–72, Chicago.

King, C. D. 1981. The evolution of Chumash society: a comparative study of artifacts used in social system maintenance in the Santa Barbara channel region before AD 1804. Ph.D. dissertation, Department of Anthropology, University of California, Davis.

King, C. D. & Casabier, D. G. 1976. *Background to historic and prehistoric resources of the east Mojave desert region.* Report prepared for the U.S. Department of the Interior, Bureau of Land Management, Riverside, Calif.

Kroeber, A. L. 1953. *Handbook of the Indians of California.* Berkeley, Calif.: California Book Co.

Laird, C. 1976. *The Chemehuevis.* Banning, Calif.: Malki Museum Press.

Leroi-Gourhan, A. & Brézillon, M. 1972. *Fouilles de Pincevent. Essai d'analysée ethnographique d'un habitat Magdalenian* (Section 36). Supplément 7, *Gallia Préhistoire.* Paris: CNRS.

Levi, J. M. 1978. Wii'ipay: the living rocks – ethnographic notes on crystal magic among some California Yumans. *Journal of California Anthropology* 5 (1): 42–52, Malki Museum, Banning, Calif.

Moeller, R. W. & Reid, J. (compilers). 1977. *Archaeological bibliography for eastern North America.* Eastern States Archaeological Federation and American Indian Archaeological Institute, Washington, Conn.

Movius, H. L., Jr., David, N. C., Bricker, H. M. & Clay, R. B. 1968. The analysis of certain major classes of Upper Palaeolithic tools. *American School of Prehistoric Research Bulletin* 26, Peabody Museum, Harvard University, Cambridge, Mass.

Ortiz, A. (vol. ed.). 1979. *Handbook of North American Indians – Southwest* 9. Washington, D.C.: Smithsonian Institution.

Rogers, M. J. n.d. Unpublished field notes on file at San Diego Museum of Man.

1939. *Early lithic industries of the Lower Basin of the Colorado River and adjacent desert areas.* San Diego Museum Papers 3, San Diego.

1966. *Ancient hunters of the Far West.* San Diego: Union-Tribune Publishing Co.

Roth, G. 1977. The Calloway Affair of 1880: Chemehuevi adaptation and Chemehuevi-Mohave relations. *Journal of California Anthropology* 4 (2): 273–86, Malki Museum, Banning, Calif.

Sample, L. L. 1950. Trade and trails in aboriginal California. *Reports of the Archaeological Survey* 8, University of California, Berkeley.

Schild, R. 1976. The final palaeolithic settlements of the European Plain. *Scientific American* 234 (2): 88–99.

Schmider, B. 1973. *Bibliographie analytique de préhistoire pour le Palaeolithique Supérior European.* Paris: CNRS.

Schroeder, A. H. 1979. Prehistory: Hakataya. In A. Ortiz, ed., *Handbook of North American Indians – Southwest,* 9:100–7, Smithsonian Institution, Washington, D.C.

Semenov, S. A. 1964. *Prehistoric technology.* London: Cory, Adams & Mackay.

Singer, C. A. 1975. The non-flint tools and other lithic artifacts from Solvieux – a preliminary analysis. Master's thesis, Department of Anthropology, University of California, Los Angeles.

1979. A preliminary report on the analysis of Calico lithics. In W. C. Schuiling, ed., *Pleistocene man at Calico. San Bernardino County Museum Quarterly* 26 (4): 55–63, Redlands, Calif.

Singer, C. A. & Ericson J. E. 1977. Quarry analysis at Bodie Hills, Mono County, California: a case study. *Exchange systems in prehistory*: 171–88, New York: Academic Press.

Strong, W. D. 1929. *Aboriginal society in southern California.* University of California Publications in American Archaeology and Ethnology 26, Berkeley.

Swanson, E. ed., 1975. *Lithic technology – making and using stone tools.* The Hague: Mouton Publishers.

Warren, C. N. ed., 1966. *The San Dieguito type site: M. J. Rogers' 1938 excavation on the San Dieguito River.* San Diego Museum Papers 5, San Diego.

Warren, E. von Till, Crabtree, Robert H., Warren, C. N., Knack, M. & McCarty, R. 1981. *A cultural resources overview of the Colorado Desert planning units.* Report prepared for the U.S. Department of the Interior, Bureau of Land Management, Riverside, Calif.

White, A. M. 1963. Analytic description of the chipped-stone industry from Snyders Site Calhoun County, Illinois. *University of*

Michigan Museum of Anthropology Papers 19: 1–70, Ann
  Arbor.
Wilke, P. & Lawton, H. W. 1975. Early observations on the cultural
  geography of Coachella Valley. *Ballena Press Anthropological
  Paper* 3: 9–36; Ramona, Calif.
Wilmsen, E. N. 1967. *Lithic analysis and cultural inference: a Palaeo-*

Indian case. Ph.D. dissertation, Department of Anthropology,
  University of Arizona, University Microfilms, Inc., Ann Arbor.
Wright, R. V. S. ed., 1977. *Stone tools as cultural markers: Change,
  evolution and complexity*. Prehistory and Material Culture
  Series no. 12, Australian Institute of Aboriginal Studies,
  Canberra.

Chapter 5

Monopoly or direct access? Industrial organization at the Melos obsidian quarries
R. Torrence

Quarry-production analysis can profitably be applied to the study of prehistoric exchange. By adopting a systems perspective, hypotheses about the nature of past human behavior at a quarry site can be derived from theories of raw material exchange and then tested against the data collected from the site. Using this innovative approach to study the obsidian quarries at Sta Nychia and Demenegaki on the island of Melos, Greece, the monopolization of source areas and/or the use of a highly organized, efficient, and specialized production technology were predicted in conjunction with commercial, market exchange of obsidian in the Aegean area. Detailed site survey and sampling strategies combined with analyses of the tools and techniques involved in quarrying obsidian and the manufacture of preform blade cores did not confirm the hypotheses. In contrast, the actual reconstruction of obsidian procurement on Melos as inefficient, unsystematic, and undertaken for short periods by nonspecialist laborers supports the opposing theory for direct access to the sources.

Introduction

The study of prehistoric obsidian exchange in the Aegean basin has been greatly facilitated by the application of a wide range of physicochemical techniques to a very substantial series of samples. These analyses have demonstrated that for all practical purposes the outcrops on the Cycladic island of Melos were the sole sources of the obsidian found in varying quantities on sites, dating from about 12,000 to 3,000 years B.P., which are distributed over the whole of the Greek peninsula and throughout the Aegean islands (Cann & Renfrew 1964; Renfrew, Cann & Dixon 1965; Dixon, Cann & Renfrew 1968; Dixon 1976; Shelford *et al.* 1982; Aspinall, Feather &

Renfrew 1972; Durrani *et al.* 1971; McDougall 1978; Perlès 1979). Unfortunately for the Aegean area the conventional methods for investigating prehistoric exchange systems by utilizing the spatial distribution patterns of the material in question, particularly in the shape of the falloff curve (e.g., Renfrew, Dixon & Cann 1968; Hodder 1974; Renfrew 1975, 1977; Sidrys 1976, 1977; Ammerman, Matessi & Cavalli-Sforza 1978); cannot be employed to illuminate the methods of obsidian exchange because the requisite quantitative data for reconstructing these patterns are not presently available for an adequate sample for sites. Nevertheless, there are other very valuable sources of data often neglected by scholars working in other parts of the world which could not be used to test hypotheses about the nature of prehistoric exchange. For the study of Aegean obsidian exchange the two very extensive obsidian quarry-workshop sites at Sta Nychia and Demenegaki on Melos (fig. 5.1) provide alternative and very important classes of data relevant to this problem. Although previous research on prehistoric exchange has ignored quarry sites, it can be argued that this class offers a tremendous potential for testing hypotheses about past exchange systems. I intend to demonstrate, by means of a case study, that the methodology employed by quarry-production analysis has a very important role to play in the study of prehistoric exchange systems.

Although numerous studies of quarries in materials suitable for the production of chipped-stone artifacts have been

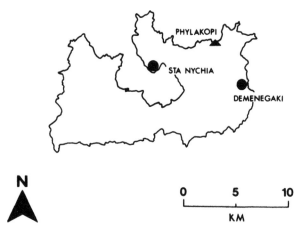

Fig. 5.1. Melos, showing locations of obsidian quarries at Sta Nychia and Demenegaki and the major Bronze Age settlement at Phylakopi.

carried out in many parts of the world (e.g., Holmes 1900, 1919; Bryan 1950; Bucy 1974; Losey 1971; Spence & Parsons 1972; McCoy & Gould 1977; Singer & Ericson 1977; Leach 1978; Engelen 1975, 1981; references in Hester & Heizer 1973), the value of this class of archaeological site for the analysis of prehistoric exchange has never been fully appreciated. This situation has arisen partly because theoretical discussions concerning quarry sites have rarely transcended the rather sterile debate about the date and function of the bifacially retouched artifacts, the 'blanks', found at many North American sites (e.g., Holmes 1894; Bryan 1950; Bucy 1974, 8−16). This state of affairs seems to be coming to an end. In a very stimulating article, Singer and Ericson (1977) have rightly stressed the value of quarries for studies of prehistoric exchange; furthermore, they were able to monitor the rate of output of obsidian at Bodie Hills Quarry in California. Although their study, along with similar work carried out by Ericson (1981), goes a long way toward exploring the potential of quarry analysis, there are still many other avenues that should be examined.

New lines of research will be possible, however, only when fresh theoretical approaches to quarries are adopted. One fairly simple perspective has been especially valuable for my research on Melos. Exchange can be envisaged as a system linking the source of a raw material with a number of consumers in any one of many possible means (e.g., Renfrew 1975, 42) with interactions or feedbacks between components of the system. Because in this way quarries, the sources for the exchanged material, have a link with all other parts of the system, much of the behavior taking place throughout the system will necessarily have had feedbacks on the behaviour at the quarries and, consequently, should be recoverable from the archaeological remains at such sites. For this reason ideal bases from which reconstruction of exchange systems can be carried out are the raw material sources. For example, commercial traders or middlemen can be expected to have extracted raw material in methods quite different from those of con-

sumers procuring their own supplies directly. Similarly, production by specialist knappers at settlement sites should also affect, for example, the methods, timing, and standardization of raw material procurement. Once the position of quarries within the exchange system has been recognized, it becomes possible to transcend the limited descriptive goals utilized in the past and to test hypotheses about past exchange. Although the results thus far have not always been completely unambiguous, I hope that the summary of my work on Melos will stimulate scholars to undertake detailed analyses of the other quarry sites and to search out improved methods for illuminating the processes of prehistoric exchange through quarry production analysis.

Theories for Aegean obsidian exchange

The nature of Bronze Age obsidian exchange was first discussed at the turn of the century by the British excavators of the site at Phylakopi on Melos (fig. 5.1). They reasoned that the growth and decline of this large, nucleated settlement with its impressive fortifications was due to fluctuations in the profits derived from control of the obsidian outcrops at Sta Nychia and Demenegaki (Bosanquet 1904; Mackenzie 1904). Although Bosanquet and Mackenzie are not explicit about the mechanisms that generated the wealth reflected in the finds from Phylakopi, it appears that they envisaged a system of obsidian trade carried out within a competitive market economy. From this model of a commercial exchange system two hypotheses can be derived to account for the supposed profits. First, the existence of some form of monopoly over access to the raw material would be necessary for Phylakopi to prevent competition from other would-be suppliers. Mere proximity to a resource need not of itself confer competitive advantage; instead, ownership or some means of control would be required. Archaeological evidence supporting the hypothesis for control of the right of access to the obsidian includes evidence of boundaries delimiting the obsidian sources and a means for enforcing restricted access, such as sentry posts, defended harbors, customs houses, and so on.

In contrast, in the absence of monopoly over supply, the value of the goods would have been regulated by consumer demand; consequently, profits could only accrue by reducing the cost of production, which in this case is most likely to have been labor. Reduction in the labor input involved in obsidian procurement could probably best be achieved by increasing either the efficiency of the technology utilized or by improving the organization of production. Therefore, the second hypothesis states that if prehistoric Aegean obsidian exchange was integrated into a commercial economic system, then there should be evidence for a highly organized and efficient industry at the quarry sites. Several archaeological expectations follow from this hypothesis. Specialized and sophisticated tools should be present. It can also be predicted that an organized industry would contain aspects of specialization which in this case would be reflected in the following: (1) method of selection for deposits to be mined, (2) specialized use of space at the sites for particular tasks, and (3) use of a specialist labor force. Finally, the consequences of craft specialization could be detected archaeologically by the presence of several characteristics: high degree of skill involved in production; low incidence of errors; small quantities of waste per unit of manufacture; standardization in methodology, and therefore in the size and shape of the output and the waste by-products; and presence of temporary or permanent shelters for laborers and their families at the site or in the near vicinity. In order for the theory of commercial trading to be supported, only one of the hypotheses needs to be found to be irrefutable but if both are disproved, the theory must be considered inadequate.

Renfrew (1969, 1972, 1973, 1975; Renfrew, Cann & Dixon 1965, 241) has adopted a view nearly diametrically opposed to that of the early British archaeologists on Melos. He has argued that obsidian was not incorporated into a commercial economy and, furthermore, that it had no effect on the rise of complex society at Phylakopi or in the Aegean at large. Instead, Renfrew feels that consumers probably traveled to Melos to obtain their own supplies of obsidian, although he also suggests that down-the-line exchange may have taken place concurrently on the Greek mainland (Renfrew 1972, 440, 442–3, 471; 1973, 85; 1975, 43; Renfrew, Cann & Dixon 1965, 241). In contrast to the earlier idea of obsidian trade, Renfrew's theory predicts that a series of unrelated, poorly organized activities took place at the obsidian quarries on Melos. The very generalized nature of his description of obsidian exchange, however, makes a detailed list of archaeological expectations difficult. Since Renfrew's direct-access model of obsidian exchange (cf. Ericson 1981) is virtually the exact opposite of the Bosanquet-Mackenzie commercial trading theory, the negation of one can be considered support for the other. In the following sections, after describing how the primary data was collected, I will briefly summarize the results of the research at Sta Nychia and Demenegaki directed toward evaluating these two theories of exchange.

Mapping and sampling procedures

Located on top of high, isolated plateaus overlooking majestic cliffs that drop off steeply to the sea, the Melos obsidian quarries are certainly very impressive sites (fig. 5.2). At both Sta Nychia and Demenegaki there are abundant quantities of obsidian and also plentiful evidence that these have been extensively exploited in the past. In each case approximately a square kilometer of land is littered with the debris from quarrying and core manufacture. Although very dense concentrations of debitage and eroded cobbles up to a meter thick in several places are found adjacent to the largest outcrops, smaller scatters can also be seen on the surrounding slopes and even on the tops of all the hills in the area (fig. 5.3). On the more gentle slopes small plots have been cleared and terrace walls built, but at Demenegaki these fields are no longer planted; the crops which are sown at Sta Nychia have to fight for survival in the stony soil which comprises mainly flakes, cores and chips.

Fig. 5.2. View of the main obsidian source area at Demenegaki. The depressions in the cliff and the pinnacle of rock (lower right) are the remains of prehistoric quarrying.

The quarries were rediscovered as early as 1836 by Fielder (1841, 2; 369–445) but the first archaeological survey of the sites was conducted by Mackenzie (1897, 77; Bosanquet 1904, 216–8). After Renfrew visited the sites for the purpose of collecting samples for characterization studies, he published simplified maps and brief descriptions of some of the sources and working areas (Renfrew, Cann & Dixon 1965; Renfrew 1973) but he did not undertake research on the abundant waste by-products at the sites. This task was not attempted until the summers of 1974 and 1975 when I carried out an extensive program of mapping and sampling at both sites, followed by a more detailed study of selected artifacts in the summers of 1976 and 1977 (Torrence 1981; 1982). The more recent fieldwork was integrated within an island-wide study of settlement and land use on Melos (Renfrew & Wagstaff 1982) organized largely to complement the findings of the concurrent excavations at the large, nucleated Bronze Age site of Phylakopi by Renfrew for the British School at Athens.

A major aim of the fieldwork undertaken at Sta Nychia and at Demenegaki in 1975 was to map the obsidian debitage which is spread so liberally over both sites. Since, for the purposes of these maps, it was not feasible to distinguish between artifacts and unmodified nodules which had either been rejected by prehistoric quarry laborers or had eroded from the outcrops, I simply plotted the density of the total ground covered by obsidian using a series of classes ranging from 0 to 100 per cent (Torrence 1981). Simultaneously, I also recorded the position of the present outcrops of obsidian and described them in terms of a series of characteristics which are reported below.

Well-delimited regions on the density maps can be translated into 'working areas' in behavioral terms, with the

Fig. 5.3. A view of the density of the obsidian debitage at Sta Nychia.

interval of 25 m over the areas of both sites which had the highest density of surface obsidian. At each intersection of the grid I counted and weighed all the material within a quarter m^2 according to debitage type and then measured t' length and width of all the flakes. These data were recorded *in situ* at the sites so that the material would be disturbed a little as possible. In this way I sampled 122 squares within six areas at Sta Nychia and 151 squares from six areas at Demenegaki (figs. 5.5, 5.7).

Since many activity areas could not be included in th systematic sampling due to time constraints, I also collected from a number of areas all the debitage from the surface of one square meter thought to be fairly representative of the area as a whole and returned these artifacts to our field laboratory on Melos for further study during 1976 and 197' Thirteen grab samples from eight activity areas at Demenega and thirteen samples from ten areas at Sta Nychia were collected (figs. 5.5, 5.7). A further collection of a total of 451 cores was made at both sites using the grid system as a reference dimension wherever possible. All in all, approximat six weeks were taken up by the mapping and collecting stage this research with an additional four weeks in the field labor tory devoted to the study and measurement of the core and debitage collections.

Structures

Since there is no evidence for any form of restriction access to the obsidian outcrops at either Sta Nychia or Demenegaki, the hypothesis predicting monopoly over the

density of the surface obsidian as a rough quantitative measure of the amount of use of each location, but in order to reconstruct the different reduction strategies which took place in each area, the debitage itself had to be sampled and studied. This was accomplished by a combination of systematic and grab sampling. In the first case I laid out a square grid with an

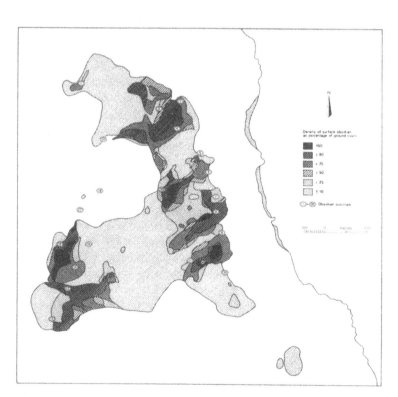

Fig. 5.4. Demenegaki. Distribution of obsidian sources and density of obsidian on the surface.

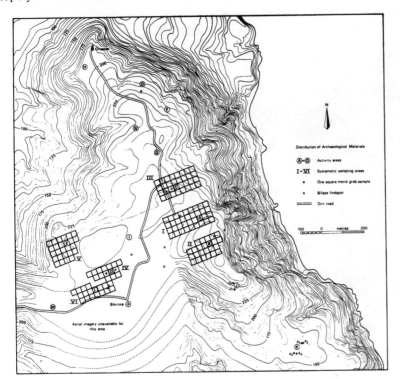

Fig. 5.5. Demenegaki. Distribution of sampling areas and other archaeological findspots.

obsidian resources as a result of commercial market exchange of the raw material cannot be supported by the data collected in the intensive survey of the sites and their immediate surroundings. Despite the substantial amount of effort invested in searching for them, no structural remains that could have housed guards, customs officials, or specialist laborers were identified at either quarry (cf. Renfrew 1972, 511). Evidence indicative of even temporary occupation at the sites during the prehistoric period, such as household refuse, pottery, or quantities of pressure-produced prismatic blades, were also absent (cf. Renfrew, Cann & Dixon 1965, 229). Finally, territorial boundaries on the periphery or within the outcrop areas signifying proprietary rights are lacking. Excavation at Sta Nychia and Demenegaki would provide the only conclusive means for determining whether structures were present, but in the meantime, it appears that the residents of Melos did not exercise ownership rights over the obsidian sources. Furthermore, the absence of structures at or near the quarries raises doubts as to whether full-time craft specialists were employed at these locations.

Obsidian sources

During the course of fieldwork at the quarries the position of all the present obsidian outcrops were mapped (figs. 5.4, 5.6) and described in terms of properties thought to have been relevant to prehistoric knappers: extent of outcrop; size, shape, and condition (fractured or corticated) of obsidian nodules; ease of extraction from the matrix; and so on (Torrence 1982). I was fortunate that Peter Shelford (1976; Shelford *et al.* 1982) of the Department of Geology

at the University of Southampton was concurrently studying many of the same outcrops and was available for consultation. Although the physical properties of the obsidian from both Sta Nychia and Demenegaki are virtually identical (Shelford *et al.* 1982), the matrix in which it occurs can be classified into four types which are markedly varied in appearance (fig. 5.8): (1) rhyolite-rhyodacite, (2) lahars, (3) calcareous ash, and (4) kaolinized rhyolite. Type 1, rhyolitic sources (fig. 5.8, top left), are composed of alternating, differentially sized bands of rhyolite, which range in color from light brown or pale pink to dark gray, and of obsidian, which is frequently very jointed, forming prismatic nodules. These sources are very similar to Type 4 deposits (fig. 5.8, bottom left), although the latter are yellow and contain bands of obsidian which tend to be considerably thicker than in Type 1 outcrops; furthermore, the Type 4 matrix is restricted to Demenegaki. Due to the generally large size and to the relative softness of Type 4 outcrops, it is likely that they would have been the most desirable and most sought after in the past. The remaining two types probably contributed much less obsidian to the total output of the quarry. Type 2 (fig. 5.8, bottom right), laharic, deposits are also yellow but the obsidian occurs as individual nodules rather than within bands. Although the laharic matrix is quite soft, so that the removal of obsidian from it is easy, the restricted extent of most such outcrops suggests that they were rarely utilized except in conjunction with adjacent rhyolitic deposits. The Type 3 (fig. 5.8, top right) matrix, white calcareous ash, is found exclusively at Sta Nychia. These outcrops are unlikely to have been valued by prehistoric quarrymen because the matrix is very hard; the

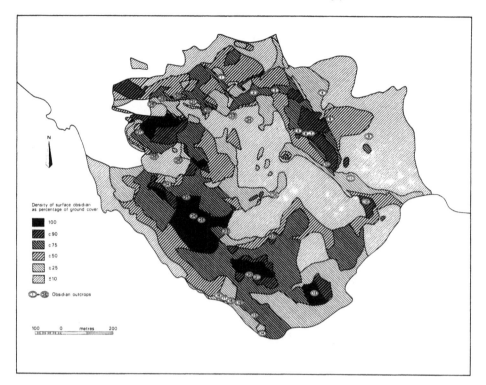

Fig. 5.6. Sta Nychia. Distribution of obsidian sources and density of obsidian on the surface.

obsidian pieces incorporated within it are rarely greater than 2 to 3 cm in diameter, and the larger nodules are often marred by a much-fractured superficial layer.

After considering all the characteristics of each outcrop, I ranked them on a scale from 1 to 5 according to their *potential* for sustained exploitation (Torrence 1981, 1982). By using the density of the debris located adjacent to each source as a measure of the *actual* degree of exploitation and by assuming that the presently observed outcrop was an adequate representation of what was available in the prehistoric period, I could next determine whether the obsidian at Sta Nychia and Demenegaki had been quarried in what I would consider as the most efficient manner. On the whole, it appears from these data that the 'best' sources had been utilized to the greatest extent; nevertheless, debitage also occurred in the vicinity of nearly every outcrop at both quarries regardless of its quality. In other words, although the sources of highest quality had contributed the most to the output of Melos obsidian, the industry at the quarries did not exclude poor quality sources. In addition, there was no evidence for the specialized use of any particular matrix type.

Technology for extraction

It is highly likely that the extraction of obsidian, particularly from matrix Types 2 and 4, required a very simple technology. In most cases the obsidian could easily be pulled out of the deposits by hand. The few traces of quarrying at the sites, a few small hollows in some rhyolitic deposits (fig. 5.9) and several pits which are revealed in the cliffs at Demenegaki (fig. 5.2) indicate that the obsidian was removed with a

minimum investment of technological skill or labor. For this reason it is also unlikely that quarrying was sustained over any appreciable length of time. When compared to the vast amount of effort that must have been required to construct the deep pits and shafts at the large flint mines in other parts of Europe (e.g., Engelen 1975, 92–4) or the extensive Mexican obsidian quarry described by Holmes (1900, 1919, 214–27), for example, the traces at the Melos quarries suggest that exploitation was not systematic and that each episode of quarry use was short-lived.

All the probable quarrying tools identified at Sta Nychia and Demenegaki are very simple and unsophisticated. Certainly, none of the forms can be compared to the very specialized and standardized equipment used by quarrymen at many past and present flint and obsidian quarries elsewhere (e.g., Skertchly 1879, 16–20; Clarke 1935, 49–51; Bordaz 1959; Gallagher 1977a, 1977b; cf. review in Torrence 1981). Possible digging implements in the form of discoidal rhyolitic artifacts have been identified at Sta Nychia by Curtis Runnels (personal communication) but these are extremely rare, largely irregular in form, and very crudely manufactured. In addition Renfrew (1972, 442) has suggested that some of the larger, irregular, unretouched obsidian flakes found at the sites could have been used for digging. His proposal is supported by extensive edge damage on the majority of these artifacts (fig. 5.10), although it is equally possible that the putative use-wear has been formed unintentionally by the trampling of more recent visitors to the sites. A third candidate for quarrying tools are bifacially retouched flakes (fig. 5.11). These artifacts, of which only fourteen examples are known, are very irregular in

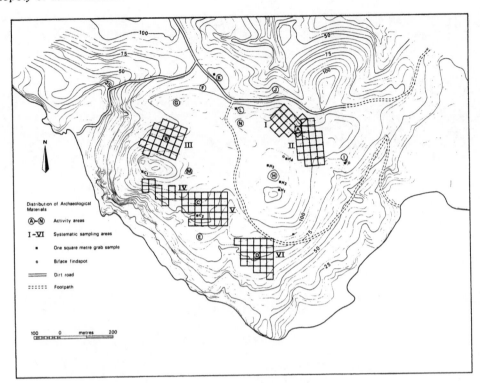

Fig. 5.7. Sta Nychia. Distribution of sampling areas and other archaeological findspots.

appearance because of the variability in the size of the hard hammer flakes used in their fabrication. Since heavy edge damage is not preserved on these tools, it is doubtful whether they were actually used to extract obsidian. It is just as plausible that their function was not as primary quarrying implements but as tools for the manufacture or maintenance of quarrying tools, such as wooden or antler picks, levers, or shovels which have since disintegrated. This extremely small sample of very crude quarrying tools, produced expediently on the spot, leads to the suggestion that small amounts of energy, largely unorganized, were invested in the extraction of obsidian at the Melos quarries.

Macrocore production

The output of production at many quarries which have been studied was one of several types of partially completed tools usually described as rough-outs or preforms (e.g., Holmes 1894, 1919; Bucy 1974; Losey 1971; Singer & Ericson 1977; cf. Mesoamerican cases listed below) and the same situation occurred at the Melos quarries. At both Sta Nychia and Demenegaki the greatest proportion of rejected, incompleted artifacts are large blade cores or macrocores (fig. 5.12) (Torrence 1979a; Renfrew 1972, pl. 26, figs. 15.5, 15.6, 15.10) which are identical in form to those recorded at Mesoamerican obsidian quarries (Hester 1972; Sheets 1972, 1975; Holmes 1900, 410–4; 1919, 220, fig. 97; Coe & Flannery 1964, fig. 2; Spence & Parsons 1972, 6; Clark 1977). The Melos macrocores appear to have been preforms for the smaller, conical, prismatic blade cores commonly found at

habitation sites throughout the Aegean (e.g., Torrence 1979b; Bosanquet 1904, 219). For this reason, it is perhaps not surprising that, although they are so common at the quarries, only two similar examples have been published from Aegean sites outside Melos (Evans & Renfrew 1968, fig. 60, p. XXXIV). Bifacially retouched flakes (noted in the previous section fig. 5.11), resembling the blanks of North American quarries, may also have functioned as preforms, but this is doubtful because there are no known obsidian artifacts in the Aegean which are likely to have been produced from a bifacial form of this type; bifaces of any kind are extremely rare in all Aegean chipped-stone assemblages.

The predominance of macrocore production can also be verified by the debitage recorded from the systematic and grab samples. By analyzing the shapes and sizes of the types of waste present on the surface of the sites, a standard model for macrocore fabrication can be reconstructed and variations from it can be described. The basic reduction strategy, identical to that described by Hester (1972, 98–9) and Sheets (1972, 19–20, 27–8; 1975, 374–6) for Mesoamerica is as follows: (1) a nodule of sufficient size was chosen; (2) a hard hammer percussion blow was struck to the side of the piece truncating the top of the nodule (fig. 5.10a, b) and thereby creating a relatively level platform which was approximately perpendicular to the side of the core; (3) further hard hammer blows were struck on the edge of the prepared platform removing flakes around the periphery of the core (fig. 5.10, c–f); (4) finally, an attempt was made to strike off long flakes or blades on the sides of the core leaving straight, narrow scars to be

Fig. 5.8. Obsidian source types. *Top left*: rhyolite-rhyodacite; *top right*: calcareous ash; *bottom left*: kaolinized rhyolite; *bottom right*: laharic outcrop. 10 cm scales. All views are approximately to the same scale except bottom right in which the size of the outcrop is *c.* 5 m from bottom to top.

used subsequently to guide the force exerted by pressure in an attempt to produce regular, prismatic blades (fig. 5.10, g–i). The largest proportion of the cores collected at the quarries, however, had been rejected at the beginning of stage 4.

　　If the macrocores had been produced in the context of an efficient industry employing full- or part-time craft specialists, it would be reasonable to expect that cores of consistent shape and size would have been manufactured using a fairly

standardized set of techniques. Although detailed ethnographic studies of specialist chipped-stone knappers are rare, the descriptions of both the Brandon gunflint knappers in England (Mitchell 1837; Skertchly 1879; Clarke 1935; cf. Torrence 1981) and of part-time obsidian knappers in Ethiopia (Gallagher 1977a, 1977b) emphasize the extent to which the output conforms to standards of shape, size, and in the technology used to produce them. For this reason it is important

Table 5.1. *Macrocore platform types.*

Platform type*	Sta Nychia		Demenegaki		Total	
	No.	%	No.	%	No.	%
1	54	73	47	64	101	69
2	11	15	16	22	27	18
3	3	4	0	0	3	2
4	4	5	2	3	6	4
5	1	1	5	7	6	4
6	1	1	3	4	4	3

*Key
1 One large flake scar
2 Two or more flake scars
3 Flake scars located solely along the edge of platform
4 Faceted flake scars along edge of platform; remainder of
  platform consisting of one or more flake scars
5 One small flake scar; most of platform is cortex
6 No platform preparation; only original surface (cortex) or
  nodule

to investigate the extent to which one main reduction sequence
was employed on Melos and whether the macrocores also
lacked variability.

Variations from the basic model of macrocore platform
preparation appear to have been fairly common. The frequency
with which all types of preparation occurred within a sample
of 190 cores studied in detail is listed in table 5.1. Since the

Fig. 5.9. Traces of quarrying obsidian from rhyolitic deposit
at Demenegaki.

Fig. 5.10. Debitage created during the production of macrocores.
a, b, primary flakes; c–f, secondary blade flakes; g–i, tertiary
blade flakes; j, crested blade.

majority of the obsidian bands at the quarries have been
extensively fractured, many of the nodules occur in the form
of nearly rectangular prisms with perpendicular faces (e.g.,
fig. 5.8). In these cases no effort was made to prepare the
platform since its angle to the core face was already appropriate for the removal of hard hammer flakes around the
periphery of the nodule (Types 5, 6). In other cases, one blow
was not sufficient to generate the correct striking angle
between the platform and the sides of the core (Type 2) and
in a very small number of cases preparation was limited to the
edge of the top of the nodules (Types 3, 4, fig. 5.12). Other
modifications of the general pattern of macrocore fabrication
involve methods for setting up long, thin blade scars on the
sides of the core (cf. Leach 1978 for an identical description
of silcrete blade core manufacture). In the majority of cases
this seems to have been accomplished by trial-and-error hard
hammer blows as described for stage 4 above. Alternatively,
one of the natural corners of the nodule was carefully
removed leaving a blade scar which was used to channel the

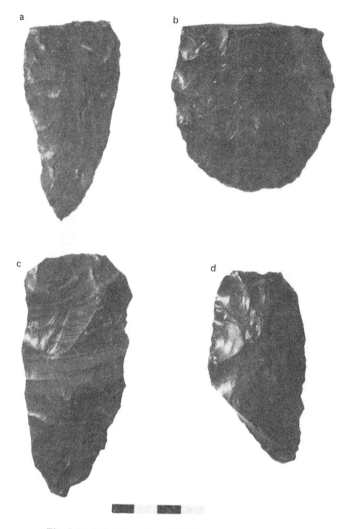

Fig. 5.11. Bifacially retouched flakes.

of manufacture are unlikely to have been subjected to the same processes of cultural selection as were the macrocores, they can be considered reliable indicators of the nature of the artifacts which were created in conjunction with them. The standard deviation and coefficient of variation for the length, width, weight, and ratio of length to width for the 7,441 flakes measured from Sta Nychia and Demenegaki are much larger than I would expect if the cores had been made by specialist knappers who worked regularly and who were dependent on their occupation for part of their subsistence (Torrence 1981, 1982). For example, the coefficient of variation for the samples taken at 25 areas on the sites ranges from 11 to 167 per cent and the mean value — i.e., the average amount of variation for the length, width, and length/width ratio of the flakes — is 60 per cent.

Comparison with modern specialist knappers would facilitate interpretation of the amount of variability recorded on the quarry debitage. Gallagher's (1977a, 1977b) ethno-

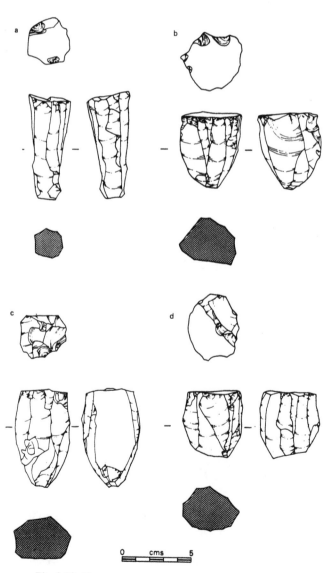

Fig. 5.12. Macrocores.

force of blows struck to it. When this was not feasible, a corner was created by striking lateral, parallel blows down the side of the piece on either one or two faces. Natural and fabricated corner flakes occur in the debitage samples (cf. Holmes 1900, 415, fig. 48; Spence & Parsons 1972, 5–6 for cases at a Mesoamerican obsidian quarry) but they are relatively rare (fig. 5.10j).

Given the variability in the techniques employed, it is not surprising that the shapes and sizes of the macrocores, summarized in table 5.2, are also far from standardized. The high values for the standard deviations and coefficients of variation for all the variables recorded, with the exception of the striking angle, suggests that they were not output by specialized craft production. On the other hand, it could be argued that the cores discarded at the quarries were substandard products and are therefore not adequate representations of those actually exported from Melos. For this reason it might be preferable to look at measurements for the shape and size of the debitage found at the quarries. As the waste by-products

Table 5.2. *Macrocore descriptive statistics.*

Variable[1]	All cores				Complete cores			
	No.	Mean	S.D.[2]	C.V.[3]	No.	Mean	S.D.	C.V.
Weight (g)	189	154.5	81.9	53.0	139	164.3	83.6	50.9
Length	190	7.2	1.9	26.1	139	7.1	1.7	23.6
Width	190	5.2	1.4	26.2	139	5.2	1.3	24.2
Thickness	185	4.0	1.1	28.5	137	4.0	1.0	25.0
Arc of flaking (degrees)	173	255.7	109.3	42.8	138	251.6	110.2	43.8
No. of scars	187	6.7	2.9	42.7	139	7.2	2.8	40.2
Platform width	146	4.9	1.4	27.7	135	4.9	1.3	26.5
Platform thickness	144	3.8	1.2	31.4	135	3.8	1.1	28.9
Striking angle (degrees)	151	84.7	9.4	11.1	135	84.6	9.5	11.2
Flake scar length	734	4.8	1.9	39.9				
Flake scar width	734	1.6	0.8	49.3				
Length/width	734	3.4	1.7	48.9				

1 Measurements in centimeters unless otherwise stated
2 Standard deviation
3 Coefficient of Variation: $C.V. = 100 \times \dfrac{S.D.}{Mean}$

graphic study of part-time leatherworkers from Ethiopia, who make obsidian scrapers for this task, is the only case documented in sufficient detail. From the means and standard deviations of the flakes he excavated from two dumps containing the waste of scraper manufacture reported by Gallagher (1977b, 277, 439), I have calculated the coefficients of variation. Since these values, which range from 34 to 45 per cent and have a mean of 32 per cent, are so much lower than the comparable statistics for the flakes at Sta Nychia and Demenegaki, it seems reasonable to conclude that the Melos debitage lacks the degree of standardization expected if manufactured by specialist craftsmen.

Although, on the basis of the evidence summarized thus far, the industrial organization of macrocore production does not appear to have been highly regulated or standardized, there is some evidence to suggest that the knappers working at the quarries were relatively skilled craftsmen. In order to calculate the rate at which failures occurred during manufacture, one can compare the number of discarded (i.e. rejected), faulty macrocores to an estimate for the total quantity of cores produced at the quarries. For several areas at Demenegaki where intensive collections of macrocores were made with reference to a grid system, it can be estimated that these macrocores represent less than one per cent of the total number of cores fabricated in these areas (see Torrence 1979a, 1981 for a complete summary of the methods used). Since several of the cores were obviously discarded because of flaws in the obsidian nodules rather than as a result of human error, the actual frequency of mistakes must have been less

than this figure, suggesting that at least in this regard the manufacturing techniques were fairly accurate and sophisticated (cf. comparable error rates for Mesoamerican production in Sheets 1978, 61). Methods for correcting errors or for the rejuvention of cores, that is, the controlled removal of the proximal or distal end of the core, can also be identified in the debitage samples, although I did not quantify the frequency of this activity.

An alternative procedure for investigating the system of production at the quarries, particularly in terms of the possibility of occupational specialists, would be to determine the total output of macrocores from the quarries as a daily or yearly rate of manufacture. Theoretically, the rate of output would set limits on the types of manpower organization which could be expected to have operated on Melos; for example, the size of yearly output would give a strong indication of the size of the labor force employed. A detailed discussion of the procedure used to estimate macrocore production at Sta Nychia and Demenegaki has been presented elsewhere (Torrence 1979a) and therefore I will only summarize the results obtained. The estimates are interesting from a methodological point of view because I had to draw on all the analytical approaches used at the quarries to obtain them: maps of the surface density of obsidian, flake counts collected in the systematic sampling, measurements of complete flakes in the grab samples, and measurements of the flake scars on macrocores collected at the sites.

The relationship between the numbers of flakes per square meter and the density of surface obsidian was determined first by means of a regression analysis using data from the systematic sampling program. After computing the total area of the site covered by each density class, the regression formulae were used to calculate the total number of flakes on the surface of the quarries: Sta Nychia *c.* 50 million; Demenegaki *c.* 32 million. The proportion of the total number of flakes resulting from macrocore production was found by measuring the size of the complete flake scars on the sides of 190 macrocores collected at the quarries. Second, it was noted that 68 per cent of the 704 complete flakes measured in the one-meter grab samples fell within two standard deviations either side of both the mean length and mean width of the macrocore scars. In the final step, 68 per cent of the total quantity of flakes was further divided by seven (the average of flake scars on the sides of a macrocore). This yielded a maximum estimate for the total number of macrocores produced at each site: Sta Nychia *c.* 4 million; Demenegaki *c.* 3 million. If the average weight of the studied macrocores is accepted as an accurate representation of finished macrocores, then the counts can also be converted into an approximation of the total weight of macrocores removed from Melos: Sta Nychia *c.* 800 metric tonnes; Demenegaki *c.* 500 metric tonnes.

Production rates can be obtained from the estimated counts by working on the archaeologically reasonable assumption that macrocores were manufactured over a period of no more than 3,000 years and assuming that one man could produce at least twenty cores per day. The period 3,000 years was chosen because macrocores could have been utilized as preforms for any of the different obsidian blade assemblages which are present in the Aegean area from the Late Neolithic to the Late Bronze Age (Torrence 1979b). Unfortunately, it is not possible to determine the length of macrocore production with greater accuracy by employing obsidian-hydration dating as in the case of Singer and Ericson's (1977) production estimates for the Bodie Hills Quarry. Applying these figures, then, a rate of 133 man-days per year is reached for the macrocore manufacture of both Demenegaki (82 man-days per year) and Sta Nychia (51 man-days per year); cf. 48 to 86 man-days per year for Bodie Hills (Singer & Ericson 1977, 185). Evaluation of the estimated rates of manufacture is not straightforward because the 133 man-days could be filled in one of several different ways. At one extreme a single part-time specialist could have worked at both quarries during the summer months only; in contrast, it is equally plausible that 133 fishermen visited the quarries in conjunction with trips to the area for the spring migration of tunnyfish (cf. Bintliff 1977, 117–25, 538–43). Although the exact structure of the labor force cannot be completely reconstructed with these data alone, the very low rates of output do not support a hypothesis for production by a team of full-time craft specialists such as might be envisaged if the Bosanquet-Mackenzie theory for commercial trading of obsidian were correct.

When considered as a whole, the data on macrocore production suggest that the cores were not manufactured within the context of an efficient, regulated industry. The wide variety of techniques employed in the reduction of the cores coupled with the low estimated discard rate suggests that the knappers were able and knowledgeable craftsmen but not specialists. Instead of turning out products with predictable shapes and sizes according to a standardized technology, the approach to their work was opportunistic. They depended on a flexible, unsystematic technology which could accommodate a wide range of nodule forms, correct for some flaws in the material or in their own flaking, and which turned out highly variable products (cf. Leach 1978). Furthermore, the relatively small numbers of macrocores that appear to have been fabricated at the quarries could not have supported either a specialist labor force or a large-scale export industry of the type which was proposed to have supported the prosperous population at Phylakopi.

Although the low rates of macrocore production indicate irregular, short-term utilization of the quarries, it is also possible that the majority of the obsidian exported from Melos was in the form of unmodified nodules and, therefore, that the core manufacturing waste at the quarries is not an adequate representation of the degree of exploitation which took place at Sta Nychia and Demenegaki. To date, my studies of the debitage at a range of Bronze Age settlement sites support this hypothesis (Torrence 1981, 1982). A further test of the hypothesis could be carried out by comparing the total weight of Melos obsidian recovered in excavations at a number of sites with the estimated weight of macrocores manufactured at the quarries. Unfortunately, there are at present no published quantitative studies of Aegean obsidian assemblages, but it is hoped that this situation will be rectified shortly.

Spatial patterning

It seems reasonable to hypothesize that if Sta Nychia and Demenegaki had been exploited for profit by the Bronze Age residents of Phylakopi, the spatial patterning of behavior at the quarries would have been organized in terms of discrete, specialized activity areas which would now be recognizable by differences in the character of the lithic debitage discarded at each location. Although the surface of both Melos quarries is strewn with flakes and chips, the rough outlines of dense concentrations of waste by-products can be detected in various places, typically adjacent to the outcrops with the highest potential yields of obsidian. The position of the working areas was noted on the maps of the density of surface obsidian; systematic and grab sampling were carried out within many of them. In order to reconstruct whether different stages of macrocore production took place in certain areas, I recorded the relative proportions of the *primary* (totally corticated) flakes, *secondary* (partially decorticated) flakes, and *tertiary* (completely decorticated) flakes in all the samples (fig. 5.10).

The results of a Ward's method Clustan analysis (Trasi 1975) of these flake data using a Euclidean distance measure enabled me to divide the activity areas into four groups. Subsequently, the statistical significance of the separation of the groups was satisfactorily confirmed by an SPSS stepwise discriminant analysis (Nie *et al.* 1975, 434–67). From these analyses it is concluded that certain areas of the quarries are differentiable on the basis of differences in the proportions of flake types. Logically, the next question is whether these differences can be accounted for as steps in macrocore production.

On the basis of examination of the scar patterns found on the macrocores collected at the quarries, I would hypothesize that during manufacturing the majority of waste consisted of secondary flakes with the remainder composed of approximately equal quantities of tertiary and primary flakes. When this model is compared to the actual distribution of flake types in the four groups, represented by the mean percentages listed in table 5.3, suggestions can be made as to the kinds of behavior which took place at the various activity areas. Following this line of reasoning, all stages of macrocore production probably took place in areas belonging to Group I. Due to the scarcity of secondary flakes in the remaining groups, it is likely that only certain stages of core manufacture were predominant in these areas. On the other hand, the very large proportions of tertiary flakes at Group III and to a lesser extent Group IV samples suggests that an additional kind of flaking, possibly retouching of flakes, occurred in these locations. These hypotheses can be summarized as follows:

Group I: all stages of macrocore production
Group II: emphasis on initial stages of macrocore production, although all stages represented
Group III: initial stages of macrocore production dominant, although all stages represented, additional manufacture of retouched flakes
Group IV: concentration of final stages in macrocore production with the possible addition of some retouching of flakes

Further analyses of the debitage in which additional variables such as size and shape of the flakes are considered are required to confirm these hypotheses. In this regard Leach's (1978) refitting techniques would be extremely valuable. On the basis of the work so far it does not appear, however, that the various stages of manufacture were regularly segregated in

Table 5.3. *Mean percentages of flake types within clustered working areas.*

| Flake type | Working area | | | |
	Group I	Group II	Group III	Group IV
Primary flakes	12.8	36.7	18.0	9.7
Secondary flakes	60.3	25.1	12.7	31.3
Tertiary flakes	26.8	38.3	69.3	58.9

space. In the first place, all stages of manufacture appear to have been carried out at three of the four groups of working areas. Second, the largest bulk of the waste by-products at the quarries are located within Group III areas where a very wide range of activities seems to have taken place. Furthermore, locations which differ from this general pattern, areas belonging to Group IV, consist of very small scatters of debitage, representing only a few exceptional instances when partially finished cores were transported away from the outcrops for the application of the final touches. The abundance of tertiary flakes in Group III areas remains somewhat of a puzzle because of the rarity of retouched flakes at Sta Nychia and Demenegaki and at most Aegean prehistoric sites with the exception, perhaps, of those belonging to the Neolithic period. The bifacially retouched flakes which were collected at the quarries were not confined to Group III areas although the artifacts may not always have been discarded at the same locality where they were made. Clearly, there is still much that needs to be learned from the data collected in the sampling program. Innovative and imaginative approaches are required but it should be possible to refine and improve my tentative interpretations of the spatial patterning of the debitage.

The lack of evidence for functional differentiation of spatially discrete areas at Sta Nychia and Demenegaki could be accounted for by the nature of macrocore production itself. In contrast to the manufacture of gunflints, for example, which was based on an assembly line of specialist craftsmen each occupying a particular area of the workshop (Mitchell 1837, 37–9; Skertchly 1879, fig. 13; cf. Torrence 1981), the process of macrocore fabrication was much simpler and required fewer different flaking techniques. Thus gains in efficiency would not have resulted from separating manufacturing stages. Nevertheless, the two vastly different activities represented at the quarries, extraction of obsidian from the outcrop and core manufacturing, were also not segregated but instead were conducted in roughly the same locations. Although the methods I have used may not be sophisticated enough to recognize spatial patterning of behavior on a small scale (cf. Leach 1978), I can conclude that the marked variation in the use of space at quarries predicted as a result of a highly efficient and tightly organized production system simply does not exist at either Sta Nychia or Demenegaki.

Summary and prospects for future research

Taken as a whole, the data summarized do not support the two hypotheses which I have derived from Bosanquet's (1904) and Mackenzie's (1904) account of Melian obsidian trade as a profitable commercial enterprise. In the first place, there is no evidence that access to the obsidian outcrops was restricted or controlled in any way. Second, neither the extraction of obsidian from the outcrops nor the reduction of nodules into large preform cores was organized and efficient. Resource procurement at the quarries was not highly specialized either in terms of the type or economic value of the outcrops. Although the sources which would have yielded the largest quantities of obsidian with the lowest input of effort were heavily utilized, all the remaining outcrops were also exploited to some degree. The very simple, unsophisticated technology employed in quarrying operations appears to have required only very crude tools which were produced on the spot as they were needed. For the most part, obsidian cobbles were gathered up and removed from the site with no modification; in some cases preform blade cores were fabricated at the same places where the nodules were found. The knappers producing the cores were skilled to the extent that they made few errors and knew how to take full advantage of the properties of the quarried obsidian; they were not the full-time employees of an organized industry manufacturing products for export.

The general picture that arises from my research at Sta Nychia and Demenegaki is that obsidian procurement was an inefficient, unsystematic occupation undertaken for short periods at irregular intervals largely by ordinary persons acquiring raw materials for their own personal use. A small number of skilled knappers also made visits to the quarries to obtain supplies but they did not support themselves by this activity. In other words, the data support Renfrew's (1975, 42) direct access theory of exchange. Once it reached the mainland, some of the obsidian obtained directly from the sources on Melos may also have traveled 'down-the-line' (Renfrew 1975, 47) by a series of balanced, reciprocal exchanges, but further studies are required to verify this proposition. Data from the quarries would also be compatible with the latter model.

The role of obsidian in the history of the settlement at Phylakopi can be fully determined only by an analysis of obsidian production at the site itself (cf. Torrence 1981), but my analysis of the quarries suggests that the apparent wealth of the site cannot be explained as the result of the monopolization and distribution of a critical resource. In fact the casual attitude adopted toward obsidian, as evidenced by the absence of structures at Sta Nychia and Demenegaki, supports Renfrew's (1972, 455) assertion that obsidian was never a sufficiently valuable resource to have supported a commercial system of exchange.

A complete reconstruction of prehistoric Aegean obsidian production and exchange can only be obtained from a combination of detailed studies of obsidian use at habitation sites as well as the Melos quarries. It would be advantageous if we had quantified data on the amount of obsidian as well as the form in which it arrived at sites throughout the Aegean; these types of data have not been forthcoming and at present the relevant knowledge is restricted to the Melos quarries. Further insights can still be achieved, however, because all the information available from Sta Nychia and Demenegaki has not been recovered. The most obvious priority for future research is the development of hydration curve (cf. Singer & Ericson 1977, 181) for Melos obsidian so that accurate dates can be obtained. Certain activity areas within Group IV could be tentatively assigned to the Neolithic period because of the

presence of small percussion blade cores (Torrence 1979b; Cherry & Torrence 1982), but the majority of the debitage at the quarries is not datable by comparisons with dated assemblages found at other sites.

Other useful research strategies within the area of experimental archaeology should be carried out. Carefully documented replication studies of both extraction and macrocore production would provide a more sound basis for the estimated rate of production. Controlled knapping experiments would yield empirical data on the relative proportion of debitage types resulting from macrocore manufacture. These data would be invaluable for interpreting the past behavior represented by the waste by-products at the working areas found at the quarries.

In order to improve quarry studies in general, the most necessary developments are not methodological but involve the theory concerning the relationship between the behavior that took place at these sites and the nature of the larger economic system in which raw material procurement was only one part. Quarries can easily be envisaged as part of an exchange system but the exact relationships between different kinds of exchange and the means for procuring the raw material involved have previously not been explored in depth. Additional theory-building could be facilitated by comparative studies of both ethnographic and archaeological situations. For instance, studies of occupational specialist stoneworkers (e.g., Gallagher 1977a, 1977b; Bordaz 1959; Mitchell 1837; Skertchly 1879; Cook 1968, 1970; cf. Irwin 1977) often contain useful information on the role of ownership of raw material resources or the effects of differing types of industrial organization on the output (cf. Torrence 1981). Further ethnographic work along these lines would be extremely valuable for achaeologists studying the organization of production.

Quarries have traditionally been studied solely as unique entities divorced both from sites incorporated into the same economic system and from other functionally equivalent phenomena. It is difficult to see how individual quarries can ever be adequately interpreted until a general understanding of the entire functional class of sites has been reached. For example, I have often been struck by the strong similarities between the debitage types present at the Melos quarries and the descriptions of certain Mesoamerican obsidian quarries (e.g., Holmes 1900, 1919; Spence & Parsons 1972). It would be extremely interesting to know to what extent these resemblances are due to the operation of similar economic systems, the exploitation of the same raw material type, or comparable transportation costs. Since there have been few detailed studies of quarries, it is unfortunately not yet possible to exploit the large potential of comparative studies of this class of site.

Studies of quarry workshops can be directed to the analysis of prehistoric exchange. Given a theory of obsidian exchange in the Aegean, one can derive several hypotheses about the kinds of behavior which should have taken place at the quarries and then test these against the abundant data from the sources at Sta Nychia and Demenegaki. I have encountered difficulties in reconstructing behavior from lithic debitage; nevertheless, the results have been extremely rewarding. Based on my experience, it seems that studies in other parts of the world could also benefit from adopting the same theoretical view in which quarries are integrated within a larger exchange system.

Acknowledgments

I am especially grateful to M. Freedman and J. Cherry for assistance with the fieldwork at the quarries. The photographs were originally taken by C. Tilley and D. Leigh; B. Pickering helped prepare the figures. Discussions with L. Binford, J. Cherry, C. Gamble, I. McBryde, C. Runnels, P. Sheets, P. Shelford, and J. Wagstaff have been extremely helpful in clearing up errors in my logic or pointing to new areas of research. The University Research Fund of Sheffield University provided travel and subsistence funds during 1977.

References

Ammerman, A. J., Matessi, C. & Cavalli-Sforza, L. L. 1978. Some new approaches to the study of obsidian trade in the Mediterranean and adjacent areas. In I. Hodder, ed., *The spatial organisation of culture*, London: Duckworth, 179–96.

Aspinall, A., Feather, S. W. & Renfrew, C. 1972. Neutron activation analysis of Aegean obsidians. *Science* 237:333–4.

Bintliff, J. L. 1977. Natural environment and human settlement in prehistoric Greece. *British Archaeological Reports, Supplementary Series* 28.

Bordaz, J. 1959. Flint flaking in Turkey. *Natural History* 78:73–9.

Bosanquet, R. C. 1904. The obsidian trade. In *Excavations at Phylakopi in Melos*, London: Macmillan, 216–33.

Bryan, R. 1950. Flint quarries: the sources of tools and, at the same time, the factories of the American Indian. *Papers of the Peabody Museum of American Archaeology and Ethnology* 17 (3).

Bucy, D. R. 1974. A technological analysis of a basalt quarry in western Idaho. *Tebiwa* 16:1–45.

Cann, J. R. & Renfrew, C. 1964. The source of the Franchthi obsidian. *Hesperia* 42:83–5.

Cherry, J. F. & Torrence, R. 1982. The earliest prehistory of Melos. In C. Renfrew & J. M. Wagstaff, eds., *An island polity: the archaeology of exploitation on Melos*, Cambridge University Press, 24–34.

Clark, J. E. 1977. A macrocore in the regional museum in Tuxtla Gutierrez, Chiapas, Mexico. *Lithic Technology* 6:30–2.

Clarke, R. 1935. The flint-knapping industry at Brandon. *Antiquity* 9: 38–56.

Coe, M. D. & Flannery, K. V. 1964. The Precolumbian obsidian industry of El Chayal, Guatemala. *American Antiquity* 30:30–2.

Cook, S. 1968. *Teitipac and its Metateros: an economic anthropological study of production and exchange in the valley of Oaxaca, Mexico*. Ph.D. dissertation, Department of Anthropology, University of Pittsburgh.

1970. Price and output variability in a peasant-artisan stoneworking industry in Oaxaca, Mexico: an analytical essay in economic anthropology. *American Anthropologist* 72:776–801.

Dixon, J. E. 1976. Obsidian characterization studies in the Mediterranean and Near East. In R. E. Taylor, ed., *Advances in obsidian glass studies*. Park Ridge, N.J.: Noyes Press, 288–333.

Dixon, J. E., Cann, J. R. & Renfrew, C. 1968. Obsidian and the origins of trade. *Scientific American* 218:38–46.

Durrani, S. A., Khan, H. A., Taj, M. & Renfrew, C. 1971. Obsidian source identification by fission track analysis. *Nature* 233: 242–5.

Engelen, F. H. C. ed. 1975. *Second International Symposium on Flint*. Maastrict, Netherlands: Netherlandse Geologische Vereniging.

1981. *Third International Symposium on Flint*. Maastrict, Netherlands: Netherlandse Geologische Vereniging.

Ericson, J. E. 1981. Exchange and production systems in Californian prehistory: the results of hydration dating and chemical characterization. *British Archaeological Reports, International Series* 110.

Evans, J. D. & Renfrew, C. 1968. *Excavations at Saliagos near Antiparos*. London: Thames & Hudson.

Fiedler, K. 1841. *Reise durch alle Teile des Konigreiches Griechenland*. Leipzig.

Gallagher, J. F. 1977a. Contemporary stone tools in Ethiopia: implications for archaeology. *Journal of Field Archaeology* 4:407–14.

1977b. *Ethnoarchaeological and prehistoric investigations in the Ethiopian Rift Valley*. Ph.D. dissertation, Department of Anthropology, Southern Methodist University, Dallas.

Hester, T. R. 1972. Notes on large obsidian blade cores and core-blade technology in Mesoamerica. *Contributions of the University of California Archaeological Research Facility* 14:95–106.

Hester, T. R. & Heizer, R. F. 1973. *Bibliography of archaeology I: experiments, lithic technology and petrography*. Reading, Mass.: Addison-Wesley.

Hodder, I. 1974. Regression analysis of some trade and marketing patterns. *World Archaeology* 6:172–89.

Holmes, W. H. 1894. Natural history of flaked stone implements. *Memoirs of the International Congress of Anthropology, Chicago* 120–39.

1900. The obsidian mines of Hidalgo, Mexico. *American Anthropologist* 2:405–16.

1919. Handbook of aboriginal American antiquities: Part I, Introductory, The lithic industries. *Bureau of American Ethnology Bulletin* 60.

Irwin, G. J. 1977. *The emergence of Mailu as a central place in the prehistory of coastal Papua*. Ph.D. dissertation, Department of Anthropology, Australian National University, Canberra.

Leach, H. M. 1978. Mind within matter: discovering the technological knowledge of early New Zealanders. Paper presented at the 43rd annual meeting of the Society for American Archaeology, Tucson, Ariz.

Losey, T. C. 1971. The Stony Plain quarry site. *Plains Anthropologist* 16:138–54.

Mackenzie, D. 1897. Ancient sites in Melos. *Annual of the British School at Athens* 3:71–88.

1904. The successive settlements of Phylakopi in their Aegeo-Cretan relations. In *Excavations at Phylakopi in Melos*. London: Macmillan, 238–72.

McCoy, P. C. & Gould, R. A. 1977. Alpine archaeology in Hawaii. *Archaeology* 30:234–43.

McDougall, J. M. 1978. *An analytical study of obsidian from Europe and the Near East by examination of magnetic parameters*. M. A. thesis, Post-graduate School of Archaeological Sciences, University of Bradford.

Mitchell, J. 1837. On the manufacture of gun-flints. *Edinburgh New Philosophical Journal* 32:36–40.

Nie, N. H., Hull, C. H., Jenkins, J. G., Steinbrenner, K. & Brent, D. H. 1975. *Statistical package for the social sciences*. New York: McGraw-Hill.

Perlès, C. 1979. Des navigateurs méditerranéens il y a 10,000 ans. *La Recherche* 10:82–3.

Renfrew, C. 1969. Trade and culture process in European prehistory. *Current Anthropology* 10:151–69.

1972. *The emergence of civilization: the Cyclades and the Aegean in the third millenium B.C.* London: Methuen.

1973. Trade and craft specialisation. In D. R. Theocharis, ed., *Neolithic Greece,* Athens: National Bank of Greece, 179–200.

1975. Trade as action at a distance: questions of integration and communication. In J. A. Sabloff & C. C. Lamberg-Karlovsky, eds., *Ancient civilization and trade.* Albuquerque: University of New Mexico Press, 3–60.

1977. Alternative models for exchange and spatial distribution. In T. K. Earle & J. E. Ericson, eds., *Exchange systems in prehistory.* New York: Academic Press, 71–90.

Renfrew, C., Cann, J. R. & Dixon, J. E. 1965. Obsidian in the Aegean. *Annual of the British School at Athens* 60:225–47.

Renfrew, C., Dixon, J. E. & Cann, J. R. 1968. Further analysis of Near Eastern obsidian. *Proceedings of the Prehistoric Society* 34: 319–31.

Renfrew, C. & Wagstaff, J. M. eds. 1982. *An island polity: the archaeology of exploitation on Melos.* Cambridge University Press.

Sheets, P. 1972. A model of Mesoamerican obsidian technology based on Preclassic workshop debris in El Salvador. *Ceramica de Cultura Maya* 8:17–33.

1975. Behavioral analysis and the structure of a prehistoric industry. *Current Anthropology* 16:369–91.

1978. From craftsman to cog: quantitative views of Mesoamerican lithic technology. In R. Sidrys, ed. *Papers on the economy and architecture of the ancient Maya.* Los Angeles, Institute of Archaeology, University of California, 40–71.

Shelford, P. H. 1976. Some aspects of the occurrence of obsidian on Melos, Cyclades, Greece. *Proceedings of the International Congress on Thermal Waters, Geothermal Energy and Vulcanism of the Mediterranean Area.*

Shelford, P., Hodson, F., Cosgrove, M. E., Warren, S. E. & Renfrew, C. 1982. The obsidian trade: the sources and characterisation of Melian obsidian. In C. Renfrew & J. M. Wagstaff, eds., *An island polity: the archaeology of exploitation on Melos.* Cambridge University Press, 182–92.

Sidrys, R. 1976. Classic Maya obsidian trade. *American Antiquity* 41: 449–64.

1977. Mass-distance measures for the Maya obsidian trade. In T. K. Earle & J. E. Ericson, eds., *Exchange systems in prehistory.* New York: Academic Press, 91–108.

Singer, C. A. & Ericson, J. E. 1977. Quarry analysis at Bodie Hills, Mono County, California: a case study. In T. K. Earle & J. E. Ericson, eds., *Exchange systems in prehistory.* New York: Academic Press, 91–108.

Skertchly, S. B. J. 1879. On the manufacture of gun-flints, the methods of excavating for flint, the age of Paleolithic man, and the connexion between Neolithic Art and the gun-flint trade. *Memoir of the Geological Survey, England and Wales.*

Spence, M. W. & Parsons, J. R. 1972. Prehistoric obsidian exploitation in central Mexico: a preliminary synthesis. *Miscellaneous Studies in Mexican Prehistory, University of Michigan, Museum of Anthropology, Anthropological Papers* 45: 1–37.

Torrence, R. 1979a. Macrocore production at the Melos obsidian quarries. *Lithic Technology* 8:51–60.

1979b. A technological approach to Cycladic blade industries. In J. L. Davis and J. F. Cherry, eds., *Papers in Cycladic prehistory.* Los Angeles, Institute of Archaeology, University of California, 66–86.

1981. *Obsidian in the Aegean: towards a methodology for the study of prehistoric exchange.* Ph.D. dissertation, Department of Anthropology, University of New Mexico, Albuquerque.

1982. The obsidian quarries and their uses, part II. In C. Renfrew & J. M. Wagstaff, eds., *An island polity: the archaeology of exploitation on Melos.* Cambridge University Press, 193–221.

Trasi, A. D. 1975. *Clustan analysis package – Clustan 1A.* Bradford, University of Bradford Computing Laboratory, Bradford.

Chapter 6

Lithic material demand and quarry production
B. E. Luedtke

The scale of demand for lithic materials in a stone-tool-using culture has implications for that culture's quarrying, transportation, and exchange activities. This chapter presents a formula for quantifying lithic demand and illustrates its use with ethnographic and archaeological data. The formula is then used to predict lithic demand in an archaeological case study of the Late Woodland cultures of the Upper Great Lakes region.

Introduction

For many prehistoric cultures, the production of stone tools was a basic economic activity which provided the necessary means for obtaining food, making clothing, and constructing shelter. In Western economic terms, a demand for lithic raw material existed and was satisfied by recourse to quarries and other sources of stone. The scale of this demand would have determined the intensity and extent of quarry activity at any given quarry, and would also have determined the amount of time and energy expended in this way as opposed to other economic and noneconomic activities. Differences between demand and locally available supply would also have affected the need to obtain stone through trade or long journeys.

Despite the significance of the demand factor as a bridge between quarrying and other activities in the cultural system, there has been little attempt in either the archaeological or ethnographic literature to quantify demand. We simply cannot say whether individuals in stone-tool-using cultures typically needed a few handfuls or several tons of stone per year,

although these extremes would have very different implications for quarrying activities. We can, however, open inquiry into this problem by examining the factors affecting demand and suggesting a formula for quantifying demand. We will then consider the formula in the light of available ethnographic data, and its utility will be tested on an archaeological case study. This study will outline what we know about lithic demand, what we need to learn, and how the concept of lithic demand can be useful in approaching ethnographic and archaeological problems.

Lithic-demand formula

Demand is here defined as the amount of lithic material necessary per fixed unit of population over a fixed period of time. Reasons for the use of the ambiguous term 'necessary' rather than the more precise 'obtained' or 'disposed of' will be discussed later. Population and time are treated as constants for the purpose of this discussion because they must be determined independently in most cases.

Demand thus defined is essentially a function of three aspects of a culture's technology: the number and frequency of activities requiring stone tools, stone-tool-production techniques, and stone-tool efficiency. With regard to the first aspect, it should be obvious that demand for stone should increase as the number of tasks requiring stone tools increases, all other factors being equal. Therefore, demand will reflect technological complexity in part, and will also be influenced by the presence or absence of functional alternatives for stone such as shell, reed, or bone tools. Not all stone-using activities need be strictly utilitarian; production of 'blanks' for trade or of stone items to be placed in graves could also be activities that increase lithic demand.

Procedures used for stone-tool production can also influence demand. As a well-known example of this, it has been calculated that, 'in the pebble tool cultures a pound of flint provided about 5 cm of cutting edge; in the hand-axe technique 20 cm; in the middle Paleolithic, 100 cm; and in the late Paleolithic, 300 to 1,200 cm' (Butzer 1964, 387). The more 'wasteful' the production technique used by a particular culture, the more raw material will be needed.

Finally, efficiency of the tools themselves is a factor in determining demand. Some tool forms keep their edge longer or break less often during use than do other forms used for the same tasks (Luedtke n.d.), and some forms can be rejuvenated more easily than others. If the average tool life-span is short, the demand for raw material will be greater.

The relationship between these factors can be expressed by a simple formula which calculates the amount of lithic material needed under specified circumstances of stone-tool production and use.

$$L = \sum_{i=1}^{n} T_i/D_i(S_i + M_i + R_i)$$

L is lithic demand, as defined above. I will use the household as the fixed unit of population, as I will be dealing primarily with societies having little craft specialization. In such societies, the household should perform nearly the full range of economic and other activities available, and the household is thus the appropriate unit for assessing lithic demand. Using the household, rather than the individual, has the additional advantage of eliminating the necessity for assuming which tasks were associated with each age and sex category in prehistoric societies. The year will be used as the fixed unit of time, as it represents one full economic cycle. Some activities take place in cycles longer than a year, however, and these must also be factored into the formula.

T_i is the amount of each task or subtask requiring stone tools of a specific type done in a year. On the average, so many animals must be butchered or arrow shafts shaped in a year, and these processes involve a number of steps performed with different stone tools (e.g., knives, scrapers, choppers). Each step counts as a separate subtask for purposes of this formula. T_i could be expressed in hours of work, number of strokes used, or other measures, but it is probably most easily calculated in terms of the number of times the task or subtask must be done each year. As a hypothetical example, if 10 deer hides are needed to meet household needs each year, then $T = 10$ for each of the tools used in processing those hides.

D_i is the discard rate, or the life-span of the specific tool type, and must be measured in the same units as T_i. Therefore, as used here, D_i is the number of times a tool can be used

for each task or subtask before it must be discarded, and is roughly a measure of tool efficiency. In reality, of course, the same tool might be used one minute to shape an arrow shaft and the next to shape a wooden bowl, but the actual life histories of individual tools are irrelevant to this formula. D_i is an abstraction, based on the length of time a tool would last if it were used for only one task. Continuing the hypothetical example above, if one end scraper can scrape two deer hides before it is worn out, then $D = 2$ for such end scrapers.

T_i/D_i, then, is the number of tools of each specific type needed each year for each task or subtask. It is equal to 5 in the hypothetical example above, and this means that each household needs five end scrapers to meet its hide-processing needs each year. End scrapers may be used for other processing activities as well, of course, but these must be calculated separately for each task.

The remainder of the formula essentially adds weight to the theoretical tools posited by the first part of the formula. S_i is the average weight of each tool type at the time it is discarded, measured in grams. M_i is the amount of unused manufacturing debris associated with the making of each tool, measured in grams. R_i is the amount of unused resharpening debris produced during the use-life of the tool, measured in grams. It should be noted that a piece of utilized manufacturing or retouch debris is counted as a tool in its own right. Thus, everything within the parentheses in this formula relates to tool-production techniques. Continuing the previous example, if the average end scraper made in the hypothetical culture weighs 5 g at the time of discard, has lost 0.5 g through resharpening, and 'costs' 7 g of waste flakes to produce, then $S + M + R = 12.5$ g. This culture required 12.5 g of raw material to produce one end scraper, and 62.5 g of stone to produce enough end scrapers to process ten deer hides each year.

This calculation must be repeated for the tools used to cut those hides and for each of the other tools used in hide preparation, and then for all the stone tools used in other activities. The total of all the resulting subtotals is L for that culture. The actual calculation of lithic demand is thus repetitive but fairly straightforward. Simply stated, the formula indicates that the amount of lithic material needed per year per household is equal to the sum of the number of stone tools needed, multiplied by the average weight of these tools plus their associated chipping debris. The formula could clearly be used for any type of stone, but throughout this chapter L will be calculated for flaked stone tools only.

The use of this formula allows a precise determination of exactly why different cultures have different demand rates for lithic raw material. T_i is clearly the most culture-specific variable, reflecting as it does the many possible technological and nontechnological uses of stone, as well as functional alternatives to stone available in different environments. There may actually be systematic and predictable relationships between T_i and environmental zones or general levels of technological or social complexity, but these relationships will have to be empirically determined.

D_i will have the narrowest range for variation of any of the factors, as it is very closely related to the mechanical properties of the stone tools and of the materials being worked with them. The type of stone being used will have an effect on use-life, however. The use-life of tools made on tough materials such as rhyolite will be longer than the same tools made on brittle materials such as obsidian. Also, different tool users may have very different ideas of when a tool is 'used up' and no longer worth resharpening, and this will affect the discard rate.

M_i is the variable most obviously under control of the stone-tool-using culture itself, and the one that can be manipulated most effectively to cope with raw-material shortages. Where raw material is abundant, large quantities of waste flakes may be left behind at quarries, and relatively wasteful production techniques may be used. Where material is less abundant, more conservative production techniques may be used and more of the resulting debitage may be utilized.

The formula as used here averages a great deal of individual variation, which could be examined by using different units of time or population. Even without marked craft specialization, some individuals make and use more stone tools than do others. Also, stone-tool use may have been markedly greater at some seasons of the year than at others (White & Peterson 1969). This level of detail and complexity may be approached with ethnographic data, but can rarely be achieved with archaeological data. In fact, the formula in general must be used differently with these different types of data.

Lithic demand and ethnographic data

Where ethnographic data are available, it should be possible to observe the actual quantities of stone material being quarried, used, and discarded, and the formula can be used descriptively. Unfortunately, ethnographic observations of this sort are virtually nonexistent. One of the first impacts made by Western culture upon the material culture of stone-tool users involved rapid replacement of stone tools by metal, and this replacement process may often have begun well before Western people themselves were encountered (Sharp 1952). Early explorers and ethnographers paid little attention to this aspect of material culture, and for most parts of the world it is much too late to ask informants questions about lithic use or demand. Some relevant data are still available, however, and it is worthwhile collecting such scattered estimates to see what light they may shed on lithic demand.

The first body of data is from Gould (1977), who has worked with the Western Desert Ngatatjara Aborigines of Australia. Some individuals of this culture still use stone tools or have used them within recent memory, and they were able to provide information on most of the elements of the lithic demand equation. Gould's information is summarized in table 6.1, which shows the quantity of lithic material used by one adult male for chipped-stone tools over the course of a

year. Again, T_i is the number of times each task was performed per year, and T_i/D_i is the number of tools needed per year for each task. No value for M_i was given, because these people apparently used nearly all of the stone they brought away from the quarries. Gould, Koster & Sontz (1971, 160–1) have stated that large quantities of unused materials are left at quarry sites. S_i and R_i are combined here because tools were either not resharpened or were weighed before use. Gould has also provided average weights for each tool type, but he cautions that the range of variation is rather wide within each category (Gould 1977, 166).

As the table indicates, an adult Ngatatjara could have been expected to use about 20 kg of lithic material in a year, mainly for maintenance tasks. Women apparently made negligible use of stone tools in this society, so this estimate is probably valid for an entire household. The desert Aborigines were highly mobile and had limited storage and transport facilities, so this figure may be considered a bare minimum for Australian Aborigines in general.

Gould's data can be compared with a similar body of data collected by Hayden from another Western Desert Aborigine group, the Pintupi (Hayden 1977 and 1979). Hayden's data (table 6.2) are based on a combination of informants' statements and his own estimates, and Hayden cautions that his estimates are probably on the liberal side. Hayden does not include exactly the same range of functions as does Gould, but the two lists are fairly close. It should be noted that the value used for the number of adzes needed for resharpening spears is taken from Gould. Hayden also includes only retouched tools, and his estimates are for an entire nuclear family. On the whole, however, the two bodies of data are generally comparable. Gould's estimates for average tool weights have been applied to Hayden's data in order to obtain estimates of the total amount of lithic material used per year, as Hayden provided no estimates of tool weights.

Comparison of tables 6.1 and 6.2 shows that Hayden's values for T_i are all considerably greater than Gould's estimates, while his D_i values are nearly always lower than Gould's values. In other words, Hayden's informants stated that most tasks were done more frequently than Gould's informants believed, and that more tools were used for each task. As a result, Hayden's total for tools needed per year is significantly larger than Gould's estimate, and the resultant L value is nearly twice as large.

Hayden supports his estimates with archaeological findings from two campsites known to have been occupied by stone-tool users of the Pintupi group 30 years previously (Hayden 1979). When Hayden collected stone artifacts from these sites and determined the length of time each site was occupied, he was able to extrapolate and arrive at estimates of 130 flaked-stone tools per person per year for the first site and 520 flaked-stone tools per person per year for the second. Since the first site was known to be the scene of considerable spear-thrower manufacturing activity and the second site was near a quarry, Hayden again feels that these

Table 6.1. *Flaked stone used by Australian Aborigines (Ngatatjara).*

Task	T_i	Tool	D_i	T_i/D_i	$S_i + R_i$	L_i
Resharpen spear tips	182	adze	20	9.1	41.4	376.7
Replace spear shafts	17.3	adze	2	8.7	41.4	360.2
Replace spear shafts	17.3	chopper	1	17.3	809.2	13,999.2
Replace spear-thrower	0.5	adze	1	0.5	41.4	20.7
Replace spear-thrower	0.5	chopper	1	0.5	809.2	404.6
Replace club	0.5	adze	2	0.25	41.4	10.35
Replace club	0.5	chopper	1	0.5	809.2	404.6
Replace throwing stick	1	adze	2	0.5	41.4	20.7
Replace throwing stick	1	chopper	1	1	809.2	809.2
Replace digging stick	2	chopper	1	2	809.2	1,618.4
Misc. ritual manufactures	3	adze	1	3	41.4	124.2
Misc. ritual manufactures	2	chopper	1	2	809.2	1,618.4
Replace wooden bowls	1	adze	1	1	41.4	41.4
Misc. cutting tasks	20	flake knives	1	20	40	800
Totals				66.35 tools/year		20,608.6 g/household/year

values are high. He estimates that 150 tools per family would be a more likely average (Hayden 1977, 182).

These two sites also provide estimates of the total lithic assemblage, including debitage (Hayden 1979). For the first site, about 1.5 pieces of debitage were found for each tool, while at the second site the ratio of debitage to tools was 5 to 1. Obviously, much of the tool manufacturing occurred elsewhere, presumably at the quarries, since much more debitage is usually found at lithic workshop sites. On the other hand, it can be expected that many of the finished tools were discarded at task-specific locations away from the campsites, and therefore the lithic materials found at the campsites may not reflect accurately the total quantities of debitage or tools discarded by these people (Hayden 1977, 182).

The differences between the Gould and Hayden estimates may be due to many factors. First, although the two

groups lived in the same general part of Australia, they are still distinct cultures and may have had somewhat different technologies. There may also have been differences in the degree of acculturation or the memories of the different informants. Certainly there appear to have been differences in the quantities of raw material available. Nevertheless, both the Gould and Hayden estimates are of about the same order of magnitude, and together they provide a range which would probably include many Australian groups.

A third body of data was provided for this study by J. P. White and C. Modjeska (personal communication 1973), and was obtained from the Duna-speaking societies of the western highlands of New Guinea. These people have not been stone-tool users since the 1950s, and thus the values given are field estimates based on informants' memories and ethnographic experiment. It was therefore not possible to

Table 6.2. *Retouched tools used by Australian Aborigines (Pintupi).*

Task	T_i	Tool	D_i	T_i/D_i	$S_i + R_i$	L_i
Replace spears	25	adze	0.5	50	41.4	2,070
Replace spears	25	chopper	2.08	12	809.2	9,710.4
Replace spears	25	flake tool	1	25	40	1,000
Resharpening spears	180	adze	20	9	41.4	372.6
Resharpening spears	180	flake tool	18	10	40	400
Replace spear-thrower	1	adze	0.07	14	41.4	579.6
Replace spear-thrower	1	chopper	0.2	5	809.2	4,046
Replace spear-thrower	1	flake tool	1	1	40	40
Replace throwing or adzing sticks	5	chopper	0.8	6	809.2	4,855.2
Replace throwing or adzing sticks	5	flake tool	1.7	3	40	120
Replace digging stick	4	adze	1	4	41.4	165.6
Replace digging stick	4	chopper	0.33	0.2	809.2	9,710.4
Replace hardwood bowl	1	chopper	0.2	5	809.2	4,046
Totals				156 tools/year		37,115.8 g/household/year

break down the data as finely as was possible for Australia, since the technology of these people has undergone considerable change. There also seems to have been a great deal of variation among individuals as to the numbers of stone tools used in a year. As White and Modjeska say (personal communication 1973). 'a few people who make arrows in some numbers for exchange probably use the greatest numbers of stone tools . . . This might be one man in 30–50 and they would contrast, at the other extreme, with people (10–20%???) who make none of the things stone tools are used for – it is possible, for instance, for a man to go for years without handling more than a few flakes.' Again, women in this culture were not stone-tool users (White & Thomas 1972), so the values given would probably apply to a household.

White and Modjeska give a very wide range for the number of stone tools that might be used in a year, and this is reflected in the wide range for the totals shown in table 6.3. In addition, a minimum case is estimated. In all cases, the tools

are miscellaneous flakes, retouched only enough so that some of them can be hafted. S_i and R_i together was estimated at 20 g per flake, based on a comparison of the size of flakes described for this area by Strathern (1969) with similar flakes measured in the course of my own research.

For all estimates, L, or the total amount of flaked stone needed by New Guineans of this area, is very low. In fact, the estimates in general are lower than for the desert Aborigines, although the New Guineans are settled horticulturalists and have no need to 'travel light' as did the Aborigines (table 6.4). Part of the reason for the low level of lithic demand is the fact that New Guineans relied on ground-edge axes (not included in the tables) for most heavy woodworking (Strathern 1969). Also, the range of tasks requiring stone tools was relatively narrow, as functional equivalents such as bamboo knives were available for many food-preparation and butchering tasks (White & Thomas 1972).

Most of the estimates for Australian and New Guinean

Table 6.3. *Flaked stone used by New Guineans (Duna-speakers).*

Task	T_i/D_i (range)	S_i	$M_i + R_i$	L_i (range)
Maximum stone-tool user				
Making arrows (50/year)	30–200	20	7	810–5,400
Drilling shells				
Drilling pig tusks				
Scraping cane for arrow bindings				
Bow making	30–600	20	7	810–16,200
Axe handle shaping				
Scraping cane for armbands and waistbands				
Misc. uses				
Totals	60–800 tools/year	g/household/year		1,620–21,600
Minimum stone tools user				
Misc. tasks	5	20	7	135 g/household/year

stone-material needs lie between 20 and 40 kg of chipped stone per household per year. Much variation appears to have existed within groups and even between similar groups. In attempting to obtain lithic-demand estimates for cultures elsewhere in the world, the margin for error is obviously great.

Lithic demand and archaeological data

It is noteworthy that all of the ethnographic data discussed above were collected by ethnoarchaeologists, or ethnographers who have worked closely with archaeologists. Stone-tool use in general has been of rather marginal interest to most ethnographers, and the process of obtaining data relevant to lithic demand is salvage ethnography at best. Archaeology, on the other hand, has demonstrated a long-term fascination with all aspects of stone tools, and it is likely to be archaeologists who will find the lithic-demand formula of most interest and relevance to their research. The formula must be used somewhat differently with archaeological data, however, and many more estimates must be used for elements in the formula. Essentially, the formula as used by archaeologists will usually be *predictive*, not *descriptive*. Few of the variables in the formula can be measured directly for prehistoric cultures, and it is difficult to verify the many necessary assumptions. However, using the formula it is possible to state how much lithic raw material would have been needed given certain conditions, and this value may prove useful for many types of analysis.

The lithic demand formula can only be put into oper-

ation by archaeologists if they already possess a certain minimum level of knowledge about the prehistoric culture in question. We may someday be able to estimate total demand on the basis of knowledge of a culture's general level of technological complexity, but the existence of regularities in the relationship between technology and demand has yet to be demonstrated. We certainly cannot generalize blithely from Austronesia to the rest of the world, and at this point it is necessary to go step by step through the formula and determine the appropriate values separately for each culture in question.

The first step is to define a region and time period

Table 6.4. *Comparison of lithic demand for three ethnographic cultures.*

Culture	Total tools/year	Lithic demand in, kg/household/year
Ngatatjara (Australia)	66.35	20.6
Pintupi (Australia)	156	37.1
Duna: maximum user	60–800	1.6–21.6
Duna: minimum user (New Guinea)	5	0.1

within which the technology remained more or less stable and lithic demand can be treated as constant per average household (though total population size may have varied). The next step is to determine the number of tasks that would have required stone tools, either directly or indirectly. A primary source for this information is the stone tools themselves, excavated from archaeological sites of the period. These tools must be analyzed in terms of use-wear as well as formal attributes, in order to link them as closely as possible with the tasks they performed (e.g. Odell 1980). Since many tools will have had multiple uses, and wear will be ambiguous, it is wise to supplement the list of tasks using other sources of information as well. For example, analysis of food remains will suggest a range of important economic activities which required the use of stone tools, either directly or for the production of other tools from materials such as wood or bone. Nonutilitarian uses of stone must also be considered.

Ethnographic analogy may sometimes suggest tool-using activities that may have left few or no direct archaeological traces. For example, bark and wooden containers must have been made by many prehistoric cultures, but remains are only rarely preserved. Such containers can probably be assumed to have existed in many cases, and they would have been produced with the use of stone tools. Similarly, the knowledge that a prehistoric people were horticulturalists will suggest the need to include stone tools used to produce wooden farming implements, though these latter may have left no direct traces.

Estimating the number of times these different tasks would have been performed in the course of a year requires a certain amount of guesswork in most cases. Ethnographic analogy will be very useful for informing these guesses, however, and information of this sort is relatively abundant in the ethnographic literature for many parts of the world.

For estimating D_i, tool use-life, there is a small amount of ethnographic data available (e.g. Osgood 1970). Evidence from short-term, single component sites may sometimes be used to generate such data (Odell 1980, 425). Another possible source of information on tool use-life is replication; tools similar to those found archaeologically can be made and used until they no longer function, and average 'life-spans' can thus be calculated (Walker 1978). It may be difficult to prove that the tools were used exactly as the prehistoric people used them, or that the same criteria are being used to determine when a tool is worn out. However, as mentioned above, D_i is assumed to be closely related to the mechanical properties of the stone tool and the material being worked, and is therefore not expected to vary as widely as some of the other variables.

S_i is perhaps the easiest variable to deal with in an archaeological study, as it can be determined by simply weighing a representative sample of each of the types of tools used by the people in question. R, the quantity of stone lost through resharpening, is less straightforward, but several means may be suggested for deriving this value. It is probably sensible to begin by examining a large number of tools of the period, in order to determine the importance of resharpening in the assemblage. If most tools show little or no evidence of resharpening, and were simply being discarded as soon as they became worn, R can safely be ignored entirely. If evidence of resharpening appears on many tools, an estimate for R must be made. In some cases, it may be possible to compare worn specimens discarded in trash pits and around living areas with unused, freshly manufactured specimens left near quarries or workshops. The average difference in weights could be used for R. The frequency of resharpening flakes in the assemblage could also be used to estimate R.

M is likely to be rather difficult to estimate, especially if much preliminary chipping was done at quarries. It could be argued, however, that quarry debris should not be counted in M, because such debris was still at the source and could potentially be used as raw material by later users of the quarry. A certain amount of stone was usually removed from the quarry and discarded as waste at habitation and activity sites, however, and this material must certainly be counted in M. If a representative sample of artifacts from a number of sites of the period in question is available, the average M for all tool types could be determined by taking the total quantity of unused debitage and dividing by the total number of finished tools. It is recognized that not all tools are discarded at habitation sites, but it is assumed that these 'missing' tools are balanced by debitage discarded away from sites, too.

As with several of the other values in the formula, replication may be a useful procedure for estimating M. Crabtree (1966, 1972) and others have shown that many useful types of information can be derived from replication experiments, including quantities of debitage generated during the manufacture of tools (Newcomer & Sieveking 1980). Estimates derived from replication experiments can at least serve as a check or comparison with estimates derived through other means.

The calculation of L is expected to be of special relevance to those involved in studies of quarries and quarrying activities. For example, in Gramly's report on the Mount Jasper quarry he calculates that 39 kg of stone were removed each year the quarry was in use (Gramly 1980, 1). Comparison of this with the minimal values for L discussed in ethnographic examples above tends to confirm Gramly's contention that Mount Jasper supplied only a small proportion of the lithic needs of the groups who exploited this region. Gramly's estimates for quantities of stone removed assume greater significance in the light of the lithic-demand formula.

Most applications of the formula will require information in addition to L, however. In particular, the time span during which the quarry was used will be especially important to nearly any application of the formula. Cross dating of artifacts will tell the general time periods of use, and radiocarbon dates may be available in some cases. For some sources, hydration rates may be used to bracket the periods of quarry exploitation rather precisely (Singer & Ericson 1977).

Table 6.5. *Comparison of tasks requiring stone tools for ethnographic and archaeological cases.*

Tasks	Australia	New Guinea	Great Lakes
Resharpen spear tips	X		X
Making spear shafts	X		X
Replace spear-throwers	X		
Making clubs	X		X
Replace throwing stick	X		
Replace digging stick	X		
Replace wooden bowls	X		X
Misc. cutting tasks	X	X	X
Misc. ritual manufacturers	X	X	X
Making arrows		X	X
Bow making		X	X
Axe-handle shaping		X	X
Making trapping and fishing equipment			X
Preparation of hide clothing			X
Food preparation			X
Making canoes			X
Making houses and shelters			X
Making mats and baskets			X

Most studies of specific quarries will also need to determine population, the other major variable affecting total lithic demand. For example, if one wished to know how much of an outcrop had been removed by a particular prehistoric culture, it would be neccessary to calculate L, multiply this by the number of years the quarry was in use, and then multiply the resulting value by the number of households using the quarry.

Population is probably best approached by first defining the territory served by a particular quarry. Frequently, there will be a core area around the quarry, within which nearly 100 per cent of archaeological assemblages are composed of material from the quarry (Luedtke 1976). In addition, there is usually a more distant zone within which only a proportion of most archaeological assemblages is made up of material from the quarry in question. The population parameter must be estimated separately for each of these zones. Once a territory is defined, population density for the territory can be estimated on the basis of ethnographic analogy or other means (Weiss 1973; Swedlund 1975). From these values, the number of households using the quarry each year can be estimated.

Archaeological case study

All possible applications of the lithic demand formula cannot be discussed here, but a specific case study will be presented as a general illustration of the usefulness of the formula. This case stems from a study of exchange and interaction patterns during the Late Woodland period in Michigan (Luedtke 1976). From about A.D. 700 to A.D. 1300, this region was inhabited by people with a range of adaptations, including sedentary horticulturalists in the south and nomadic hunter/gatherer/fishers in the north. The study was concerned with the extent to which exchange and interaction took place across ecological and cultural boundaries, and lithic materials were used as the primary index of interaction. It was found that stone materials were transported long distances from the quarry sources during this period, either through exchange or other interaction processes, but it was not clear why this occurred. If stone was acquired by people far from the source because of economic necessity, then the distribution and quantities of the material at archaeological sites would reflect primarily underlying geological patterns of raw-material availability. However, if stone was being exchanged as an accompaniment to a variety of other social processes, then distributions and quantities of raw materials should be a reflection of total social interaction.

The problem, then, was fairly straightforward: could locally available sources of stone meet the needs of the populations resident in the different parts of Michigan? If the answer was yes, then lithic exchange must have been determined by factors other than pure economic necessity. If local supplies of stone could not meet demand, however, then necessity had to be considered as a strong motive for trade.

The first step in determining demand was to assess the range of stone-tool functions for Upper Great Lakes people of this time period. Since the Late Woodland is also the period of first European contact, there is a great deal of ethnohistoric data available on the activities of people in this area. Blair

Table 6.6. *Estimate of flaked stone used by Great Lakes Indians.*

Task	T_i	Tool	D_i	T_i/D_i	S_i	$M_i + R_i$	L_i
Making bows	1	scraper	0.33	3	10	300	930
Making arrows	40	scraper	2	20	10	300	6,200
Tipping arrows	40	projectile point	1	40	2.5	100	4,100
Making clubs	1	scraper	0.5	2	10	300	620
Making spears	5	scraper	0.5	10	10	300	3,100
Making bark and wooden containers	5	scraper	1	5	10	300	1,550
Making snares, traps, fishing gear, snowshoes, and misc. equipment	25	knife, scraper	0.5	50	10	300	15,500
Preparation of clothing	20	knife, scraper	1	20	10	300	6,200
Making bone and shell beads	15	drill, scraper	5	3	5	150	465
Food preparation	90	chopper, knife	3	30	20	300	9,600
Construction of canoes	5	scraper, knife (axe)	0.5	10	20	600	6,200
House, shelter, and village construction	0.2	(axe), heavy chopper	0.05	4	100	200	1,200
Cutting reeds for mats and baskets	10	knife, scraper	2	5	10	300	1,550
Totals				202 tools/year			57,215 g/household/year

(1911), Kinietz (1940), and Thwaites (1897) were used as major sources for information on activities.

In addition, the range of tools found at archaeological sites of this period was considered, and attempts were made to relate tools to activities. Unfortunately, no thorough use-wear studies have been performed on Upper Great Lakes tool types thus far, so it is difficult to say exactly how many tools were used. For example, we do not know whether end scrapers were used for woodworking, hide preparation, fish scaling, or combinations of these and other possible functions. Until use-wear studies such as those performed in other regions have been performed on Michigan assemblages (Odell 1980; Keeley 1977), it will be impossible to relate specific tools to specific activities with complete confidence. However, general morphological categories of tools can at least be assigned to general categories of activities.

It was immediately apparent that the range of tasks calling for stone tools was considerably greater in this region than it had been for either Australia or New Guinea, primarily because of the colder climate and the consequent need for more substantial shelter and clothing (table 6.5). Of course, there would have been variation between the various tribes as to the kinds of tasks performed, but it was assumed that the total number would be reasonably similar for all groups in the region. While wood, bone, and antler tools were common functional alternatives to stone in this area, they all required stone tools for their manufacture. Ground-stone axes were made in this area during the Late Woodland period and were probably used for much of the heavy woodworking and fire-wood chopping. Ground-stone tools have not been included in the material totals in table 6.6, but they are mentioned in parentheses under some categories of activity where they were undoubtedly used. Hoes are also not included because they were not used by all Late Woodland groups of this area and because functional equivalents to stone were probably more important as hoe blades. Utilized flakes were classified as 'scraper' or 'knife', depending on how they were used.

Estimates for the number of times different activities were done each year came from the meager ethnohistoric data on this subject, from ethnographic analogy, and sometimes from pure speculation. Estimates for D_i, tool use-life, were derived from replication experiments (Luedtke n.d.) and ethnographic analogy. All of these estimates were deliberately conservative, and are subject to revision as better data become available.

The remaining values in table 6.6 are based on measurements taken from actual Late Woodland assemblages in the course of the larger study (Luedtke 1976) and are therefore likely to be quite valid. S_i is an average value based on the weights of archaeological examples of each tool type, while $M_i + R_i$ is based on the ratio of debitage to artifacts at the 54 sites used in the study (fig. 6.1), adjusted somewhat for different tool types. Resharpening does not appear to be very significant for most tools in these assemblages. Again, a possible source of error for these estimates is the quantity of lithic material deposited in places other than habitation sites (cf. Hayden 1978). It can only be hoped that the various sources of possible error in these estimates will cancel each other out, rather than compound the total error.

The resulting estimate of stone-tool material needed per family per year is about 50 kg (110 pounds), which seems reasonable when compared with the values for Australia and New Guinea. The Australian tool kit was generalized and individual, as it included items that every man had to have at all times. The New Guinea tool kit was more specialized, and there was therefore much more variation in the quantities needed per person. Although men were probably the primary users of stone tools in the Great Lakes area, as in the other areas considered, women also used knives, scrapers, and choppers in their daily activities to a considerable extent. Therefore, men and women in the Great Lakes area would probably have had personal or family tool kits somewhat larger than those of the Australian Aborigines because of the wider range of functions for which they used stone tools. In addition, Great Lakes Indians also probably had specialized tool kits for some of the periodic tasks shown in table 6.6.

The Great Lakes tools are generally quite a bit smaller than the Australian tools, perhaps due in part to the small size of the nodular and tabular chert available in Michigan. Nodules and chunks of Michigan chert are rarely greater than 10 cm in thickness, and this limits the size of any tools made on this raw material. Also, the quantity of debitage on Michigan sites is considerably greater than on the Australian sites described by Hayden. Hayden found ratios of tools to debitage of 1:5 and 1:1.5. For the 54 Michigan sites in this study, ratios of tools to debitage ranged from 1:1.5 to 1:345, with the median at 1:20. This suggests somewhat different patterns

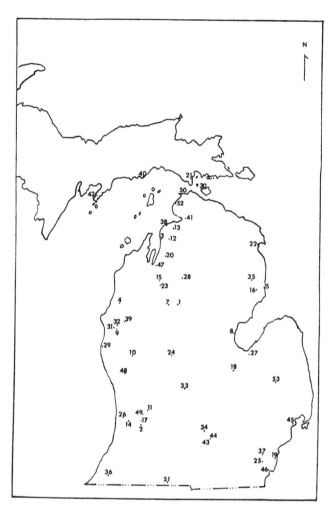

Fig. 6.1. Locations of Michigan prehistoric sites used in this study.

of lithic material procurement, processing, and disposal. An alternative explanation, testable with use-wear studies, is that the Michigan 'debitage' actually contains many utilized flakes with microscopic wear.

The results of calculation of the lithic-demand formula for Great Lakes groups indicate that one very heavy pack load or one canoe load of stone could have satisfied a family's needs for a year. There are a number of stone-quarry sources in the region which could have been exploited (fig. 6.2), and usable chert is also available almost universally in the glacial gravels that blanket the state. Timed pickup of chert pebbles from gravel banks in several parts of the state indicated that at least two usable pebbles could be found in a minute. If the pebbles are assumed to weigh 50 g, a minimal figure, then the total stone needed by a family could have been acquired from gravels alone in slightly more than eight hours. It is likely that prehistoric people went directly to quarries when they were in the vicinity, because of the larger quantities and higher quality of the cherts there, but it is unlikely that they would procure all of the needed chert for a year in a single trip, as this would require considerable transportation of a heavy and bulky

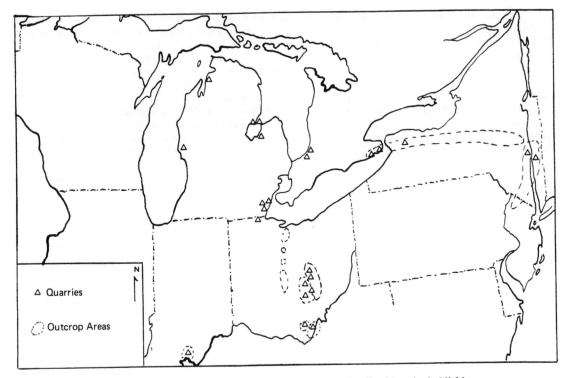

Fig. 6.2. Locations of major quarries exploited, directly or indirectly, by Late Woodland Peoples in Michigan.

commodity. Common sense, and analysis of archaeological assemblages, suggest that most groups used a mixed chert-procurement strategy, including occasional trips to quarries as well as the casual collection of pebbles from gravel banks and stream beds during the course of other activities.

Given this scale of lithic demand, and the readily available supply of stone, it is unlikely that stone was traded for purely economic reasons during the Late Woodland period in Michigan. It can be concluded that lithic exchange occurred primarily for social and political reasons during this period.

Conclusions

Consideration of the factor of lithic demand can provide a useful means for understanding lithic procurement strategies, quarrying practices, and other aspects of prehistoric economic and social adaptations. While many applications of the lithic-demand formula are possible, a single example has been presented to demonstrate its utility.

I hope that this article will stimulate responses of two types. First, if additional ethnographic data relevant to 'ithic demand exist in the literature, in unpublished field notes, or in fieldworkers' or informants' memories, it should be reported. Second, I hope that others will help to refine the various values used in the demand formula so that it will reflect Upper Great Lakes prehistoric reality more accurately, and so that the formula can be applied with greater security to other archaeological cases.

Acknowledgments

A somewhat different version of this chapter was published in the *Midcontinental Journal of Archaeology* 4. The author is especially grateful to D. Braun for his comments on the earlier version, and to J. E. Ericson for his suggestions on revisions. R. Gould, B. Hayden, J. P. White, and C. Modjeska very kindly provided the unpublished data upon which earlier drafts of this work were based, and their help is greatly appreciated.

References

Blair, E. H. ed. and trans. 1911. *The Indian tribes of the Upper Mississippi Valley and the Great Lakes regions.* Cleveland: Arthur J. Clark.

Butzer, K. W. 1964. *Environment and archaeology.* Chicago: Aldine.

Crabtree, D. E. 1966. A stoneworker's approach to analyzing and replicating the Lindenmeier Folsom. *Tebiwa* 9:3–39.

1972. *An introduction to flintworking.* Occasional Papers of the Idaho State University Museum no. 28, Pocatello.

Gould, R. A. 1977. Ethnoarchaeology; or, where do models come from? In R. V. S. Wright ed., *Stone tools as cultural markers.* Australian Institute of Aboriginal Studies, Canberra, 162–8.

Gould, R. A., Koster, D. & Sontz, A. H. 1971. The lithic assemblage of the Western Desert Aborigines of Australia. *American Antiquity* 36:149–69.

Gramly, R. M. 1980. Prehistoric industry at the Mt Jasper mine, northern New Hampshire. *Man in the Northeast* 20:1–24.

Hayden, B. 1977. Stone tool functions in the Western Desert. In R. V. S. Wright, ed., *Stone tools as cultural markers.* Australian Institute of Aboriginal Studies, Canberra, 178–88.

1978. Snarks in archaeology; or, inter-assemblage variability in lithics (a view from the antipodes). In D. D. Davis, ed., *Lithics and subsistence.* Vanderbilt University Publications in Anthropology no. 20, Nashville, 179–98.

1979 *Paleolithic reflections: lithic technolgoy of the Australian Western Desert.* Australian Institute of Aboriginal Studies, in press.

Keeley, L. H. 1977. The functions of Paleolithic stone tools. *Scientific American* 237 (5): 108–26.

Kinietz, W. V. 1940. *The Indians of the western Great Lakes, 1615–1760.* Occasional Contributions of the Museum of Anthropology no. 10, University of Michigan, Ann Arbor.

Luedtke, B. E. 1976. Lithic material distributions and interaction patterns during the Late Woodland period in Michigan. Ph.D. dissertation, Department of Anthropology, University of Michigan, Ann Arbor.

n.d. The determination of functions of stone implements. Unpublished Ms., University of Michigan Museum of Anthropology.

Newcomer, M. H. & Sieveking, G. de G. 1980. Experimental flake scatter-patterns: a new interpretive technique. *Journal of Field Archaeology* 7:345–52.

Odell, G. H. 1980. Toward a more behavioral approach to archaeological lithic concentrations. *American Antiquity* 45:404–31.

Osgood, C. 1970. *Ingalik material culture.* Yale University Publications in Anthropology 22 (1940), reprinted by Human Relations Area Files Press, New Haven, Conn.

Sharp, L. 1952. Steel axes for stone age Australians. In Edward H. Spicer, ed., *Human problems in technological change: a casebook.* New York: The Russel Sage Foundation.

Singer, C. A. & J. E. Ericson. 1977. Quarry analysis at Bodie Hills, Mono County, California: a case study. In Timothy K. Earle and Jonathon E. Ericson, eds., *Exchange systems in prehistory,* New York: Academic Press, 171–87.

Strathern, M. 1969. Stone axes and flake tools; evaluations from two New Guinea Highlands societies. *Proceedings of the Prehistoric Society* 35:311–29.

Swedlund, A. ed. 1975. *Population studies in archaeology and biological anthropology: a symposium.* Memoirs of the Society for American Archaeology 30, Washington, D.C.

Thwaites, R. G. ed. 1897. *The Jesuit relations and allied documents.* Cleveland: Burrows Brothers.

Walker, P. L. 1978. Butchering and stone tool function. *American Antiquity* 43:710–15.

Weiss, K. M. 1973. *Demographic models for anthropology.* Memoirs of the Society for American Archaeology 27, Washington, D.C.

White, C. & N. Peterson, 1969. Ethnographic interpretations of the prehistory of western Arnhem Land. *Southwestern Journal of Anthropology* 25:1–23.

White, J. P. & Thomas, D. H. 1972. What mean these stones? Ethno-taxonomic models and archaeological interpretations in the New Guinea Highlands. In D. L. Clarke, ed., *Models in archaeology,* London: Methuen, 275–308.

Chapter 7

**Economic aspects of prehistoric quarry use:
a case study in the American southwest**
F. J. Findlow and M. Bolognese

Quarry use at the Hermanas Ruin, a San Luis Phase community in southwestern New Mexico, is analyzed in light of modern optimization theory. Initial results of this analysis suggest that many of the changes in lithic use at this site resulted from a process of optimizing the procurement of five different lithic materials, so that all related costs were minimized. This research has broad implications for archaeological quarry analysis as it suggests that economic analyses of multiple material lithic procurement systems will provide insights into prehistoric quarry use not apparent in traditional quarry analyses.

Introduction

Although reports on 'quarry analysis' are appearing with increased frequency in the archaeological literature, only a small fraction of these reports involve economic analyses. An even fewer number of studies have sought to analyze the total lithic procurement strategy of prehistoric societies. With a small number of exceptions (cf. Ericson 1977; Bettinger n.d.), most quarry analysts have focused their attention on quarrying procedures and subsequent manufacturing activities at single quarry sites (cf. Singer & Ericson 1977). Economic analyses of lithic procurement strategies involving multiple raw materials have generally remained outside the scope of quarry analysis.

Of particular interest in this analysis is a subject which is often overlooked, namely, to understand the ways in which prehistoric groups scheduled their quarry activities when multiple raw materials with different quarry locales were needed. Specifically, how were such quarrying-related costs as

transport, preform preparation, and the actual quarrying balanced as a single economic activity? Likewise, what sort of decision processes were involved when a society had access to competing raw materials such as chert or obsidian when procurement costs were roughly equivalent?

In many ways the lack of an economic component in most archaeological quarry analyses is surprising since archaeologists often imply that the quarry activities they study are governed by the 'costs' and 'benefits' involved in the use of a particular raw material (cf. Ericson 1977). Such assumptions, however, have generally remained just that; and very few analyses have incorporated tests that would allow such assumptions to be confirmed or rejected. This lack of testing is even more remarkable if one considers how much of archaeological/ anthropological theory depends on optimization principles (cf. Harris 1968).

In this chapter we examine the cross-temporal changes in the lithic procurement strategies found at a single prehistoric community, the Hermanas Ruin in southwestern New Mexico. Our primary objective is to assess the degree to which the sequence of changes in lithic raw material preference at that site represented directional movements toward more optimal procurement patterns. Specifically, we are attempting to show that the changes in lithic material use at Hermanas Ruin marked an attempt on the part of its former inhabitants to simultaneously minimize transport costs and waste rates across their entire lithic procurement system, while maximizing the benefits they derived from the use of a series of different raw materials, each with its own particular physical characteristics.

Data for the present analysis come from the Hermanas Ruin excavation report published by Fitting (1971) and from collections made during the course of Columbia University's Hidalgo Archaeological Research Project (Findlow & DeAtley 1976; Findlow 1980). The analyses reported on here involve changes in the use of five different lithic materials during the roughly 100-year occupancy of Hermanas Ruin. The research methods are based primarily on the use of linear programming techniques (Dorfman, Samuelson & Solow 1958).

Hermanas Ruin

The Hermanas Ruin is a small San Luis Phase (Mimbres) site located just west of Hermanas in Luna County, New Mexico (fig. 7.1). First recorded by Kidder *et al.* (1949), the site has received intermittent attention both from professional archaeologists and pot hunters. The data used in this study were collected in 1970 during excavations in undamaged portions of the site (Fitting 1971). Based on a comparison of the data collected by Fitting (1971) and data collected on a number of similar sites in the area (Findlow & DeAtley 1976; Findlow 1980), it is now evident that the Hermanas Ruin represents a brief, though apparently continuous, San Luis Phase occupation, spanning the period from the end of the eleventh century to the end of the twelfth century. Despite the short occupation, deposits on the site reveal a clear stratigraphic sequence.

Three factors were of primary importance in the decision to use data from the Hermanas Ruin in this analysis: (1) the clear evidence that the site represents a single component occupation, free from breaks; (2) the comprehensive body of data available on the use of a series of lithic raw materials by the site's occupants (Fitting 1971); (3) good stratigraphic control that allowed patterns of lithic raw materials use to be assessed at different points during the site's occupation. In combination, these three factors produced an ideal body of data that allowed the decisions made concerning the use of different lithic raw materials to be isolated.

The geologic setting of Hermanas Ruin

An examination of figure 7.2 reveals that Hermanas Ruin is located in an area of great geological diversity. Within relatively short distances are outcrops producing basalts, chert, and agate, all within seven miles of the site. Obsidian from the Antelope Wells source in Hidalgo County is available 64 miles southwest of the site. In this study we are concerned with five raw materials that combined make up over 95.7 per cent of the total lithic assemblage at Hermanas Ruin (Fitting 1971). In order of relative frequency these materials include: basalt, which is available in formations within one mile of the site; Pauley chert (fine-grained rhyolite), available within six miles of the site; Pauley jasper (another rhyolite), also available

Fig. 7.1. The location of Hermanas Ruin.

within six miles of the site; agate, which occurs in outcrops roughly seven miles from the site; and Antelope Wells obsidian, which occurs 64 miles from Hermanas Ruin.

An examination of these five materials allows them to be evaluated in terms of their general utility as components in the Hermanas Ruin lithic technology. In the simplest terms, the benefits of each can be ranked according to their relative efficiency in producing the edges necessary for particular tools (table 7.1). Likewise, each can also be ranked in accordance with the costs each involves in procurement and production (table 7.2).

Even a cursory examination of tables 7.1 and 7.2 makes it apparent that the occupants of Hermanas Ruin were confronted with a number of important decisions concerning what balance should be maintained between the costs and benefits of using the five raw materials. For example, would the relatively cheap procurement costs associated with basalt make up for its low efficiency as a tool-producing material? Or could the high procurement costs of obsidian be offset by the efficiency of the material in producing sharp edges?

From the variety of lithic raw materials at Hermanas Ruin it is apparent that all of the five raw materials were not fully interchangeable. Obsidian could not always be substituted for basalt, and vice versa. Elements such as the size of the finished tool and the frequency with which it had to be replaced must have reduced the interchangeability of these materials and helped to ensure that none of them could be dropped from the assemblage without incurring some additional costs (cf. Jones 1980, 153–65). As a result, the prehistoric occupants were confronted with a two-fold problem.

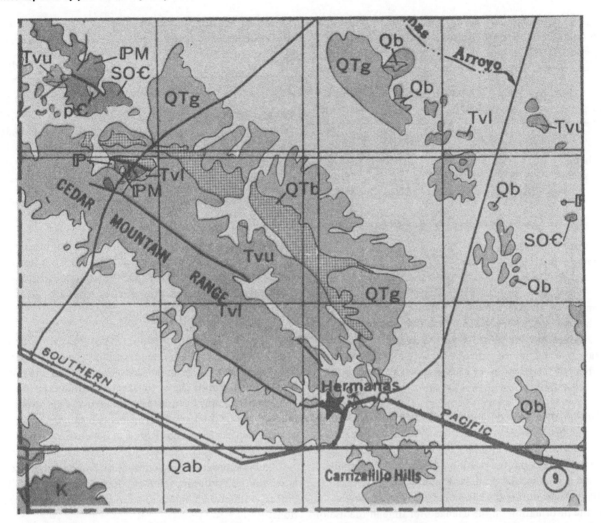

Fig. 7.2. Geological setting of Hermanas Ruin. Qb represents basalt flows; QTg, Gila conglomerate; QTb, basalt/andesite flows; Tvu, quartz latite, latite, and andesite; Tvl, quartz latite, rhyolite, and andesite; IPM, Pennsylvanian and Mississippian rocks; OP, Pennsylvanian rocks; SOC, Silurian, Ordovician, and Cambrian rocks; and Qab, alluvium and other surface deposits. Pauley cherts and Pauley jasper derive from quarries in the Cedar Mountains (Tvl); Agate quarries were also located in the Cedar Mountains (Tvu). Obsidian was obtained from the Antelope Wells source 64 miles southwest of the site (not shown).

Table 7.1. *Relative costs of lithic materials.*

Material	Weight[1] per tool	Distance[2] to source	Adjusted[3] distance	Percentage of waste per unit	Trips per unit of material[4]
Basalt	35.00	1.0	430	92	12.5
Pauley chert	25.00	6.0	1,500	90	10.0
Pauley jasper	14.33	6.0	860	90	10.0
Agate	4.00	7.0	280	90	10.0
Obsidian	1.00	64.00	109	57	2.3

1 Weight in grams

2 Distance in miles

3 Distance in miles multiplied by the average weight needed per tool

4 i.e. 1.0/percentage of waste

Table 7.2. *Relative edge sharpness of Hermanas Ruin lithic raw materials and the number of tools produced per kilogram of raw material.*

Material	Sharpness rank[1]	Tools per kilogram[2]
Basalt	4	2.28
Pauley chert	3	4.00
Pauley jasper	2	6.98
Agate	2	25.00
Obsidian	1	100.00

1 Sharpness of edges
2 After removing the waste flakes

On the one hand, they required a certain minimum amount of each of the five raw materials, something that placed rather rigid constraints on their ability to vary their overall procurement strategy while, on the other hand, they had to deal with the cost/benefit relationships of each material as a part of a total (five-material) procurement system.

Chronological changes in lithic use at Hermanas Ruin

During his excavations at Hermanas Ruin, Fitting (1971) collected data within five arbitrary 0.5-foot levels. As level 5 was found only on a limited portion of the site, he combined levels 4 and 5 in reporting his data. Representing as they do sequential periods during the site's occupancy, these levels preserve the information on the change over time in the use of lithic raw materials. Table 7.3 shows the percentages of each material within each of Fitting's levels (1971). Table 7.4 illustrates the average use together with the maximum and minimum use for each material.

An examination of these tables shows that the pattern of use among the five lithic raw materials was quite variable from level to level. In the case of some materials, such as agate and Pauley chert, clear patterns of change can be observed during the site's occupation. For others, such as obsidian and

Table 7.3. *Raw material used by level.*[1]

Material	Level 1	Level 2	Level 3	Levels 4—5
Basalt	0.261	0.190	0.183	0.223
Pauley chert	0.150	0.202	0.223	0.254
Pauley jasper	0.438	0.440	0.422	0.363
Agate	0.142	0.147	0.150	0.156
Obsidian	0.009	0.021	0.012	0.004

1 All values represent percentages of the total lithic assemblage

Table 7.4. *The use of lithic materials at Hermanas Ruin.*

Material	Mean[1]	Maximum	Minimum
Basalt	0.214	0.261	0.183
Pauley chert	0.210	0.254	0.150
Pauley jasper	0.416	0.440	0.363
Agate	0.149	0.142	0.156
Obsidian	0.012	0.021	0.004

1 All values represent percentages of the lithic assemblage

basalt, the trends are less clear. While the exact meaning of the observed changes cannot be determined from the patterning, nevertheless it is evident that the site's occupants rather frequently adjusted their procurement strategy.

Methodology

The methodology used in this study involves the use of standard linear programming procedures (Dorfman, Samuelson & Solow 1958). In the most general sense linear programming is used to determine the optimal mix of lithic resources used at Hermanas Ruin. In turn the optimal usage discovered in this manner will be used as a base against which changes in lithic procurement at Hermanas Ruin can be measured and interpreted.

Linear programming consists of finding either the maximum or minimum value of a linear function, called an objective function, subject to a series of constraints or restrictions:

1. Objective function

$$f(x) = C_1 X_1 + C_2 X_2 + \ldots + C_N X_N. \qquad (1)$$

2. Constraints

$$A_{11} X_1 + A_{12} X_2 + \ldots + A_{1N} X_N \leqslant b_1$$
$$A_{21} X_1 + A_{22} X_2 + \ldots + A_{2n} X_n \leqslant b_2$$

$$\qquad (2)$$

$$A_{M1} X_1 + A_{M2} X_2 + \ldots + A_{MN} X_n \leqslant b_M$$

Where feasible, solutions represent all points that solve (1) over the set (2), and optimal solutions are those points where (f) takes on a maximum or minimum value (Dorfman, Samuelson & Solow 1958).

In this chapter we make use of linear programming to find the optimal use for each of the five lithic raw materials used at Hermanas Ruin. Specifically, we find the pattern of

Table 7.5. *Optimal and observed lithic use.*[1]

Material	Optimal use	Level 1	Level 2	Level 3	Levels 4—5
Basalt	0.223	0.261	0.190	0.183	0.223
Pauley chert	0.161	0.150	0.202	0.223	0.254
Pauley Jasper	0.439	0.438	0.440	0.422	0.363
Agate	0.156	0.142	0.147	0.150	0.156
Obsidian	0.021	0.009	0.021	0.012	0.004

1 All values represent percentages of the total lithic assemblage, optimal use based on the results of the linear programming analysis

use among the materials that will minimize all of the costs listed in table 7.1 while under the constraint that each material must be used. For each raw material the latter constraints are determined from the variation in observed use found at the site. For each material the upper and lower bounds of the constraints on usage were determined from the maximum and minimum use observed at the site (table 7.4). For example, the constraints on the use of basalt were an upper bound of 0.261 per cent and a lower bound of 0.183 per cent.

The cost associated with the use of each raw material was the amount of material needed to manufacture an average tool made from that material multiplied by the distance to the source of the material. For example, the average weight of a tool made from agate was 4 g and 90 per cent of all agate ended up as waste flakes. The distance to the agate quarry is seven miles. Consequently, 4 g represents 10 per cent of the total amount of agate needed by weight to make the average agate tool; 10 per cent equals 4 g and the total necessary 40 g; 40 multiplied by the distance to the quarry equals 280. The cost of using agate is therefore 280. Table 7.1 lists the costs for each material.

Analysis and results

Using the maximum and minimum values observed for each raw material within the Hermanas Ruin lithic assemblage as the upper and lower bounds on the constraints for each material, and the costs associated with the procurement of each material (tables 7.1—7.4), a linear program was run to find the optimal use level for each of the five raw materials. Table 7.5 shows the results of this analysis and provides a comparison of this optimal usage of the five raw materials with the actual values found in the stratigraphic levels of each site. Table 7.6 illustrates the derivation of the observed values for each raw material in each level from the optimal value.

Based on these analyses a number of general trends in use of lithics at Hermanas Ruin are evident. Most important is the clear evidence that the changes in lithic procurement involved a reduction in the total costs associated with the

quarrying, transport, and manufacture of stone tools. It is clear that in the 100 or so years of occupation, a steady reduction in deviation from the optimal pattern took place.

Also apparent from these analyses is the fact that the changes that led toward a more optimal procurement strategy at Hermanas Ruin involved several major shifts in the pattern of lithic use over time. As tables 7.5 and 7.6 show, the trend toward greater optimality did not occur uniformly across all five of the lithic materials. Indeed in some instances (Pauley chert, obsidian) the trend seems to be erratic. While it is not completely clear from the analysis, it appears that the Hermanas Ruin inhabitants were attempting to achieve a stable use pattern, by first finding the optimal use level for those materials required in the greatest absolute bulk, i.e., basalt and Pauley jasper. In both of these cases, values near optimal are reached rather quickly during the site's occupation and then maintained. This appears to have been accomplished by reducing the use of materials used in small quantities to the lowest possible amount, even if this meant using them less than optimally, i.e., agate, Pauley chert, and obsidian. This may also have been due to the prehistoric inhabitant's perception of costs as a direct function of distance to the quarry,

Table 7.6. *Deviations from optimal lithic use.*[1]

Material	Level 1	Level 2	Level 3	Levels 4—5
Basalt	0.038	0.033	0.040	0.000
Pauley chert	0.011	0.041	0.072	0.093
Pauley jasper	0.001	0.001	0.017	0.076
Agate	0.014	0.009	0.006	0.000
Obsidian	0.012	0.000	0.009	0.017
Total Deviation	0.077	0.083	0.145	0.187

1 All values represent percentages of the total lithic assemblage

since obsidian, Pauley chert, and agate are all derived from quarries at greater distances than apparently functionally similar materials of basalt and Pauley jasper.

While it cannot be concluded that the use of raw materials at Hermanas Ruin would have achieved a perfectly optimal pattern, these analyses do indicate that the changes that occurred prehistorically were focused on that goal. Had the Hermanas Ruin been occupied longer it is likely that the deviation from the optimal use of raw materials would have continued to be gradually reduced.

Discussion and conclusions

The importance of this study lies not in the demonstration that quarry use at Hermanas Ruin became increasingly optimal over time, but rather in the support it provides for the use of cost-benefit analysis methods in archaeological quarry analysis. Of specific importance to all archaeologists studying prehistoric quarry use is the evidence these analyses provide, illustrating that changes in the use of a particular raw material may have been predicated not so much by physical characteristics as by the need to use a variety of lithic resources. It is clear from the use of lithics at the Hermanas Ruin that the economic factors that regulate quarry use cannot be understood through reference to the quarrying and procurement of any single lithic resource. The unit of analysis must be the full range of raw materials used by prehistoric community if changes in the use of any particular raw material are going to be understood. In short, prehistoric populations, like modern ones, were involved in economic behavior that was systematic in the true sense of the word. Consequently, if archaeologists are going to understand the quarry usage of prehistoric groups they must analyze the whole range of economic factors that influenced prehistoric decisions about quarry use.

On a more specific level, the analyses reported here shed light on the meaning of lithic use at Hermanas Ruin. When Fitting (1971, 33) summarized his finding about lithic use at the ruin he concluded: 'The earliest occupation seems to have been represented by an industry (lithic) using coarser raw materials and manufacturing larger tools and projectile points . . . This gave way, over time, to a wider variety of raw materials, more exotic raw materials and an increase in smaller objects, particularly smaller projectile points and preforms.'

From these analyses it is now apparent that the trends Fitting recognized were a product of the gradual adjustment on the part of the Hermanas Ruin population in their lithic procurement strategy. Such shifts resulted in a reduction in procurement costs through the use of raw materials that allowed for more tools per unit of raw material and that allowed other procurement costs to be reduced. The clear movement of the use of the five raw materials toward a pattern that minimized all procurement costs provides rather conclusive evidence that the trend observed by Fitting had real economic meaning to the prehistoric inhabitants of Hermanas Ruin.

References

Bettinger, R. L. n.d. Prehistoric territoriality in Owens Valley: Fish Springs obsidian distribution, manuscript.

Dorfman, R., Samuelson, P. A. & Solow, R. M. 1958. *Linear programming and economic analysis*. New York: McGraw-Hill.

Ericson, J. E. 1977. Egalitarian exchange systems in California: a preliminary view. In T. K. Earle & J. E. Ericson, eds., *Exchange systems in prehistory*. New York: Academic Press, 109–26.

Findlow, F. J. 1980. A catchment analysis of San Luis Phase and Animas Phase sites in southwestern New Mexico. In F. J. Findlow & J. E. Ericson, eds., *Catchment analysis essays on prehistoric resource space, Anthropology, UCLA* 10 (142): 157–78.

Findlow, F. J. & DeAtley, S. P. 1976. Prehistoric land use patterns in the Animas Valley: a first approximation. *Anthropology, UCLA* 6 (2):1–57.

Fitting, J. E. 1971. The Hermanas Ruin, Luna County, New Mexico. *Southwestern New Mexico Research Reports* 3, Department of Anthropology, Case Western Reserve University, Cleveland.

Harris, M. 1968. *The rise of anthropological theory*. New York: Crowell.

Jones, P. R. 1980. Experimental butchery with modern stone tools and its relevance for Paleolithic archaeology. *World Archaeology* 12 (2):153–65.

Kidder, A. V., Cosgrove, H. S. & Cosgrove, C. B. 1949. The Pendleton Ruin, Hidalgo County, New Mexico. *Contribution to American Anthropology and History*, Washington, D.C.: Carnegie Institution, 50:108–52.

Singer, C. A. & Ericson, J. E. 1977. Quarry analysis at Bodie Hills, Mono County, California: a case study. In T. K. Earle & J. E. Ericson, eds., *Exchange systems in prehistory*. New York: Academic Press, 171–90.

Chapter 8

Preliminary report on the obsidian mines at Pico de Orizaba, Veracruz
T. L. Stocker and R. H. Cobean

The obsidian mines at Pico de Orizaba, Veracruz, are important to the study of Mexico's prehistory for at least four reasons: (1) They are some of the best preserved pre-Hispanic mines in the New World, never having been damaged by looters. (2) Due to the unlooted nature of these mines, they provide a highly detailed record of ancient technology in Mexico. (3) They are among the few pre-Hispanic obsidian quarries which can be at least partially dated with considerable confidence. (4) On the basis of results from trace-element analyses, it is very likely that obsidian from the general area of the Pico de Orizaba mines was exploited and traded by Mexico's ancient peoples for thousands of years.

Introduction

Until recently, very few Mesoamerican obsidian quarries have been surveyed or excavated by archaeologists. Most of this chapter will be devoted to describing our fieldwork at the Pico de Orizaba, Veracruz, obsidian mines including the excavations done there by Stocker in 1973 which are still unpublished (Stocker, Cobean & Swibel 1974). To our knowledge the only excavation of a Mesoamerican obsidian quarry previous to the work reported here was done by W. H. Holmes (1900) in his pioneering research at the Sierra de Pachuca in Hidalgo during the late nineteenth century. The results of our fieldwork, especially the excavations, are extremely modest, but we would like to use them to emphasize that much more rigorous excavation and survey programs need to be done at Mesoamerican quarry sites before archaeologists can begin to understand the mechanisms of pre-Hispanic obsidian exploitation in any detail.

The data which we have recovered for the Pico de Orizaba mines is very incomplete and only can be analyzed and reported in a tentative manner. We never had the resources to pursue a long-term intensive field program at this quarry. Most of our data was collected during brief visits while we were in Mexico working on archaeological projects that did not deal directly with obsidian studies.

The obsidian mines at Pico de Orizaba are important to the study of Mexico's prehistory for at least four reasons. First, they are some of the best-preserved pre-Hispanic mines in the New World. No part of them has been damaged by looters, unlike the obsidian quarries of Central Mexico (especially in the Sierra de Pachuca, Hidalgo, and at Otumba, Estado de Mexico) which have been extensively destroyed by local people seeking obsidian to make souvenirs for tourists.

Secondly, due to the unlooted nature of the Pico de Orizaba mines, they provide a highly detailed record of ancient technology in Mexico. Many components of the pre-Hispanic quarrying operation are still preserved in place where the Indian miners left them at least five centuries ago. There are at least four unblocked prehistoric mine shafts, most of which contain the original wooden ladders used by the miners along with stacks of processed high-quality obsidian and some mining tools in place. Near the mine shafts there are standing walls and foundation stones for buildings where the miners lived and worked. Enormous amounts of obsidian flakes and other quarrying and knapping debris form large taluses below each mine entrance (fig. 8.1).

Thirdly, these mines are among the few pre-Hispanic obsidian quarries which can be at least partially dated with considerable confidence. As will be described below, significant amounts of Late Postclassic (*c.* A.D. 1350–1520) Aztec pottery have been found associated with the Pico de Orizaba mines.

Lastly, it is very likely that obsidian from the general area of the Pico de Orizaba mines was exploited and traded by Mexico's ancient peoples for thousands of years. Trace-element analyses by a number of investigators have shown that obsidian from outcrops on or near Orizaba volcano was being used extensively by peoples in southern Mexico at least as early as 1500 B.C. (Cobean *et al.* 1971; Pires-Ferreira 1975; Hester, Jack & Heizer 1971; Zeitlin 1979; Zeitlin & Heimbuch 1978), but the widespread use of Orizaba volcano obsidian probably started long before this. The Yale University obsidian program analyzed a Midland point from the El Riego phase in the Tehuacan Valley, Puebla (dating to shortly after 6500 B.C.) and found it to be made with obsidian from a flow on Orizaba volcano near Guadalupe Victoria, Puebla (Cobean *et al.* 1971, 668).

Background

Pico de Orizaba volcano at 5,700 m is the third highest mountain in North America and the highest peak in Mexico. The Aztecs called it Citlaltepetl, 'Mountain of the Star'. It is capped by glaciers and covered by snow year-round. Orizaba volcano is located 200 km southeast of Mexico City and is situated almost exactly on the border between the states of Veracruz and Puebla. The borderline bisects the volcano and its slopes into eastern (Veracruz side) and western (Puebla side) sectors.

At least four obsidian outcrops have been reported to date in areas on or near the slopes of Pico de Orizaba. On the western slopes (Puebla side) of the volcano, the most extensive obsidian deposits found so far are near the town of Guadalupe Victoria, Puebla. This obsidian source was discovered nearly twenty years ago by J. L. Lorenzo of the Departamento de Prehistoria del Instituto Nacional de Antropologia e Historia (INAH) during his archaeological surveys of Mexican volcanoes (Lorenzo 1969, personal communication). The Guadalupe Victoria source consists of great numbers of obsidian cobbles which have been exposed in barrancas and stream beds along the alluvial sand dunes and lower foothills at the base of Orizaba volcano. No primary obsidian flows have been found exposed in the Guadalupe Victoria source area. It may be that this is actually a secondary source because the obsidian cobbles found in the area may have been transported by streams and erosional processes from higher regions on the slopes of Orizaba volcano.

The densest concentration of obsidian cobbles found so far is in a large barranca on the south edge of the town of Guadalupe Victoria. This barranca runs southeast-northwest and is about 20 to 30 m wide and varies from 5 to 10 m deep. Dense concentrations of obsidian cobbles extend along the bottom of the barranca for at least 4 km beyond the edge of the town to the southeast. No obsidian mine shafts or debitage taluses have been found in the Guadalupe Victoria source area, although there are light concentrations of obsidian fragments in the sand dunes for about a 5-km radius surrounding the town, which in some cases may be remains of ancient obsidian workshops.

A second source of obsidian, which we have not yet visited, is reported by Ramirez (1976, 10) on the south flank

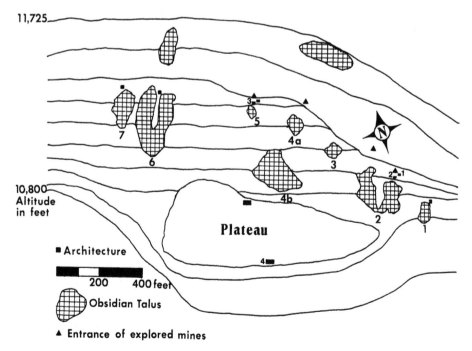

Fig. 8.1. Taluses 1–7 (large figures). The small figures 1–4 denote structures excavated by Stocker in 1973.

of Orizaba volcano about 30 km southeast of Ciudad Serdan, Puebla. Ramirez (1976, 10) calls the location of this source 'La Montana de Arena'. From his brief description, it is not clear if this source area contains actual obsidian flows or just concentrations of cobbles.

A third Orizaba volcano obsidian source is described by C. H. Berendt, a nineteenth-century German anthropologist, in a letter published by Rau (1873, 359) and reprinted in Hester, Jack and Heizer (1971, 102–3). The source which Berendt visited in the 1850s appears to be on the eastern slope of Pico de Orizaba very near the mines which we will describe here. Berendt's source is about 4.5 miles north of the village of Alpatlahua (near Coscomatepec, Veracruz), which places it approximately 10 miles east of the mines that we have investigated. Berendt describes a 'cave' with an entrance about 50 feet high and an interior 'grotto' filled with heaps of obsidian chips (Rau 1873, 359). These features are almost certainly parts of a pre-Hispanic mining system, but they are not like the mines that we found on Pico de Orizaba, which have very narrow entrances that are usually less than 2 m wide.

Both Berendt's letter and the report by Rau in which it is found were translated from a German journal and republished in English in the Smithsonian Institution *Annual Report* for 1872. The original German version of Berendt's letter may contain important details which were lost or distorted in the English translation. Stocker has spent a number of days surveying areas near Alpatlahua, Veracruz, but we have not yet found the mines which Berendt visited.

The Valle del Ixtetal mines

The only extensive pre-Hispanic obsidian mines which we have located so far in our surveys near Pico de Orizaba are on the north slope of the volcano in a valley which farmers in the nearest settlements call the 'Valle del Ixtetal,' the Valley of Obsidian. This valley lies about 20 km northeast of Coscomatepec, Veracruz, near the Puebla border. The obsidian mines in the Valle del Ixtetal are often called 'Cerro Minas' by people in the nearest communities downslope. We first were told about the existence of these mines in 1969 by F. Beverido of the Universidad Veracruzana in Jalapa and by A. Barges of Córdoba, Veracruz.

The Valle del Ixtetal mines are situated in a densely forested region about 4,000 m above sea level (fig. 8.1). They consist of a series of quarry shafts and debitage taluses placed along a steep canyon wall at the base of a cliff. Seven of the debitage taluses are very well preserved, containing hundreds of thousands of obsidian fragments. Some of the taluses are as much as 120 m long and 50 m wide. At the top of each talus is a horizontal mine shaft going into the base of the cliff. At least four of these shafts are relatively free of rubble and contain extensive tunnel systems carved into an enormous obsidian flow inside the canyon wall.

We have found two badly damaged taluses on the mountainside above the seven principal ones (fig. 8.1). These upper taluses appear to be older than the seven lower ones.

The obsidian flakes in the upper taluses are often badly weathered. Much of the original surface of the taluses is covered by soil and vegetation. No mine shafts have been found associated with the two upper taluses, but their entrances may have been covered long ago by erosion or quarrying debris.

There are ruins of small structures at the top of each of the lower seven taluses. These ruins are small rectangular buildings, which have remnants of walls consisting of two or three layers of roughly hewn stone blocks. The majority of these buildings were directly connected to the mine entrances by stone-walled passageways. The buildings and passageways probably had roofs so that the miners could work more comfortably in the cold wet climate of this region. On the plateau below the seven principal taluses are two large architectural units (fig. 8.1), which are characterized by a single layer of roughly hewn stone blocks about 30 cm high. These blocks may have been foundation stones for wooden buildings.

Excavations

In 1973 Stocker excavated four 1-by-1 m test pits in structures at the Valle del Ixtetal mines (fig. 8.1). These excavations were dug in 10 cm arbitrary levels. One pit (Pozo 1) was excavated in the southeast corner of structure no. 2 above Talus 2, and another pit (Pozo 2) was excavated in the southwest corner of structure no. 3 above Talus 5. Two pits were made in structure no. 4 on the plateau below the mines: one (Pozo 3) in the northwest corner and the other (Pozo 4) in the center of the building (Stocker, Cobean & Swibel 1974).

Only three eroded unidentifiable surface sherds were recovered from the excavations in structures 2 and 3, which were terminated at a depth of 70 cm. The fill of both these test pits consisted almost entirely of obsidian debitage, which will be described in a separate publication by Stocker.

The two test pits in structure no. 4 on the plateau produced 47 potsherds, most of which are badly eroded. These excavations were ended at 80 cm because ceramics were encountered only in the upper 30 cm and no lithic remains occurred below 50 cm. In addition to the pottery recovered in the excavations of structure no. 4, over 100 potsherds were found on the surface on or near the seven principal mine taluses (see table 8.1):

The eroded condition of most of the pottery from both the excavations and the surface collections make it impossible to identify confidently the cultural affiliations of the people who built the Valle del Ixtetal mines. On the basis of trace-element analysis results cited above, we suspect that these mines were exploited for a number of centuries, but the few sherds of clearly identifiable pottery which we recovered all date to the same period – the Late Postclassic (c. A.D. 1350–1520). All of these sherds are pure Aztec in style and manufacture (Griffin & Espejo 1947, 1950; Parsons 1966; Charlton 1972). They are probably imports from in or near the Basin of Mexico. All the major attributes of these sherds including slip, paste, and firing are visually identical with the same features

Table 8.1.

Pottery from the excavations

Pozo 1, Surface: 1 eroded unidentifiable sherd
Pozo 2, Surface: 2 eroded unidentifiable sherds
Pozo 3, Surface: 3 eroded unidentifiable sherds
      Level 1: 1 eroded unidentifiable body sherd
      Level 2: 3 eroded unidentifiable body sherds
             1 local Gulf Coast redware sherd
      Level 3: 2 eroded unidentifiable body sherds

Total   10 sherds

Pozo 4, Surface: 1 eroded unidentifiable sherd
      Level 1: 18 eroded unidentifiable sherds
             2 possible Aztec comal rims
      Level 2: 13 eroded unidentifiable sherds
             1 Aztec comal rim
             1 probable Aztec comal rim
             1 possible Aztec stamped incensario rim

Total   37 sherds

Pottery from the surface on or near the mine taluses

Talus 1: 7 eroded unidentifiable sherds
         1 possible local Gulf Coast thin brownware rim
         1 possible local Gulf Coast reddish brownware rim

Total   9 sherds

Talus 2: 66 eroded unidentifiable sherds
         4 eroded olla rims
         1 Aztec III black on orange dish rim
         1 Aztec Texcoco black on red rim
         1 probable Aztec stamped incensario rim
         1 possible Aztec stamped incensario sherd
         1 possible local Gulf Coast incised orangeware sherd

Total   75 sherds

Talus 3: 4 eroded unidentifiable brown olla sherds
         4 eroded unidentifiable orangeware sherds
         1 eroded unidentifiable grayware jar rim
         1 probable Gulf Coast red on orange dish rim

Total   10 sherds

Talus 4: 5 eroded unidentifiable olla sherds
         1 eroded unidentifiable bowl sherd

Total   6 sherds

Note: Paste descriptions and illustrations of the excavated and surface pottery from the Valle del Ixtetal mines will be presented in a future report.

on Aztec pottery in the Basin of Mexico. In addition, about 30 per cent of the 'eroded unidentifiable' sherds from the excavations and surface collections have fine pinkish orange paste which is similar or identical to the paste of most Basin of Mexico Aztec orangeware.

On the basis of the limited ceramic data (table 8.1), we postulate that during the Late Postclassic the Valle del Ixtetal mines were exploited by people who had close ties with the Aztec state. The mines may have been under direct Aztec control. Sixteenth-century Spanish *Relaciónes geográficas* indicate that there was an Aztec imperial garrison and granary complex at Coscomatepec only 20 km downslope from the mines (Gerhard 1972, 83). It may well have been that the Aztecs administered the Valle del Ixtetal mines from their base in Coscomatepec (Stocker 1981). Aztec control of the mines could not have lasted very long, however, because their conquest of this part of Veracruz came late. Aztec tribute records indicate that the region containing Coscomatepec and the Valle del Ixtetal was not conquered until the reign of Axayactl, *c.* A.D. 1469–1481 (Gibson 1971, 379–81).

We possess little data to indicate who controlled the Valle del Ixtetal mines before the Aztec conquest of the area, but we assume that they were worked mainly by local Gulf Coast people. During surveys of the eastern slopes of Orizaba volcano, Stocker found an extensive obsidian workshop site at Calcahualco, Veracruz, about 15 km downslope from the mines. Ceramics from this site indicate that it has a sequence of occupations by local Gulf Coast people spanning from the Middle Formative to the Late Postclassic (A. Medellin Zenil 1973, personal communication). It is very likely that much of the obsidian being worked at Calcahualco came from the Valle del Ixtetal and that local people controlled the obsidian-production system on the slopes of Orizaba volcano for centuries or millennia.

Our excavations did not produce much information concerning the functions of the structures associated with the Valle del Ixtetal mines. Most of the ceramics recovered, including the Aztec sherds, are from utilitarian or 'domestic' vessels that probably were employed for cooking and serving food.

The two excavated structures above the taluses contained large amounts of obsidian knapping debris, while the building excavated on the plateau contained only small quantities of debris. It is likely that the structures above the taluses were used as knapping areas to process obsidian. We do not know if all the structures functioned as living places for the miners. The scarcity of pottery in the two buildings located above Taluses 2 and 5 suggests that they may not have been used frequently as living areas. The major residences for the miners may have been the two large structures on the plateau below the taluses (fig. 8.1).

The geological context of the mine tunnels

Probably the most important feature of the Valle del Ixtetal obsidian mines is that they contain a number of tunnel systems which have not been damaged by looters and possess many components of the pre-Hispanic mining operation in place where the miners left them centuries ago. To date we have surveyed the tunnel systems for four of the mines: the mine above Talus 5, the mine above Talus 4a, the mine above the western half of Talus 2 and the mine above the eastern half of Talus 2 (see map 8.1).

Before describing the mine tunnels it is worthwhile discussing some aspects of their geological context in the Valle del Ixtetal and some of the general problems involved with trying to reconstruct the principal techniques used by the prehistoric miners to extract obsidian from the flows in this region. The geology of most areas of Orizaba volcano including the Valle del Ixtetal never has been studied in much detail. This situation soon will be improved considerably by the publication of the Mexican government geological maps for Veracruz and Puebla. What is needed, however, is a detailed geological survey of the volcanic activity in this region so that it can be determined how many separate obsidian flows were produced by Orizaba volcano and what their stratigraphic sequence is. The 'geological contexts' which we discuss here are our amateur observations concerning various aspects of the Valle del Ixtetal obsidian-flow system. We hope to collaborate with a professional geologist in order to produce an adequate study of this subject soon.

As was noted earlier, the Valle del Ixtetal taluses and mine shafts are located in the central portion of a steep canyon wall about 4,000 m above sea level on the northern slopes of Orizaba volcano. This canyon is oriented northwest-southeast. The mines and taluses are on the northern side of the canyon. The southern side of the canyon is the primary slope of Orizaba volcano. On clear days the cone of the volcano is visible directly across the canyon from the mines, with the snow line starting several hundred meters above the level of the tunnel entrances.

The north side of the canyon is a narrow ridge (probably less than 2 km wide at its base) running northwest-southeast across the slope of the volcano. Most of the ridge appears to be composed of rhyolite formations and one or more massive flows of obsidian. The top of this ridge above Taluses 1–4 (fig. 8.1) consists of columnlike masses of rhyolite which form an extensive series of cliffs. Much of the interior of the ridge beneath these cliffs appears to be nearly solid obsidian. All or most of the ancient mine tunnels excavated into the ridge expose obsidian formations at least 10 to 15 m thick.

Only small parts of the obsidian-flow system are exposed on the surface of the ridge near the mines. There are small exposures (usually less than 1 m wide) of obsidian in a rhyolite matrix at the base of the cliff and at several places farther west on the ridge side, but most areas on the south side of the ridge lack surface outcrops of obsidian. In contrast, on the north side of the ridge opposite the mines is an enormous outcrop of obsidian cobbles mixed with volcanic ash extending for several kilometers. We found no prehistoric mining or workshop sites associated with this large cobble outcrop. It is likely that the ancient Mexicans preferred to mine the massive flow system on the opposite side of the ridge and never bothered to process large amounts of the surface cobbles on the north side of the ridge.

Despite the well-preserved state of the Valle del Ixtetal

mines, we still cannot reconstruct in much detail many of the techniques which the Indians used to excavate the mine tunnels. It is extremely impressive that the miners were able to cut passageways over 70 m long into nearly solid obsidian without employing metal tools, explosives, or any of the other technology used in modern mining operations. We think that a key factor which helped determine ancient mining technology in the Valle del Ixtetal is that the obsidian flow system there is only 'nearly solid'. Massive fractures formed in the flow when it was deposited. These fracture planes made it much easier to break up the obsidian and construct tunnels. This probably explains why the tunnels often are not straight. The miners followed the 'path of least resistance' along fractures in the flow, creating a tunnel system of differing elevations and directions.

On the basis of our surveys inside the tunnels we postulate that the principal mining tools used by the Indians were wooden levers. We found a probable level pole inside the mine above Talus 4a, and fragments of several other poles which may have been levers were found in some of the other mines. The pole found in the Talus 4a mine is made from a heavy pine log about 15 cm in diameter and 2 m long. It has a wedge-shaped sharpened end. A sharpened pole like this would be an effective tool for tunneling into the obsidian flow. In addition to fractures, most parts of the flow system exposed inside the Valle del Ixtetal mines possess numerous bands of crystalline inclusions and other defects which can be used as starting points for breaking up the obsidian with a lever pole. The sharpened point of the pole could have been inserted in fractures on the surface of the flow, and then large chunks of obsidian could be broken off by applying leverage to the pole either vertically or laterally. This technique would make it possible to excavate tunnels into the flow and to extract blocks of high-quality obsidian for making artifacts without employing any tools more sophisticated than sharpened poles and hammerstones.

The only potential mining tools besides the probable wooden levers that we found in the tunnels are small hammerstones usually between 7 and 10 cm in diameter made from dense rhyolite or some other kind of volcanic rock. We are certain that these hammerstones were employed extensively in the mining process because they appear to be too small to have been used to break off large chunks of the flow. It also should be observed that we found no evidence for the use of other 'preindustrial' mining techniques in conjunction with the probable lever poles. None of the mine tunnels and chambers is coated with carbon residue or burned areas, which suggests that fire was not employed to help break up the flow. In addition, we found no remains of wooden wedges like the ones sometimes used (along with water or hammers) in the Old World to quarry stone.

The quality and texture of the obsidian in the Valle del Ixtetal usually varies greatly within individual tunnels and chambers. As we mentioned, there are many parts of the obsidian-flow system which contain defects: crystalline inclusions, fractures from internal stresses, zones of brittle perlitic glass, zones of coarse-textured glass, and so on. In general, high-quality obsidian suitable for making artifacts occurs only in relatively narrow horizontal bands with much of the rest of the flow being defective. In the mines that we surveyed, the bands of high-quality obsidian were usually approximately 30 cm to 1 m thick, but occasionally they exceeded 2 m in thickness. An essential part of the mining operation appears to have consisted of breaking away the defective obsidian above and below a band of high-quality obsidian, and then breaking up the high-quality band into blocks which were initially stored in piles inside the mines. As will be described later, these blocks eventually were taken out of the mines and then in most cases processed into large blade cores (Hester 1972; Sheets 1975; Clark 1977). The large blade cores were probably transported to workshop sites downslope from the Valle del Ixtetal where they were finally used to produce prismatic blades and other finished artifacts.

The quality of the obsidian also varies considerably horizontally within the flow system. It is almost certain that the main reason that the pre-Hispanic miners took the trouble to dig shafts deep into the canyon wall was to maximize the amount of high-quality obsidian that they could recover. Most narrow tunnels in the mines were cut through zones of defective obsidian, while most of the large chambers were excavated into zones having substantial amounts of high-quality obsidian. It seems obvious that the main purpose for the miners carving the larger chambers was to exploit an extensive zone of high-quality obsidian.

An aspect of this reconstruction of techniques used by the pre-Hispanic miners, which will be an important factor later in our discussion of the lithic technology of the Valle del Ixtetal quarries, is that a substantial proportion of the debris in the mine taluses is merely 'shatter' or waste fragments of low-quality obsidian produced while the miners were excavating tunnels and chambers in the flow. A key problem in analyzing the lithic technology of these mines is trying to identify which fragments in the taluses are shatter and which are flakes made while forming large blade cores and other products that eventually were turned into artifacts.

It is worthwhile noting that 'high quality' Valle del Ixtetal obsidian still contains some defects. In particular, it almost always possesses tiny crystalline inclusions dispersed throughout its glassy matrix. Cobean *et al.* (1971, 668) suggested that these inclusions probably made Orizaba volcano obsidian unsuitable for making prismatic blades. This is not true. The workshop which Stocker found at Calcahualco, Veracruz (about 15 km downslope from the Valle del Ixtetal mines), contains thousands of prismatic blades made from Orizaba volcano obsidian. Most of the obsidian which we have seen in Orizaba volcano (including both the Valle del Ixtetal mines and the Guadalupe Victoria, Puebla outcrops) is cloudy gray with numerous fine dark gray or black bands running throughout its glassy matrix. The Valle del Ixtetal obsidian generally appears to be slightly more trans-

parent (less cloudy) than the Guadalupe Victoria, Puebla, obsidian. Nearly all the obsidian which we have seen on Orizaba volcano contains the tiny crystalline inclusions mentioned above. Probably in part due to these inclusions, Orizaba volcano obsidian tends to have relatively coarse texture when compared with obsidian from some of the major Central Mexican sources such as the Sierra de Pachuca in Hidalgo (Holmes 1900; Spence & Parson 1972; García-Bárcena 1975; Lopez *et al.* 1979). Orizaba volcano obsidian, however, is not as brittle as the famous fine-textured 'bottle green' Sierra de Pachuca obsidian.

The four surveyed mine tunnels

The data that we obtained from our explorations of four mine tunnels is very preliminary and incomplete. We have spent only three days exploring the tunnels, and several months of continuous fieldwork would be necessary in order to study them with adequate detail. All seven of the lower mine taluses in the Valle del Ixtetal have at least one tunnel entrance excavated into the hillside above them. It is very likely that all of these tunnel systems are in good enough condition to be explored. Our major criterion for deciding to explore the four mines reported here is that their entrances were relatively free of rubble and other debris. It is possible that the entrances for some additional mine shafts are buried beneath the piles of obsidian fragments in the taluses. In addition, the entrance of a mine about 30 m east of Talus 3 has been blocked by a huge boulder which fell from the cliffs above some time in the past.

Most of the mine entrances are small, usually about 1 m wide and 1.5 to 2 m high. They are cut directly into the rhyolite formation which composes the bulk of the ridge on the north side of the Valle del Ixtetal. Usually there are only small patches of obsidian exposed in the rhyolite matrix outside the entrances of the mines. Within a few meters of the entrances inside the mines, however, the tunnels enter zones of nearly pure obsidian. As we emphasized earlier, the obsidian-flow system inside the mines always contains extensive fractures which probably formed as the flows cooled. The patterns of these fractures very likely determined many aspects of how the Indians constructed the mines. The layouts of each of the four mines which we explored are different in many ways. Apparently the miners did not have a predetermined 'standard plan' for excavating the chambers and tunnels, but instead constructed the mines according to the specific nature of the obsidian flow. Tunnels generally appear to follow large fractures within the flow. As we suggested above, it is very probable that the miners' chief reason for carving out a chamber was to exploit a zone of unusually high-quality obsidian.

The mine above Talus 5

The entrance of this mine is about 1.5 m high and 1 m wide (fig. 8.2). It is at the top of a vertical shaft 2.5 m deep. At the bottom of the shaft is the upper part of a steep talus of obsidian fragments. This talus goes down another 2.5 m.

Beyond the base of the talus are the entrances to two separate passages. The passage to the west ends within 17 m, but the passage to the east is the beginning of a system of tunnels and chambers extending over 70 m into the immense obsidian flow at the center of the ridge. This system involves a total descent from the level of the mine entrance of nearly 14 m by the time the final chamber is reached.

The ceiling of the first part of the long tunnel system is low – 70 cm or less in most areas. The floor is covered with small thin fragments of obsidian. The walls are composed of fractured segments of the obsidian flow exposed by the Indian miners' levers and hammerstones. This initial passage is approximately 14 m long and ends in a narrow chamber about 2.5 m wide, which has a shaft cut into its floor that leads to the lower sections of the mine.

The vertical shaft is about 2 m deep. Resting against its south wall is a pre-Hispanic ladder, which probably is in place where the miners left it at least 500 years ago. The ladder is hewn from a single pine log about 20 cm in diameter and 2.5 m long. Groovelike steps for the miners' feet were carved on one side of the log. All the ancient ladders which we have seen inside the Valle del Ixtetal mines are made from single pine logs in this simple fashion.

At the bottom of the ladder is a narrow (1.5 m wide) passage about 6 m long which leads to a small irregularly

shaped chamber about 6 m long and 2.5 to 3 m wide with a ceiling between 1.7 and 2.5 m high. Along the walls of this chamber are neatly stacked piles of blocks of high-quality obsidian. These blocks generally are roughly rectangular in shape and measure between 15 and 30 cm long and 10 to 15 cm wide. They are probably the chief products of the mining operation. Normally, the Indian miners eventually would have removed the blocks from the mine so that they could be transformed into large blade cores for making prismatic blades and other artifacts. In many areas of the chamber, the stacks of obsidian blocks reach the ceiling.

The obsidian exposed in the walls of this chamber appears to be of high quality, much better than the obsidian occurring in the preceding tunnels which often contains bands of crystalline inclusions and other defects. One wall of this chamber has a completely smooth surface consisting of a band of high-quality obsidian nearly 1 m thick.

The next chamber is reached through a passage about 3.5 m long and 2 m wide. There is a 1.7 m drop at the end of the passage which leads directly into the chamber. This is the largest room in the mine. It is roughly circular with a 3.3 m diameter and a ceiling 3.3 m high in most areas. There are a number of grottolike subchambers cut into the walls of this room, some of which are nearly 2 m in diameter. The miners probably were exploiting a particularly high-grade vein of obsidian in these recessed areas.

Beyond this large chamber there is only one small room before the tunnel system ends. It is reached through a narrow passage about 2.5 m long which starts at the north end of the large chamber. This passage drops about 2 m before entering the small room, which is about 2.2 m wide and 2.5 m long with a 1.3 m ceiling.

The mine above Talus 4a

This mine was not mapped. We can only include here some brief impressions of our exploration of its tunnel system, which is much less extensive than that of the mine above Talus 5. The first chamber of this mine contains a pile of high-quality obsidian blocks stacked against one wall. In the second room we found the sharpened pine pole already described, which very likely was used as a lever to break up the obsidian formation and excavate tunnels. The third (and last) major chamber has a pool of water covering part of its floor.

The mine above the western half of Talus 2

The entrance of this mine (fig. 8.3) consists of a vertical shaft which is about 7 m deep. At the bottom of this shaft is a pre-Hispanic ladder braced against the wall in its original position. It is hewn from a single pine log like the ladder that we found in the Talus 5 mine. The major chamber of the mine begins at the bottom of the shaft. It is 10 m long and 4 to 6 m wide with a ceiling varying between 1.7 and 2.7 m. The floor of most parts of this room is slanted downward at approximately a 45° angle. There is a talus of obsidian fragments about 5 m long in the upper part of the room starting at the

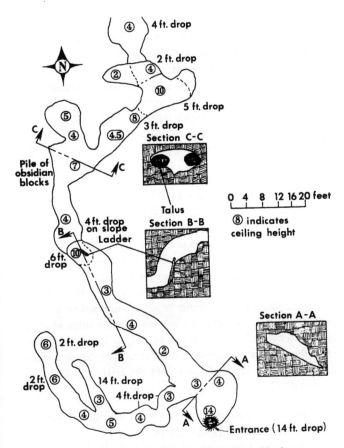

Fig. 8.2. Talus 5 mine, Pico de Orizaba mines, Mexico.

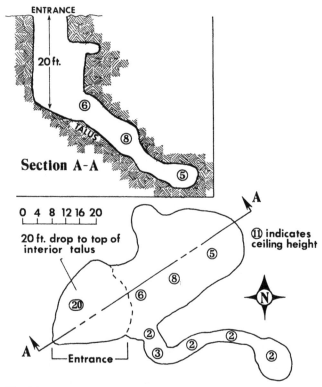

Fig. 8.3. Mine above Talus 2, Pico de Orizaba mines, Mexico.

at the base of the entrance shaft in the east wall of the main chamber. This passage is 1 to 1.3 m wide and about 10 m long. It leads to a small round subchamber about 2.7 m in diameter with a ceiling 0.7 m high.

The mine above the eastern half of Talus 2

We can present only a preliminary description of this mine because it has not been mapped yet. It appears to be nearly as large as the mine above Talus 5.

This mine has a steep shaft (inclined at about a 45° angle going downward) starting at its entrance and continuing for about 15 m. At the bottom of the shaft is a small hole less than 50 cm high which leads to the rest of the mine. It is strange that the miners never widened this low passage area, which must have hindered considerably the removal of obsidian from the mine.

The low crawl-way extends for several meters, after which a large straight tunnel begins which has a ceiling nearly 2 m high. At various points along the tunnel are neatly stacked piles containing blocks of high-quality obsidian. Most of this tunnel inclines upward. At two places along it there are steep taluses of obsidian flakes and debris, with the passage continuing at the top of each talus.

Above the first talus there is a small circular hole cut into the tunnel wall. This small entrance appears to be literally knapped into the obsidian flow, with its edges having flake scars similar to those found on large obsidian bifaces. It leads to a small shaft a few meters long which goes parallel to the main tunnel.

After the second interior talus, the main tunnel continues to climb until it terminates in another large talus of obsidian fragments. At one side of this talus there is a small hammerstone left by the miners.

Further comments

The Valle del Ixtetal quarry has some of the most extensive tunnel systems known for pre-Hispanic Mesoamerican obsidian mines. The only obsidian mine tunnels which we have seen that probably are substantially larger than these are in the Sierra de Pachuca, Hidalgo (Holmes 1900; Breton 1902; Spence & Parsons 1972; García-Bárcena 1975; Lopez, Nieto & Cobean 1979). The ancient quarrying system used in the Sierra de Pachuca appears to have been different from that of the Valle del Ixtetal mines in that the entrance shafts of the Sierra de Pachuca mines are completely vertical with initial drops sometimes in excess of 15 m. The Sierra de Pachuca mines also appear to have more sophisticated tunnel designs than those of the Valle del Ixtetal, including probable passages over 70 m long with ventilation holes and multiple entrance shafts. Other Mesoamerican obsidian sources possessing at least some tunnel or shaft systems include the mine on Orizaba volcano described by C. H. Berendt (letter published by Rau 1873, 359) cited above; the mines at Zinapécuaro, Michoacán, described by Breton (1902), which have probably been destroyed; and the mines at Otumba, Estado de México (Lopez & Nieto 1981). Very extensive pre-Hispanic tunnel systems have also been reported for a number of products other than obsidian in Mexico: metals in Guerrero (Hendrichs 1941), semiprecious stones in Zacatecas (Weigand 1968), and cinnabar in the Sierra de Querétaro (Langenscheidt 1970) to cite a few important examples. As will be emphasized in the final section of this chapter, ancient mines constitute extremely important sources of information for reconstructing key features of Mexico's pre-Hispanic economies. Obsidian is only one of many prehistoric mining products which needs to be investigated.

Two additional topics should be mentioned before ending this section. First, there is a potential for obtaining more exact dates for the main period when the Valle del Ixtetal mines were being used by taking radiocarbon samples from the wooden ladders found in the mine tunnels. In the near future, we hope to obtain a permit to collect these samples and produce a series of carbon-14 dates for the mines.

Secondly, it is very surprising that we did not find any remains of pre-Hispanic torches or other illumination devices inside the mines. The miners must have needed some kind of lighting device to work inside the tunnels. It is very likely that when the mines are surveyed more thoroughly, torches and a number of other kinds of equipment and artifacts will be recovered.

Preliminary comments concerning the lithic technology of the Valle del Ixtetal mines

The lithic technology of the Valle del Ixtetal mines will be presented in a separate report by Stocker. Here we will describe briefly a few of the most important aspects of the manufacturing processes which took place at the mines. As we stated, on the basis of our fieldwork and the reports of a number of other archaeologists who are investigating ancient Mesoamerican lithic technology, we have concluded that the main products of the Valle del Ixtetal mines were large blade cores. These blade cores appear to have varied considerably in size and shape. The larger ones (which are rare but sometimes are in excess of 20 cm long) probably are what many investigators call 'macrocores' (Hester 1972; Sheets 1975; Clark 1977), and the smaller ones (approximately 7 to 10 cm in length) may be the equivalent of Clark's (1977, 1979) 'large polyhedral cores'. We postulate that the blocks of high-quality obsidian quarried from the Valle del Ixtetal flow system were knapped into large blade cores at the mines, and that these large blade cores were then taken to workshop sites (such as the one which Stocker found at Calcahualco, Veracruz) where they were used to produce prismatic blades and other finished artifacts.

This reconstruction is based on a variety of factors. It appears that very few finished tools or artifacts were being produced at the Valle del Ixtetal mines. During our surveys of the mines and the areas near the taluses, we encountered fewer than 20 finished artifacts (mainly bifaces with knifelike or scraper forms) among the hundreds of thousands of obsidian flakes. In our studies of the obsidian debitage associated with the mines, we found that these bifacially worked artifacts were not being produced in large numbers because there is very little typical debris from biface manufacture, such as thinning flakes (Crabtree 1972, 94) or broken biface fragments, in the taluses. We have tentatively divided the obsidian fragments in the taluses into two general categories: 'shatter' and waste fragments produced by the miners when they excavated the tunnels and chambers into the obsidian flow; and debitage produced by processing blocks of high-quality obsidian into large blade cores or (in rare cases) into some other kinds of 'preforms' for making artifacts.

As we mentioned, it is often difficult to distinguish 'shatter' and waste fragments produced during the mining operation from actual debitage. We define 'shatter' as pieces of obsidian that were broken off and discarded by the miners as they were excavating into the flow. These pieces possess clearly distinguishable fracture scars on their surfaces. We define 'waste fragments' as small 'natural' unbroken pieces of obsidian which the miners appear to have found lying loose in the fracture systems of the flow as they excavated, and which they subsequently discarded into the taluses. Much of the shatter and waste fragments consists of low-quality obsidian, but some small pieces of high-quality obsidian also occur in these subcategories. Our preliminary estimate is that well over half of the obsidian fragments in the taluses are shatter or waste fragments, but this really is only a guess.

The nature of the debitage at the Valle del Ixtetal mines will be described in considerable detail by Stocker in a separate publication. Here we will discuss only one of the most important types of flakes produced at the mines: the ridge flake. In the analysis of the debitage, we have identified large numbers of most of the types of large flakes and blades which Crabtree (1968, 1972), Hester (1972), Hester, Jack and Heizer (1971), Sheets (1975), Clark (1977, 1979) and others have described as being produced in the initial steps of making blade cores. It is important to point out, however, that ridge flakes generally have not been given much importance in the reports of Sheets (1972, 1975) or other 'behavioral' analyses of Mesoamerican lithics because most of these investigations done to date have been based on the analysis of debitage from ancient workshops located well away from the areas where the obsidian was quarried. These workshops usually were devoted to producing finished artifacts from large blade cores or 'preforms' which had been partially processed at the quarries before being transported to the workshop sites. While some kinds of ridge flakes do occur at workshop sites (Hester, Jack & Heizer 1971, 81; Sheets 1972; Kerley 1981; Healan 1980, personal communication), they appear to be much more common and diagnostic at ancient Mesoamerican quarry sites devoted to the production of large blade cores.

The concept of ridge flakes was introduced into Mesoamerican lithic studies by Hester, Jack and Heizer (1971, 81) in their analysis of obsidian artifacts from Tres Zapotes, Veracruz. These flakes have also been called 'lame à crête', 'corner trimming flakes', 'crested ridge flakes', and 'lascas con cresta' among other names (Bordes & Crabtree 1969; Crabtree 1968; 1972; Healan 1979; Stocker, Cobean & Swibel 1974; Lopez, Nieto & Cobean 1979). Ridge flakes occur in many parts of the world associated with lithic industries devoted to producing blade cores of various kinds. They were described over a century ago by Evans (1872, 25, 248) in his study of prehistoric European stone-tool industries. An excellent analysis of ridge flakes in the core-blade technology of Alberta, Canada, was recently presented by Sanger (1968), whose definitions formed part of the basis for Hester, Jack and Heizer's (1971) study of similar flakes at Tres Zapotes.

The ridge flakes (fig. 8.4) at the Valle del Ixtetal quarries were formed during core manufacture in order to facilitate the production of blades with straight edges. They were probably often the first large flake removed from the quarried block of obsidian in the process of forming a large blade core. The ancient knappers made a straight ridge along the length of the quarry block by removing a series of small flakes to form two nearly parallel narrow facets which intersect at an acute angle longitudinally along the block's surface. The knappers then struck the upper surface of the block (which was going to be used as a platform) at a point slightly behind the upper part of the ridge (Sanger 1968, 197). This removed the ridge flake and left a straight flake scar along the length of the block which could be used to produce a series of successively straighter flakes in forming the large blade core. The ridge flakes have a triangular transverse cross-section. At the Valle del Ixtetal mines they generally have many small flake scars perpendicular to their length on both their dorsal facets, but

I

II

Fig. 8.4. Debitage and ridge flake from Pico de Orizaba mines, Mexico. I. Ventral surfaces: (A) Typical small debitage from the taluses. (B) Ridge flake. II. Dorsal surfaces of (A) and (B).

there are occasional examples which possess flake scars on only one dorsal facet.

We believe that the 'ridge-flake technique' was one of the major methods which the knappers at the Valle del Ixtetal mines employed to produce large blade cores. The mine taluses contain thousands of ridge flakes, which probably constitute between 5 and 10 per cent of the flakes over 10 cm long in the debitage at this quarry. Ridge flakes also appear to be common at many other Mesoamerican obsidian quarries. They are very common at the Sierra de Pachuca, Hidalgo mines, where they have been reported by Holmes (1919, 225, fig. 100), Spence and Parsons (1972, 5–6), Stocker, Cobean and Swibel (1974), and Lopez, Nieto and Cobean (1979). In our surveys of Mesoamerican obsidian sources over the past eleven years, we have found substantial numbers of ridge flakes at El Chayal, Guatemala; Otumba, Estado de México; Ucareo, Michoacán; Oyameles, Puebla; and Zacualtipán, Hidalgo along with lesser quantities of these flakes at several other sources (Stocker 1981). It is almost certain that most of the ridge flakes at these quarries were produced in the manufacture of large blade cores.

The ridge-flake technique, however, is not the only method which can produce blade cores with straight facets. Stocker has reconstructed several alternative core-preparation sequences at the Valle del Ixtetal mines which probably did not involve making ridge flakes. (These sequences will be described in a future report.) Recent experiments by J. Clark (1980, personal communication) and by D. M. Healan and

J. Flenniken (1981, personal communication) have shown that high-quality blade cores can be produced without making ridge flakes. Despite this, the ridge-flake technique was probably an important method for manufacturing large blade cores in many areas of ancient Mesoamerica.

The ridge flakes at the Valle del Ixtetal quarries generally vary from between 6 and 20 cm long and 1.5 and 5 cm wide, with flakes between about 12 and 15 cm long and about 2 and 4 cm wide being most common. Because ridge flakes probably were the first flakes to be removed in forming a blade core, their length provides an index of the original maximum core size. In the Valle del Ixtetal quarries, the cores which we found associated with the mines are generally considerably smaller than most of the ridge flakes.

The Valle del Ixtetal cores will be treated in detail in a separate report. Here we will include only a few observations concerning them. Most of the cores are between 7 and 12 cm long, with some rare examples over 20 cm long. They are generally between 6 and 8 cm in diameter, but cores with diameters in excess of 10 cm occur occasionally. Most cores are roughly cylindrical in shape but some, especially the smaller ones, are conical. Most cores possess between seven and ten longitudinal flake scars. Most of these scars are very irregular in outline, and often only one or two of them extend the entire length of the core. Many of the cores are 'bipolar' in that one or two of the flakes were struck off their distal ends. Their platforms generally are multifaceted, with at least three to six flake scars. 'Natural surfaces' unaltered by flaking base of the pre-Hispanic ladder. A narrow passageway is carved often occur on one-fourth to one-half of the surface of the cores.

We think that most of the cores that we found at the Valle del Ixtetal mines are not representative of the large blade cores which probably were the chief products of the quarrying operation. The majority of the cores that we recovered have major defects, such as step fractures or other knapping errors, or extensive bands of crystalline inclusions. They are probably rejects that were discarded by the ancient knappers. Cores also are much rarer than ridge flakes. We found between 120 and 150 blade cores at the mines, while there are thousands of ridge flakes in the taluses. We assume that cores are relatively rare at the mines because they were probably transported to workshop sites away from the quarry area where they were used to produce prismatic blades and other finished artifacts. We have seen no evidence of extensive prismatic blade production at the Valle del Ixtetal mines. We recovered only three or four prismatic blades and no exhausted polyhedral cores during our surveys of the mines. In contrast, Stocker found dozens of exhausted poly-hedral cores and thousands of prismatic blade fragments on the surface of the workshop site at Calcahualco, Veracruz, about 15 km downslope from the mines. The Valle del Ixtetal mines probably were supplying large blade cores to a number of such workshop sites.

Concluding comments

Much more archaeological research needs to be done at the Valle del Ixtetal mines and in the areas near them before their origins and development can be reconstructed in any detail. Very little has been published so far concerning the archaeology of the Pico de Orizaba region. The major public-ation which we have found is a report by H. Lehmann (1952) on a group of figurines and ceramic statues from Orizaba, Veracruz, which was collected in the late nineteenth century and now is in the Musée de l'Homme in Paris. This collection contains a number of different art styles spanning several periods between the Formative and the Postclassic, and even includes some Olmec figurines. We have located a number of important sites in our preliminary surveys on both the Puebla and Veracruz slopes of Orizaba volcano (Stocker, Cobean & Swibel 1974), but detailed settlement-pattern surveys covering most of the volcano slopes are needed before we can begin to understand many aspects of the local obsidian-exploitation system. We especially need to locate more obsidian-workshop sites downslope from the mines and to investigate the work-shop at Calcahualco in detail.

An intensive systematic survey and excavation program at the Valle del Ixtetal mines would produce large amounts of data on many topics which we only can speculate about now, such as the probable existence of pre-Aztec occupations at the mines, and the nature of the social and economic organization of the miners. Did the miners live at the mines year-round or did they work on a seasonal basis? How was the labor force organized at the mines? Did different groups of people excavate the mine shafts and knap the blade cores?

The ceramic and ethnohistorical evidence suggesting that the Valle del Ixtetal mines were integrated into the Aztec empire is especially interesting. Archival studies and other ethnohistorical investigations are needed to recover more information concerning the Aztec conquest and administration of this area. In conjunction with these studies it would be especially important to survey and excavate the Aztec settle-ment at Coscomatepec, Veracruz.

The Mesoamerican obsidian program at the University of Missouri Research Reactor Facility will soon produce substan-tial amounts of new data concerning the patterns of obsidian exploitation and trade in the Orizaba volcano region. During 1980 we collected over 130 obsidian source samples from the Valle del Ixtetal and several other areas on the slopes of Pico de Orizaba. These samples are currently being analyzed via neutron-activation analysis by J. R. Vogt, C. C. Graham, and M. D. Glascock of the Missouri reactor staff. The Missouri project is also analyzing over 100 artifacts from the important Olmec center of San Lorenzo Tenochtitlán, Veracruz (Coe & Diehl 1980), which was a major importer of Orizaba volcano obsidian (Cobean *et al.* 1971).

Before closing we would like to emphasize the need for long-term intensive excavation and survey projects at Meso-american obsidian quarries. In the last decade a number of important quarry investigations have been undertaken (including Abascal 1981; Charlton 1978; García-Bárcena 1975; Gaxiola & Guevara 1981; Lopez, Nieto & Cobean 1979; Lopez & Nieto 1981; Sidrys, Andreson & Marcucci 1975; Soto 1981; and Weigand & Spence 1981). In addition, recently there has been an impressive increase in the number of projects surveying or excavating Mesoamerican obsidian workshops (Casteneda 1981; Healan 1979, 1981; Kerley 1981; Neivens & Libbey 1976; Pastrana 1977; Rattray 1980; Sheets 1972, 1975a). Before archaeologists can reconstruct the specific mechanisms and roles of obsidian mining and trade in the economics of ancient Mesoamerica, it will be necessary to integrate data from a wide variety of research fields in con-junction with intensive studies of quarries and workshops (Charlton 1978; Spence 1978; Santley in press). Research in ethnohistory concerning ancient systems of trade, tribute, and markets, and trace-element analysis projects involving large numbers of obsidian-source samples and artifacts are especially necessary for achieving this goal.

Another factor which greatly increases the need for investigating Mesoamerican obsidian quarries in the near future is the problem of looting. Of the nearly twenty Mexican and Guatemalan quarries which we have visited, only three have not been badly damaged by looters. There is not much time left to examine what remains of these quarries. Obsidian mines were among the first archaeological sites in Mesoamerica to be studied scientifically. (Humboldt [1814] and Tylor [1861] both give accounts of the Sierra de Pachuca, Hidalgo, quarries.)

It would be ironic and sad if most of these sites ceased to exist without ever being studied thoroughly.

Acknowledgments

The research reported here was done in intermittent periods over the last 11 years and was supported by a number of grants and institutions: the Department of Anthropology, Yale University; the Department of Anthropology, University of Illinois; the University of Missouri Research Reactor Facility; the National Science Foundation (grant NSF BNS 79 15409); and the Explorers Club of New York. Our fieldwork would not have been possible without the encouragement and cooperation of a number of archaeologists in Mexico's Instituto Nacional de Antropologia e Historia (INAH), especially E. Matos Moctezuma and A. Garcia Cook who supplied us with research permits.

Over the years we have been helped by many people in our investigations at Orizaba volcano. M. D. Coe (Yale University), K. K. Turekian (Yale University) and D. C. Grove (University of Illinois) greatly inspired and aided us during our initial research in ancient Mexican obsidian mining and trade. J. L. Lorenzo (INAH), F. Beverido (Universidad Veracruzana), and A. Barges provided us with crucially important information for locating major obsidian outcrops in the Pico de Orizaba region. A. Medellin Zenil (Universidad Veracruzana) helped us greatly in the analysis of the ceramics. R. A. Diehl (University of Missouri), M. W. Spence (University of Western Ontario), and T. H. Charlton (University of Iowa) advised us in important ways during both our fieldwork and laboratory analyses. We also very much want to thank J. L. King and L. Vargas of the Instituto de Investigaciones Antropologicas (UNAM) along with J. R. Vogt, R. M. Brugger, and D. M. Alger of the University of Missouri Research Reactor Facility for research support given to Cobean during the later part of our investigations.

References

Abascal Macias, R. 1981. Yacimientos y telleres prehispanicos de obsidiana en Zacualtipan, Hidalgo: ensayo metodologico. Paper presented at the symposium 'La Obsidiana en Mesoamerica', Centro Regional Hidalgo, INAH, Pachuca, Hidalgo.

Bordes, F. & Crabtree, D. 1969. The Corbiac blade technique and other experiments. *Tebiwa* 12:1–21.

Breton, A. C. 1902. Some obsidian workings in Mexico. *Thirteenth International Congress of Americanists, New York.*

Casteneda, C. 1981. Manufactura de la talla de obsidiana en la region comprendida entre los sitios arquelogicos de San Bartolo Agua Caliente, Guanajuato y El Pueblito, Queretaro. Paper presented at the symposium 'La Obsidiana en Mesoamerica', Centro Regional Hidalgo, INAH, Pachuca, Hidalgo.

Charlton, T. H. 1972. Population trends in the Teotihuacan Valley, A.D. 1400–1969. *World Archaeology* 4:11, 106–23.

1978. Teotihuacan, Tepeapulco, and obsidian exploitation. *Science* 200:1227–36.

Clark, J. E. 1977. Large polyhedral cores from Mesoamerica. *Katunob* 10 (4): 79–93.

1979. A method for the analysis of Mesoamerican lithic industries: an application to the obsidian industry of La Libertad, Chiapas, Mexico. M.A. thesis, Department of Anthropology, Brigham Young University, Provo, Utah.

Cobean, R. H., Coe, M. D., Perry, E. A. & Kharkar, D. P. 1971. Obsidian trade at San Lorenzo Tenochtitlan, Mexico. *Science* 174: 666–71.

Coe, M. D. & Diehl, R. A. 1980. *In the land of the Olmec.* Austin: University of Texas Press.

Crabtree, D. E. 1968. Mesoamerican polyhedral cores and prismatic blades. *American Antiquity* 33:446–78.

1972. An introduction to flintworking. *Occasional Papers of the Museum, Idaho State University* 28.

Evans, J. 1872. *The ancient stone implements, weapons, and ornaments of Great Britain.* New York: Appleton and Company.

García-Bárcena, J. 1975. Las minas de obsidiana de la Sierra de las Navajas, Hidalgo, Mexico. *Actas del XLI Congreso Internacional de Americanistas, Mexico, D. F.* 1:369–77.

Gaxiola, M. & Guevara, J. 1981. Un Conjunto habitacional especializado en la talla de obsidiana en Huapalcalco, Hidalgo. Paper presented at the symposium 'La Obsidiana en Mesoamerica', Centro Regional Hidalgo, INAH, Pachuca, Hidalgo.

Gerhard, P. 1972. *A guide to the historical geography of New Spain.* Cambridge University Press.

Gibson, C. 1971. Structure of the Aztec empire. In R. Wauchope, ed., *Handbook of Middle American Indians* 10, Austin: University of Texas Press, 376–94.

Griffin, J. & Espejo, A. 1947. La alfareria correspondiente al ultimo periodo de occupacion Nahua del Valle de Mexico I. *Memorias del Academia Mexicana de Historia* 6:131–47. Mexico.

1950. La alfareria del ultimo periodo de occupacion Nahua del Valle de Mexico II. *Memorias del Academia Mexicana de Historia* 9:118–67. Mexico.

Healan, D. M. 1979. Functional, technological, and developmental aspects of obsidian workshop production at Tula, Mexico. Proposal to the National Science Foundation, Department of Anthropology, Tulane University, New Orleans.

1981. Especializaction de talleres liticos. Paper presented at the symposium 'Perspectivas en el Estudio de la Litica', Instituto de Investigaciones Antropologicas, UNAM, Mexico, D.F.

Hendrichs, P. 1941. Datos sobre la tecnica minera prehispanica. *El Mexico Antiquo* 5:148–60.

Hester, T. R. 1972. Notes on large obsidian blade cores and core-blade technology in Mesoamerica. *Contributions of the University of California Archaeological Research Facility* 14:95–106.

Hester, T. R., Jack, R. N. & Heizer, R. F. 1971. The obsidian of Tres Zapotes, Veracruz, Mexico. *Contributions of the University of California Archaeological Research Facility* 13:65–131.

Holmes, W. H. 1900. The obsidian mines of Hidalgo. *American Anthropologist* 2: 405–16.

1919. Handbook of aboriginal American antiquities, part 1: The lithic industries. *Bureau of American Ethnology Bulletin* 60. Washington, D.C.

Humboldt, A. 1814. *Researches concerning the institutions and monuments of the ancient inhabitants of America, with descriptions and views of some of the most striking scenes of the Cordilleras.* London.

Kerley, J. M. 1981. Un taller de obsidiana tolteca del Postclasico temprano en Tula de Allende, Hidalgo. Paper presented at the symposium 'La Obsidiana en Mesoamerica', Centro Regional Hidalgo, INAH, Pachuca, Hidalgo.

Langenscheidt, A. 1970. Las Minas y la mineria prehispanicas. *Mineria Prehispanica en la Sierra de Queretaro.* Secretaria del Patrimonio Nacional. Mexico, D. F.

Lehmann, H. 1952. L'archéologie d'Orizaba Mexique. *Journal Société des Américanistes* 41: 1–20.

Lopez, F. & Nieto, R. 1981. Los yacimientos y talleres de obsidiana de Otumba. Paper presented at the symposium 'La Obsidiana en Mesoamerica', Centro Regional Hidalgo, INAH, Pachuca, Hidalgo.

Lopez, F., Nieto, R. & Cobean, R. 1979. La producción prehispanica de obsidiana en el sur de Hidalgo. Paper presented at the 1979 Mesa Redonda, Sociedad Mexicana de Antropologia, Saltillo.

Neivens, M. & Libbey, D. 1976. An obsidian workshop at El Pozito, Northern Belize. In T. R. Hester & N. Hammond, eds., *Maya Lithic Studies: papers from the 1976 Belize Field Symposium.* Center for Archaeological Research, University of Texas at San Antonio, 137–49.

Parsons, J. R. 1966. *The Aztec ceramic sequence in the Teotihuacan Valley, Mexico.* Doctoral dissertation, Department of Anthropology, University of Michigan, Ann Arbor.

Pastrana Cruz, A. 1977. *Producción de instrumentos en obsidiana – division del trabajo.* Thesis, Escuela Nacional de Antropologia e Historia, Mexico, D. F.

Pires-Ferreira, J. W. 1975. Formative Mesoamerican exchange networks with special reference to the Valley of Oaxaca, *Memoirs of the Museum of Anthropology, University of Michigan* 7.

Ramirez, G. 1976. *Chemical characterization of volcanic glass and its application to archaeological studies.* M. A. thesis, Department of Geology, University of New Orleans.

Rattray, E. C. 1980. Informe al INAH de las investigaciónes en la Hacienda Metepec, Teotihuacan, Estado de México. Excavation report, Instituto de Investigaciones Antropologicas, UNAM, Mexico, D.F.

Rau, C. 1873. Ancient aboriginal trade in North America. *Annual Report, Smithsonian Institution* (for 1872) 348–94.

Sanger, D. 1968. The High River microblade industry, Alberta. *Plains Anthropologist* 13:190–208.

Santley, R. S. In press. Obsidian trade and Teotihuacan influence in Mesoamerica. In A. Miller, ed., *Interdisciplinary approaches to the study of highland-lowland interaction.* Dumbarton Oaks Research Library, Washington, D.C.

Sheets, P. D. 1972. A model of Mesoamerican obsidian technology based on Preclassic workshop debris in El Salvador. *Cerámica de Cultura Maya* 8: 17–33.

1975. Behavioral analysis and the structure of a prehistoric industry. *Current Anthropology* 16:369–91.

Sidrys, R., Andresen J. & Marcucci, D. 1975. Obsidian sources in the Maya area. *Journal of New World Archaeology* 1 (5): 1–14.

Spence, M. W. 1978. The archaeological objectives of obsidian characterization studies in Mesoamerica. Paper presented at the symposium 'Obsidian Characterization and Exchange Systems in Prehistory', cosponsored by the National Bureau of Standards, U.S. Department of Commerce, and the Smithsonian Institution, Washington, D.C.

Spence, M. W. & Parsons, J. R. 1972. Prehispanic obsidian exploitation in central Mexico: a preliminary synthesis. In M. W. Spence, J. R. Parsons, M. H. Parsons, eds., *Miscellaneous studies in Mexican prehistory, Anthropological Papers of the Museum of Anthropology, University of Michigan* 45: 1–33.

Stocker, T. 1981. Obsidian technology in Mexico. *Explorers Journal* 59 (4): 176–181.

Stocker, T., Cobean, R. & Swibel, S. 1974. Research report on excavations at the Pico de Orizaba, Veracruz, Mexico obsidian quarries. Paper presented at the Annual Meeting, Society for American Archaeology, Washington, D.C.

Tylor, E. B. 1861. *Anahuac: Mexico and the Mexicans: ancient and modern.* London.

Weigand, P. C. 1968. The mines and mining techniques of the Chalchihuites culture. *American Antiquity* 33: 45–61.

Weigand, P. C. & Spence, M. 1981. El complejo de minas de obsidiana en La Joya, Jalisco, Mexico. Paper presented at the symposium 'La Obsidiana en Mesoamerica', Centro Regional Hidalgo, INAH, Pachuca, Hidalgo.

Zeitlin, R. N. 1979. *Prehistoric long-distance exchange on the southern Isthmus of Tehauntepec.* Ph.D. dissertation, Department of Anthropology, Yale University, New Haven, Conn.

Zeitlin, R. N. & Heimbuch, R. C. 1978. Trace element analysis and the archaeological study of obsidian procurement in Pre-Columbian Mesoamerica. In D. D. Davis, ed., Lithics and subsistence: the analysis of stone tool use in prehistoric economies. *Vanderbilt University Publications in Anthropology* 20: 117–59.

Chapter 9

State-controlled procurement and the obsidian workshops of Teotihuacán, Mexico
M. W. Spence, J. Kimberlin and G. Harbottle

The inhabitants of Teotihuacán, a major pre-Hispanic urban center, imported huge quantities of obsidian from the Sierra de las Navajas region 50 km to the northeast. Within the city this material was distributed in a highly equitable fashion among the numerous workshops. Trace-element analysis reveals that each workshop area included material from a number of distinct loci of exploitation in the source region. These data indicate that the obsidian was exploited and transported to Teotihuacán through a procurement network organized and maintained by the Teotihuacán state. With the collapse of the state about A.D. 750, the flow of Navajas material into Teotihuacán largely ceased.

Introduction

Teotihuacán, one of the two largest urban centers in the pre-Hispanic New World, lies a short distance northeast of Mexico City. At its height, about A.D. 200–600, it had a population of 150,000 and controlled much of the central Mexico region (Bernal 1966; Millon 1973). At that time it must have been importing enormous quantities of raw materials, both to supply its own huge population and to fuel the widespread trade network that it dominated. This raises a number of questions about the mechanisms involved in the exploitation and transportation of these resources. It is important to determine the role played by the Teotihuacán state in procurement, the scope and stability of the networks that were established, and the effects of these networks on the political and economic structures of both Teotihuacán and the source regions. Beyond that, there are implications for the more general debate over the degree to which resource exploitation and trade in the Archaic civilizations were managed by the state (cf. Polanyi, Arensberg & Pearson 1957; Adams 1974; Lamberg-Karlovsky 1975; Kohl 1978).

The production and distribution of obsidian artifacts was one of the basic features of Teotihuacán's economy. Very large quantities of obsidian, coming principally from two sources, were processed through the numerous workshops of the city. Gray obsidian, used primarily in the manufacture of bifacial artifacts and some scrapers, came from quarries in the Otumba region 17 km east of the city (fig. 9.1), and from deposits of water-carried nodules in the intervening area and within the city itself. The green obsidian, dedicated largely to the production of cores, blades, and some end scrapers, is from the Sierra de las Navajas region, about 50 km northeast of Teotihuacán (Spence & Parsons 1972). Although good prismatic cores and blades can be produced from gray obsidian, the finer structure of the Navajas obsidian demands less skill and ensures a higher rate of success, making it the preferred material for core-blade manufacture. Other obsidians, like those of Otumba and Pizarrin, frequently have a secondary fracture pattern, created by stress prior to final solidification, that makes blade production more difficult (Fraunfelter, in Spence & Parsons 1972, 31).

The obsidian workshops of Teotihuacán are generally clustered together into larger workshop areas that represent corporate social groups (Spence 1974). These areas fall into three categories – local, regional, and precinct. The local workshop areas include a wide range, from small peripheral areas of only a few workshop sites to large areas often located on major arteries closer to the city's heart. Most local areas were probably oriented toward production for that part of the city in which they were situated. The component workshop sites generally produced a wide range of artifacts, only occasionally showing evidence of subspecialization. The regional workshop areas, on the other hand, were larger and often located in the center of the city adjacent to the major civic-ceremonial structures. In several cases these areas were either devoted exclusively to the production of one item or divided into subspecialized zones. The products of this subspecialization were cores and blades of green obsidian and bifacial blanks of gray obsidian. The intensity of production in these regional areas and the paucity of evidence for the consumption of the blanks within Teotihuacán indicates that they were largely oriented toward production for distribution beyond the city. The precinct workshop-area category is represented by two workshop zones that were located within the precincts of major public structures. The Moon precinct zone consisted of a series of workshops by the Moon Pyramid where bifacial implements were produced. The Great Compound precinct zone was a core-blade manufacturing zone extending along the west edge of the Great Compound precinct. The craftsmen in these precinct zones were probably producing artifacts under the supervision of state officials to satisfy a levy imposed by the state.

The distribution of green obsidian

Surveys of Teotihuacán's obsidian sources and the intervening regions have produced some evidence about the nature

Fig. 9.1. Obsidian sources and archaeological sites of central Mexico.

of the city's procurement systems. Extensive Teotihuacán period workings have not yet been identified (Spence & Parsons 1972; Charlton 1969; González Rul 1972; García-Bárcena 1975), although the recent discovery by T. Stocker of a Teotihuacán sherd in an Aztec obsidian waste heap in the Navajas source region indicates their presence there. Surveys and excavations to the north of Teotihuacán, between the city and the source region, have been conducted by A. García Cook (1967), E. Matos Moctezuma (1976), T. Charlton (1978), W. Sanders and his colleagues (Sanders, Parsons & Santley 1979), and R. Mora López (1981). Tepeapulco, the focal point for several of these studies, is somewhat east of the region that might be expected to provide information about direct Navajas–Teotihuacán traffic (fig. 9.1), but Mora López's work to the west and north of Tepeapulco has resulted in some relevant discoveries. Of fifteen Teotihuacán period sites that he has identified south of the source region, only one, Casacoalco, has evidence of workshop activity focused on the processing of Navajas macrocores (Mora López 1981). Consisting of some 40 habitation structures, Casacoalco may have played an important role in Teotihuacán's exploitation of the Navajas region (R. Mora López personal communication 1981).

The workshop sites within Teotihuacán that were involved to a significant extent in core-blade manufacture show uniformly high proportions of green obsidian, rarely less than 90 per cent among cores and blades (table 9.1). This is the rule even for workshops that are relatively isolated and peripheral, like those of squares N3E2 and N3E3 of the Teotihuacán map (Millon, Drewitt & Cowgill 1973). One exception, site 23:N5W3, has a large quantity of earlier Tzacualli phase ceramics on the surface. The obsidian collection may thus include preworkshop Tzacualli material that would swell the gray-obsidian count disproportionately. The other exception involves an unspecialized zone in the large workshop area which lies immediately northwest of the Moon Pyramid (Spence 1967, fig. 1, no. 6). Here the proportion of green obsidian among blades and cores drops to 83.2 per cent and 87.4 per cent respectively, while in the adjacent core-blade specialized zone the proportions are 90.1 per cent and 96.7 per cent (table 9.1). This variability may be due to the internal distribution mechanisms operating in the workshop area, rather than to any problem of supply. The evidence thus indicates that large quantities of green obsidian entered the city, to be distributed without bias to all the workshops involved in core-blade production.

Most of the green obsidian recovered in Teotihuacán represents a point well advanced in core refinement. The cortex, the original surface of the obsidian, is rarely seen. The vast majority of polyhedral cores found in Teotihuacán workshops are exhausted or nearly exhausted, while cores in the early stages of use are very rare (cf. Hester 1972). 'Crested ridge flakes' or 'core block corners' which result from the straightening of core edges early in the manufacturing process (Crabtree 1968, 455, 460; Spence & Parsons 1972, 5–6) are

Table 9.1. *Green obsidian proportions among cores and blades.*

Workshop	Blades		Cores	
	no.	green	no.	green
Minor local workshop areas				
* 10–11:S1E2	303	98.7	19	100.0
* 29,36–39,47:N3W3	967	90.7	167	97.0
* 25:N3E2;18,20:N3E3	102	90.2	22	95.5
* 3–4:N2E5	392	94.4	46	97.8
23:N5W3	481	77.8	28	85.7
Major local workshop areas				
Santa Maria	1612	89.2	279	93.5
San Juan	2521	89.2	458	96.1
Regional workshop areas				
* Great Compound	783	93.6	276	97.5
Ciudadela	3821	93.3	515	95.9
* Moon (core-blade zone)	779	90.1	274	96.7
Moon (unspecialized)	1167	83.2	127	87.4
San Martin	3380	90.7	284	93.3
* N1E6–N1E7 area	3427	92.1	472	93.4
* S3E1–S4E1 area	877	97.7	174	97.7
Precinct workshops				
* Great Compound precinct	958	95.9	102	100.0

*Devoted exclusively to core-blade production.

not common, nor are the large flake blades that characterize the early stages of core refinement. Apparently the initial preparation of cores occurred elsewhere, to reduce the weight to be transported and to expose any structural flaws that would have rendered them unsuitable. Later Aztec quarrying in the Sierra de las Navajas region followed the same procedures (Spence & Parsons 1972).

One area in Teotihuacán seems to have been an exception to this pattern. Sites 13:D,F,H:N1W1, a group of room complexes on the south platform of the Great Compound, produced a collection of 53 obsidian cores, of which 49 (92.5 per cent) were of Navajas obsidian. Present also were two crested ridge flakes, an exhausted core that retained the original cortex on one side (unsuitable for marketing?), and a core blank with a faceted platform that had been accidentally split in half before it had reached the point of regular, controlled blade production. The size and nature of this core assemblage, plus the paucity of blades and waste, suggest that these room complexes might have been storage facilities where core blanks entering the city were kept, and perhaps further refined, before distribution to the workshop areas. However, this will have to be tested by excavations in the rooms.

There seem to have been no Teotihuacán period obsidian workshops in the Valley of Mexico beyond Teotihuacán. In fact, there have been no reports of extensive workshop activity involving green obsidian anywhere to the south, west, or east of the city. Despite this, green obsidian was consumed in quantity in many parts of central Mexico and even appears frequently well beyond the region. Green obsidian artifacts form a large proportion of the obsidian from Classic period sites in eastern Morelos, an area under Teotihuacán's control at that time, and about one quarter of a sample from Early Classic contexts in the Valley of Oaxaca (Hirth 1980, 70; Appel 1979). Further afield, they make up 1.6 per cent of a sample from Tikal and 7.9 per cent of the obsidian from Solano, a Teotihuacán-related site in highland Guatemala (Moholy-Nagy 1975, 511, 514; Brown 1977, 420). The absence of green obsidian workshops beyond the city and the concomitant dependence of much of the central Mexico region on Teotihuacán for artifacts of this material indicate the existence of some constraints on the movement of Navajas obsidian. If these other areas had had unimpeded access to it, we would have expected its wider distribution as raw material and the development of workshops in areas not within easy reach of Teotihuacán. The nature of these constraints is uncertain but they must have originated in Teotihuacán, since it controlled access from these areas to the source and had large quantities of green obsidian in its own workshops.

To the north of Teotihuacán the situation may have been somewhat different. Tepeapulco, an important site some 30 km northeast of Teotihuacán and 30 km south of the Sierra de las Navajas source region (fig. 9.1), was an obsidian-production center from at least the Tezoyuca-Patlachique period (Charlton 1978). Through much of this span there was a growing emphasis there upon the Navajas material. Charlton suggests that Tepeapulco was dominated by Teotihuacán, and that Teotihuacán had developed it as a subsidiary center to control production and trade to the north, east, and southeast. However, the common occurrence in the Tepeapulco workshops of obsidian from the Paredon source (fig. 9.1), coupled with its absence in Classic period contexts in Teotihuacán, reveal that products and raw materials from the Tepeapulco system did not flow back into Teotihuacán or the Valley of Mexico (Charlton 1978, 1233). The city's supply of green obsidian probably followed a more direct route from the source region, not passing through Tepeapulco. The Casacoalco site may have been involved in this movement, as might the Cempoala site (fig. 9.1). Since Cempoala is located roughly halfway between Teotihuacán and the source region, the Teotihuacán period site there may have served as a way station (R. Nieto Calleja, personal communication 1981). No Teotihuacán period workshop debris occurs there (Mora López 1981), but such debris would not be expected if the site served principally as a storage and transshipment point.

Trace-element analysis

Detailed analyses of California and Guatemalan obsidian sources have shown that there can be consistent and measurable geochemical variation within a single source region (Bowman, Asaro & Perlman 1973; Hurtado de Mendoza & Jester 1978). There is reason to believe that such variation exists within the Sierra de las Navajas source region, and that wide-spectrum trace-element analyses and the appropriate statistical techniques can reveal it (García-Bárcena 1975; Zeitlin & Heimbuch 1978, 139). If so, material from different sectors of the source region can be identified and its distribution among the Teotihuacán workshops traced, data that could provide important information on the city's procurement networks. Unfortunately we do not have obsidian from a carefully designed sampling program of the source region itself (although R. Cobean and J. Vogt of the University of Missouri are presently conducting such a study). It was decided instead to analyze a number of specimens from Teotihuacán workshops, in the expectation that groups could be statistically separated that would correspond to geochemically distinguishable sectors of the source region, that is, to separate loci of exploitation. To this end 56 exhausted green obsidian cores from six Teotihuacán workshops were submitted for analysis at the Brookhaven National Laboratory. The sample consists of:

1. Seven cores from site 14:N1W2, a workshop in the large Great Compound regional workshop area, a core-blade specialized area lying immediately to the west of the Great Compound. This was probably the parent area for the craftsmen who worked in the Great Compound precinct workshop zone.

2. Nine cores from site 46:N1E2, a workshop in the large, unspecialized Ciudadela regional workshop area (Spence 1967, 510, fig. 1, no. 8).

3. Ten cores from site 2:N6W1, a workshop in the core-blade specialized zone of the Moon regional workshop area (Spence 1967, 510, fig. 1, no. 6).

4. Ten cores from site 23:N5W3, a small, unspecialized, and relatively isolated local workshop in the Old City section of Teotihuacán.

5. Ten cores from site 17:N1E7, a workshop in the N1E6-N1E7 core-blade specialized regional workshop area near the east edge of the city (Spence 1967, 510, fig. 1, no. 5).

6. Ten cores from site 17:A:S3E1, a core-blade specialized workshop in the regional workshop area in squares S3E1 and S4E1, in the southern part of the city (Spence 1967, 510–11, fig. 1, no. 11).

The specimens were subjected to neutron activation analysis at the Brookhaven facilities. All were prepared alike and irradiated in close proximity to one another, thereby reducing the effect of any mechanical errors that might have occurred. Twenty-one elements were measured for each of the 56 cores (table 9.2). The results were first submitted to cluster analysis (AGCLUS) to form groups, which were then refined using stepwise discriminant analysis (SPSS) in an iterative manner. Four groups were distinguished. These distinctions seem based particularly on elements Fe, Zn, Ce, Hf, and Th, all measured with a high degree of accuracy. Using these five

elements, the group separations were tested with analysis of variance. The results indicate that the intergroup differences are significant ($F[3, 52] = 156.201$ [Fe], 46.849 [Zn], 85.856 [Ce], 91.001 [Hf], 98,884 [Th], $p < 0.001$ for each). Then the Scheffe procedure was applied to test the separation of each element. The separations were consistently assigned a confidence level of 0.95 or better, with the single exception of the separation of groups 1 and 4 on the basis of Zn. Even this separation, though, was confirmed with the other four elements (and with Zn by the less demanding LSD and Tukey-HSD procedures). Although these results cannot be said to demonstrate conclusively the reality of the four groups, the consistently high confidence levels do suggest that the separations are valid. Presumably, then, each group represents a geochemically distinguishable part of the source deposit, and thus a separate locus of Teotihuacán period exploitation. It is also possible that a series of vertically overlapping flows in one locality could account for such variation, but this seems unlikely. While observations made at one mine shaft in the region raise the possibility of two layers of obsidian (P. Weigand, personal communication 1981), this would not be enough to explain all four groups. Also, there is some evidence to suggest that only the lower flow was exploited intensively.

The groups are distributed among the various workshops in an apparently random fashion (table 9.3). Each workshop produced specimens of at least two and usually all four groups. Similarly, each group was represented in at least five of the workshops. This indicates that the material derived from each of the four loci of exploitation flowed through the same node at some point between the source and the workshops, to be then passed on to the workshop areas without regard to its original provenience (cf. Pires-Ferreira 1975, 31). This suggestion is reinforced by a study of the Mean Euclidean Distance values. These values provide a measure of the degree of geochemical difference between any two of the cores. A very low value indicates that the two cores involved in that comparison were probably derived from very similar geological contexts, perhaps the same quarrying operation or even the same block of obsidian. There were 12 comparisons which produced strikingly low values (0.001–0.002). Of these, all but three involved the comparison of cores collected from different workshops. The evidence suggests, therefore, that material quarried at a particular locale did not generally end up in the same workshop, which in turn implies some form of pooling before the final disposition of the cores.

There is still the question of contemporaneity. It could be that each source locale was exploited in a different period. If so, their overlapping distributions in Teotihuacán might merely reflect the long time spans of the workshops. This possibility was tested by submitting the specimens to C. Meighan for hydration analysis at the University of California, Los Angeles, Obsidian Hydration Laboratory. The variations in chemical composition among the four groups are too minor to have had a significant effect on the hydration rate. Hydration measurements were obtained for 48 of the

Table 9.2. *Element values by group.*

Element	Group 1 Mean	SD	Group 2 Mean	SD	Group 3 Mean	SD	Group 4 Mean	SD
Zr	764.90	24.46	751.29	27.72	734.07	17.51	785.06	32.56
Hf	25.20	0.17	24.91	0.16	24.39	0.20	25.63	0.21
Ta	5.55	0.08	5.54	0.08	5.39	0.11	5.69	0.11
Sb	0.22	0.06	0.21	0.07	0.20	0.05	0.23	0.05
Se	16.83	0.30	16.56	0.29	16.22	0.17	17.01	0.24
Th	20.43	0.13	20.09	0.22	19.64	0.16	20.77	0.13
Zn	227.24	1.66	223.16	2.66	217.85	3.16	229.82	2.80
La	45.11	1.33	43.86	0.88	43.14	0.41	46.21	1.25
Ce	87.99	0.51	86.81	1.09	84.46	0.75	89.63	0.69
Nd	55.52	2.81	53.63	1.88	52.62	2.06	55.71	1.87
Eu	1.73	0.02	1.72	0.02	1.68	0.02	1.77	0.02
Gd	3.97	0.06	3.92	0.07	3.79	0.08	4.08	0.07
Tb	2.83	0.07	2.81	0.06	2.82	0.10	2.89	0.09
Tm	1.22	0.14	1.19	0.14	1.12	0.12	1.37	0.19
Yb	15.05	0.49	14.88	0.46	14.82	0.71	15.19	0.37
Lu	1.88	0.02	1.85	0.02	1.81	0.03	1.91	0.02
Rb	200.30	3.62	198.08	3.46	192.48	2.41	204.50	3.34
Cs	4.11	0.09	4.01	0.10	3.89	0.09	4.19	0.18
Ba	82.14	13.17	74.52	11.45	77.76	11.16	81.66	9.81
Sc	3.84	0.76	3.60	0.02	3.53	0.02	3.70	0.02
Fe	1.65	0.00	1.63	0.01	1.60	0.01	1.68	0.01

Fe in %, all other elements in ppm.

cores. In four cases two distinct measurements were obtained from a single core: 3.0 and 3.9 microns on a group 1 specimen from site 2:N6W1, 3.6 and 4.4 for a group 1 core from 17:A: S3E1, 3.6 and 4.1 for a group 4 core from 14:N1W2, and 3.7 and 4.1 for a group 4 core from 23:N5W3. Only the earlier (larger) of these measurements were included in table 9.3, since these presumably reflect the time of manufacture and early use of the core. The more recently developed hydration bands probably represent later reuse or accidental breakage.

Within the limits imposed by the small size of the sample, the four groups seem to have been at least partially contemporaneous. The overlap is primarily in the 3.4–4.2 micron span, where most of the measurements cluster. A lineal hydration rate of about 1 micron/400 years, which seems at the moment to be the most acceptable rate for Teotihuacán green obsidian (Spence 1978), would place this span roughly between A.D. 300 and A.D. 600, in the Tlamimilolpa and Xolalpan phases of the Teotihuacán chronology (table 9.4). This finding is what one would expect, since these phases encompass the peak period of the city. The hydration analysis, then, indicates that the four loci were exploited contemporaneously during the height of Teotihuacán.

Table 9.3. *Teotihuacán obsidian cores by group and workshop.*

Workshop	Group 1	Group 2	Group 3	Group 4
14:N1W2	2	2	1	2
2:N6W1	2	4	1	3
46:N1E2		5	4	
17:A:S3E1	2	2	1	5
23:N5W3	2	3	1	4
17:N1E7	4	1		5

Discussion

Three possible models can be suggested for Teotihuacán's procurement of Navajas obsidian. It must be noted that these models really represent the extremes of a range of possible alternatives. They are somewhat oversimplified, do not exhaust the possibilities, and may not even be mutually exclusive. Elements of each could have been combined in one system, but they do provide a framework within which the data can be examined.

In model 1, which represents the 'entrepreneurial' extreme, each workshop area developed its own procurement

Table 9.4. *Teotihuacán obsidian hydration measurements.*

Microns	Group 1	Group 2	Group 3	Group 4	Phase
2.0				1	
2.1					
2.2					
2.3					
2.4					
2.5	1				
2.6				1	
2.7		1			
2.8			1		
2.9					
3.0				1	
3.1		2			
3.2	1			1	
3.3		2			. . . .
3.4		1		2	
3.5					Xolalpan
3.6		1	2	2	phase
3.7		3		3	. . . .
3.8	2	2			
3.9	3		1	1	
4.0					Tlamimilolpa
4.1		1		3	phase
4.2	1		1		
4.3					. . . .
4.4	1			1	
4.5	1				
4.6				1	
4.7					
4.8	1				
4.9			1		
5.0					
5.1					
5.2					
5.3		1			

network, either mounting its own mining expeditions to the source region or establishing independent contact with a particular indigenous group there that mined the material, refined it, and then passed it to the representatives of the workshop area. The latter alternative seems somewhat more likely, since the scale of obsidian use in Teotihuacán and its importance to the city's economy imply a more stable flow than periodic small quarrying expeditions from the city could have ensured.

Model 2 represents the opposite extreme, a state-controlled procurement system. The source region may have been fully absorbed into the Teotihuacán state, with the quarrying of obsidian conducted by local inhabitants under state direction, or the state may have organized direct mining

expeditions to the source region. In either case, the material was obtained under state aegis, entered the city through a state conduit of some sort, and was distributed to the workshop areas as the state officials saw fit. With model 3, another variant of the entrepreneurial end of the range, traders would have been responsible for obtaining the obsidian in the source region and transporting it to Teotihuacán. Independent of the state and acting largely in their own self-interest, these entrepreneurs would have traded for the obsidian with the inhabitants of the source region and then passed it on to the workshop areas as opportunity and profit dictated.

A procurement system like that outlined in model 1, with each area developing its own network, would have required considerable effort and expense by the workshop-area corporate groups. It should be reflected in striking inequities in the distribution of Navajas obsidian within Teotihuacán, since only the larger areas would have been able to command the resources and personnel necessary to develop and maintain effective procurement networks. The green obsidian of each workshop area should constitute a single homogeneous trace-element group, distinguishable from those of other workshop areas, since each area would establish its own set of contacts in the source region. Furthermore, one might expect that a number of Classic period communities in or near the source region would have been involved in obsidian quarrying and processing, each passing its output along to one or a few workshop groups. The actual evidence suggests the contrary. Large quantities of green obsidian entered Teotihuacán and were distributed very equitably among the workshop areas, with each area obtaining material from several different locales in the source region. Furthermore, the survey by Mora López (1981) indicates that only one of the Teotihuacán period sites near the source region, Casacoalco, has evidence of obsidian macrocore processing. Model 1, in the extreme form in which it has been presented, must be rejected.

In model 2, the state-controlled system, one would expect those workshops most closely associated with the major public structures, the precinct workshops and the nearby regional workshop areas, to show somewhat higher proportions of green obsidian. Furthermore, the green obsidian in any particular workshop area should have a variable trace-element composition, reflecting its derivation from several exploitation loci whose output had become mixed in transit through the state system. There should also be storage facilities for the core blanks, probably associated with one of the major public structures in the heart of the city.

The evidence seems largely to substantiate model 2, although there are still some discrepancies. The geochemical variability of the obsidian in each workshop area conforms to the expected pattern, as does the presence of a possible storage facility within the Great Compound precinct. On the other hand, the green obsidian entering the city was distributed equally to all of the workshop areas, with no apparent bias toward those with the closest state associations. This seems to contradict the expectation derived from model 2, but it is not necessarily incompatible with the model itself. Such a distribution could occur if supplies were so plentiful that state officials were not forced to discriminate, or if the state recognized some responsibility toward even the smaller and more isolated local areas. It is also possible that there was some bias in assignment, and that the local workshop areas responded to this by restricting their core-blade output to a level where they could maintain high proportions of Navajas obsidian.

Model 3 presupposes a set of independent traders mediating between the source-region inhabitants and the Teotihuacán craftsmen. Such a system might well have resulted in the variable composition of the obsidian from each workshop area, if particular traders and particular workshop areas had not forged exclusive relationships. On the other hand, there should be more marked variation in the proportions of green obsidian, with the larger and richer workshop areas taking the lion's share of the material. One might also expect relatively widespread evidence of Teotihuacán period obsidian processing near the source region, since a relatively open system of this sort would have involved a number of local communities. The apparent restriction of macrocore processing to Casacoalco is at variance with this expectation. By the same token, in an entrepreneurial system green obsidian as a raw material should have circulated more widely beyond the city, with the concomitant development of workshop areas elsewhere in the Valley of Mexico and beyond. The absence of such rival developments suggests that, if traders were involved, they were operating under some rather rigid constraints imposed by the state. To that degree, then, they may have been more agents of the state than independent entrepreneurs.

In sum, the evidence from Teotihuacán suggests a green-obsidian-procurement system dominated to a considerable extent by the state, with little or no opportunity for entre-preneurial behavior by either traders or the corporate groups of the workshop areas. This is not unexpected. It is unlikely that Teotihuacán would have permitted a highly *laissez-faire* approach to the supply of a material as vital, in terms of both trade and the production of other commodities, as the Navajas obsidian. The distance between the source region and the city would have made it more difficult to ensure a regular and copious flow of obsidian through a series of independent networks, and to exclude rival polities from access to the material.

In the Tzacualli phase (A.D. 0–150) Navajas obsidian entered Teotihuacán in much smaller quantities and was more erratically distributed (Spence, in press). The proportion of green obsidian among blades in city workshops of that period ranged from 20.3 per cent to 81.2 per cent, and it was not very common in contexts suggesting state associations. Apparently each workshop area developed its own system for obtaining green obsidian, the state was not overtly involved in procurement, and links with the source area were not strong enough to obtain and transport large quantities.

Some time in the Miccaotli (A.D. 150–A.D. 200) or Tlamimilolpa (A.D. 200–A.D. 450) phase, the amount of green obsidian entering Teotihuacán increased enormously and all workshop areas, even the smaller and more marginal ones, gained unimpeded access to all that they required (table 9.1). A number of different sectors of the Navajas region were being exploited. There had clearly been some major changes in the situation. One of these was the direct involvement of the state in the exploitation and transportation of the obsidian. In fact, the area immediately to the south of the Navajas region was probably first extensively settled and absorbed into the Teotihuacán empire at this time (Mora López 1981), its population playing a major part in the state procurement system.

The control and trade of the fine Sierra de las Navajas obsidian probably did not play an important role in Teotihuacán's development into a state. It had already become a state in the Tzacualli phase, when green obsidian was available only in limited quantities and was not linked to state institutions of any kind. In fact, a secure supply of Navajas obsidian was only made possible through the intervention of the already thriving state.

Control of the Navajas material did play an important part in the expansion of the city's obsidian industry. The most striking area of growth was in the core-blade production sector. Even then, much of the basic structure of the industry, including its division into local and regional workshop areas, had been set in the Tzacualli phase (Spence, in press). The influx of Navajas obsidian resulted in an increase in the scope of the industry and must have meant a greatly expanded market for its output, but it was handled through an elaboration of the existing pattern rather than through any fundamental structural changes.

Conclusions

The fact that green obsidian procurement was largely an administered system does not necessarily inform us about Teotihuacán's economy in general. In some other cases, like the exploitation of cinnabar in Querétaro, the state may have played a major role (Millon 1973, 61–2). On the other hand, the procurement of gray obsidian seems to have been handled independently by each workshop area, with little or no state intervention. Each material must be studied independently, since each may represent a distinct set of relationships, procedures, and even goals. The nature of any particular procurement system might have depended on a variety of factors: the distance to the sources, the importance of the material in Teotihuacán's economy, the political relationships between the city and the source region, the particular role played by the material in Teotihuacán's social system, and so on. It may be misleading for an archaeologist working outside Teotihuacán to view the city as a monolith with a large, undifferentiated impact upon his area of investigation. He may be dealing sometimes with a highly integrated and tightly focused foreign presence, but in other situations Teotihuacán's influence may have been mediated through a series of different and even competing units, each developing its own set of links within the local society.

By the same token different kinds of procurement systems will have had different effects on Teotihuacán itself. Those that relied on state involvement for their successful operation (tribute systems, state-organized mining expeditions, etc.) were probably capable of obtaining and transporting considerable quantities of material with a high degree of stability. The deterioration of the state or its withdrawal from the source region, however, may have led to the total collapse of such a system. If the material were vital to the society, the collapse could have aggravated the difficulties that the state was experiencing. A series of relatively independent networks, like those suggested for gray obsidian procurement in Teotihuacán, would probably not have been able to obtain such large quantities of material and would have been subject to some irregularity as individual networks encountered difficulties. On the other hand, the disruption of political ties with the source region or the deterioration of the state would not necessarily have halted the flow of material. With a number of somewhat repetitive and overlapping networks, independent of the state and of each other, the systemic pathology that Flannery (1972) has termed hyper-coherence would have been avoided. The effects of any disruptions would have been muted, with some networks suffering and others, buffered from them, surviving and even expanding. The little that we know of obsidian production in the Coyotlatelco phase (A.D. 750–A.D. 950), which immediately followed the collapse of Teotihuacán, provides some support for this hypothesis. Recent excavations by E. Rattray (1979) reveal that the Metepec Hacienda workshop area, several sites in the east end of Teotihuacán that were devoted to the production of gray obsidian bifacial blanks, dates largely to the Coyotlatelco phase. Evidently raw material was still being imported in quantity from the Otumba source region. On the other hand, we have not yet identified any Coyotlatelco-phase green-obsidian workshops in Teotihuacán, and green obsidian seems to have been sparse on Coyotlatelco-phase occupation sites elsewhere in the Valley of Mexico (Rattray 1966, 130, and personal communication 1979). Perhaps the collapse of Teotihuacán destroyed the highly centralized Navajas procurement network but did not totally disrupt the more flexible Otumba networks.

Acknowledgments

This work was supported in part by a Canada Council Research Grant. The Brookhaven National Laboratory facilities were used for the neutron-activation analysis and C. Meighan, director of the University of California, Los Angeles, Obsidian Hydration Laboratory, kindly undertook the hydration analysis. We also thank T. Charlton and N. Hammond for their comments on an earlier version of this paper, and M. Green, C. Creider, I. Spence, and J. Baskerville for help with various statistical matters. The generous assistance of R. Mora López, F. López Aguilar, and R. Nieto Calleja, of the INAH Centro Regional de Hidalgo, is gratefully acknowledged.

References

Adams, R. M. 1974. Anthropological perspectives on ancient trade. *Current Anthropology* 15:239–58.

Appel, J. 1979. Lithic production in the Valley of Oaxaca, Mexico. Paper presented at the 44th Annual Meeting, Society for American Archaeology, Vancouver.

Bernal, I. 1966. Teotihuacán: capital de imperio? *Revista Mexicana de Estudios Antropológicos* 20:95–110.

Bowman, H. R., Asaro, F. & Perlman, I. 1973. Composition variations in obsidian sources and the archaeological implications. *Archaeometry* 15:123–7.

Brown, K. L. 1977. Toward a systematic explanation of culture change within the Middle Classic period of the Valley of Guatemala. In W. T. Sanders & J. W. Michels, eds., *Teotihuacan and Kaminaljuyu: a study in prehistoric culture contact.* University Park: Pennsylvania State University Press, 411–40.

Charlton, T. A. 1969. On the identification of prehispanic obsidian mines in southern Hidalgo. *American Antiquity* 34:176–7.

1978. Teotihuacan, Tepeapulco, and obsidian exploitation. *Science* 200:1227–36.

Crabtree, D. E. 1968. Mesoamerican polyhedral cores and prismatic blades. *American Antiquity* 33:446–78.

Flannery, K. V. 1972. The cultural evolution of civilizations. *Annual Review of Ecology and Systematics* 3:399–426.

García-Bárcena, J. 1975. Las minas de obsidiana de la Sierra de las Navajas. Hgo., México. *Actas del XLI Congreso Internacional de Americanistas*, 1:369–77. Instituto Nacional de Antropología e Historia, Mexico City.

García Cook, A. 1967. Análisis Tipológico de artefactos. *Instituto Nacional de Antropología e Historia Investigaciones* 12.

González Rul, F. 1972. Sobre las minas de obsidiana de Cerro Pelón, Hgo. *Instituto Nacional de Antropología e Historia Boletín* 3:11–16.

Hester, T. R. 1972. Notes on large obsidian blade cores and core-blade technology in Mesoamerica. *Contributions of the University of California Archaeological Research Facility* 14:95–105.

Hirth, K. 1980. Eastern Morelos and Teotihuacán: a settlement survey. *Vanderbilt University Publications in Anthropology* 25.

Hurtado de Mendoza, L. & Jester, W. A. 1978. Obsidian sources in Guatemala: a regional approach. *American Antiquity* 43: 424–35.

Kohl, P. 1978. The balance of trade in southwestern Asia in the mid-third millennium B.C. *Current Anthropology* 19:463–92.

Lamberg-Karlovsky, C. C. 1975. Third millennium modes of exchange and modes of production. In J. A. Sabloff & C. C. Lamberg-Karlovsky, eds., *Ancient civilization and trade.* Albuquerque: University of New Mexico Press, 341–68.

Matos Moctezuma, E. 1976. Relationships between Tepeapolco and Teotihuacán. Paper presented at the 41st Annual Meeting of the Society for American Archaeology, St Louis.

Millon, R. 1973. *Urbanization at Teotihuacán, Mexico, vol. I: The Teotihuacan map, part 1: Text.* Austin: University of Texas Press.

Millon, R.; Drewitt, R. B. & Cowgill, G. 1973. *Urbanization at Teotihuacan, Mexico, vol. I: The Teotihuacán map, part 2: Maps.* Austin: University of Texas Press.

Moholy-Nagy, H. 1975. Obsidian at Tikal, Guatemala. *Actas del XLI Congreso Internacional de Americanistas* 1:511–18.

Mora López, R. 1981. La división social del trabajo de la obsidiana en el sureste del estado de Hidalgo. Paper presented at the Simposio la Obsidiana en Mesoamérica, Pachuca.

Pires-Ferreira, J. 1975. Formative Mesoamerican exchange networks with special reference to the Valley of Oaxaca. *University of Michigan Museum of Anthropology Memoir* 7.

Polanyi, K. Arensberg, C. & Pearson, H. eds. 1957. *Trade and market in early empires.* Glencoe, Ill.: The Free Press.

Rattray, E. 1966. An archaeological and stylistic study of Coyotlatelco pottery. *Mesoamerican Notes* 7–8:87–193.

1979. Craft production in Teotihuacan in the Coyotlatelco phase. Paper presented at the 44th Annual Meeting, Society for American Archaeology, Vancouver.

Sanders, W. T., Parsons, J. R. & Santley, R. S. 1979. *The Basin of Mexico: ecological processes in the evolution of a civilization.* New York: Academic Press.

Spence, M. W. 1967. The obsidian industry of Teotihuacán. *American Antiquity* 32:507–14.

1974. Residential practices and the distribution of skeletal traits in Teotihuacán, Mexico. *Man* (n.s.) 9:262–73.

1978. Comments on the Teotihuacán obsidian hydration measurements. In C. Meighan and P. I. Vanderhoeven, eds., Obsidian dates II: a compendium of the obsidian hydration determinations made at the UCLA Obsidian Hydration Laboratory. *University of California, Los Angeles, Institute of Archaeology Monograph* VI, 162–4.

In press. Craft production and polity in early Teotihuacán. In K. Hirth, ed., *Trade and exchange in early Mesoamerica.* Albuquerque: University of New Mexico Press.

Spence, M. W. & Parsons, J. R. 1972. Prehispanic obsidian exploitation in central Mexico: a preliminary synthesis. *University of Michigan Museum of Anthropology Anthropological Papers* 45:1–43.

Zeitlin, R. & Heimbuch, R. C. 1978. Trace element analysis and the archaeological study of obsidian procurement in precolumbian Mesoamerica. In D. Davis, ed., Lithics and subsistence: the analysis of stone tool use in prehistoric economies. *Vanderbilt University Publications in Anthropology* 20:117–59.

PART THREE

Technology and techniques

Chapter 10

Jigsaw: reconstructive lithic technology
H. M. Leach

The reassembling of original parent blocks from the scattered waste flakes, blades, and cores recovered from working floors may be likened to attempting a three-dimensional jigsaw puzzle which is known to be incomplete. Nevertheless, reconstruction of only a small number of blocks may reveal valuable details of the actual manufacturing processes. The method was applied to the problem of the technological affinities of anomalous blade knives used by early East Polynesian settlers in southern New Zealand. It enabled a comparison to be made of the reduction sequences at a blade-making site and an adze manufactory, and demonstrated that the technical knowledge required for adze-making at this period encompassed the techniques necessary for successful production of blade knives.

Introduction

In the south of the South Island of New Zealand (fig. 10.1), East Polynesian migrants established themselves about 1,000 years ago during a period of comparatively rapid exploration of their new home. Most of their settlements were concentrated along the coast at the mouths of streams and rivers where they could pull up large double canoes, exploit the resources of the sea (ranging in size from sea elephants to cockles), and use the waterways to gain access to forests and a rich avifauna. Among the stone tools which are found on their sites are adzes of typical East Polynesian types, quadrangular, triangular, and trapezoidal in cross-section. These are commonly interpreted as woodworking tools (Best 1977). They are made in two main materials: metamorphosed argillites available at Bluff Harbour and Riverton, and basalts from several points along the coast near Brighton Island. In addition to the adzes, large retouched silcrete (orthoquartzite) blades are found, especially in the earliest levels of these sites. This raw material occurs *in situ* in parts of Central Otago such as Oturehua, but was also carried down to the coast by river action.

Three problems, raised by the presence of these blades, have been the subject of much discussion. One is their function – were they linked to the processing of the bones of the large flightless moas, since they both disappear from the sites at about the same period (Simmons 1973)? The second is their distribution – they occur in South Island sites, especially the southern half, but nowhere in the North Island, with which the south had extensive trade networks (B. F. Leach 1969a). The third, which is the subject of this chapter, is their technological affinities. They were made and used by East Polynesians soon after their arrival from a presumed homeland in the Society or Marquesas Islands. No blades were recognized from any tropical Polynesian assemblage until the 1970s. These recently reported finds, which are too few to constitute evidence of a blade industry, are of obsidian micro-blades from Easter Island (McCoy 1976), trachytic glass micro-blades from Molokai, Hawaiian Islands (Kirch & Kelly 1975), and some larger Marquesan artifacts which may include adze preforms as well as blade tools (Gerard 1976). In the absence of a well-established East Polynesian blade *industry,* several prehistorians have debated whether the technique of blade-making could have been perfected in one or or two centuries in New Zealand by modifying adze-making procedures (B. F. Leach 1969a; Jones 1972; Simmons 1973). I would like to present important evidence in support of this view.

Oturehua blade quarry workshop

In 1966 a new prehistoric quarry site with associated working floors was discovered on the flanks of the Ida Valley, near the town of Oturehua (fig. 10.1). Other silcrete quarry workshops were known in Central Otago but none were quite so suitable for archaeological investigation. At the Oturehua site discarded blades, decortication flakes, and reject cores marked the positions of workshops lying within an area of 50 acres on a north-facing slope. On a broad ridge and adjacent hollow, just above the main workshop area, numerous quarry pits were located. In a surveyed area 60-by-60 m, 49 subrectangular pits were plotted up to 8.5-by-2.5 m in size, but commonly about 3 by 2 m. They were usually 20 to 25 cm deep with a broad face on the uphill side and a terrace of worked-over boulders on the downhill side. In several places piles of fine-grained material, already split open and tested for quality, were stacked up ready for removal to the workshops. Although the surface of the hillside is littered with silcrete boulders, they are deeply weathered and have a sugary texture quite unsuitable for flaking. Since the material taken to the working floor and that found in the pits displays a much thinner cortex, it is clear that the quarry pits were for the extraction of less-weathered pieces.

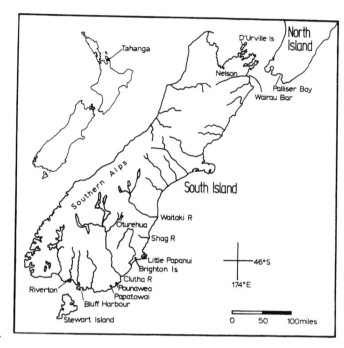

Fig. 10.1. Geographical location of South Island, New Zealand.

After surveying some of the workshops and the quarry-pit areas, excavations were undertaken in 1967 which were designed to recover material for technological analysis. The director of the project, B. F. Leach, hoped to reassemble sufficient flakes, blades, and cores to reveal the techniques of blade manufacture and throw some light on the question of technological affinities. Accordingly all the worked silcrete from the single cultural level was removed from an area of 6 by 10 m, and recorded spatially by 20-by-20 cm divisions. After steam cleaning the 6,208 flakes larger than 2 g and 140 reject cores, and counting, weighing, and boxing 7,713 flakes and chips less than 2 g, the larger items (greater than 2 g) were set out on a gridded floor and the task of reassembly begun. Through most of 1968, during lunch hours and weekends, reconstruction took place despite the knowledge that some of the pieces had fallen or been thrown outside the excavated area and that others had been removed by the prehistoric blade-makers. At the conclusion of the exercise, which it seemed appropriate to term 'jigsaw' reconstruction, 785 or 12.4 per cent of the 6,348 pieces laid out had been reassembled. By weight this represented nearly 30 per cent of the total assemblage of 14,061 items.

The next stage of the analysis was to examine the spatial patterns of debris dispersal in the workshop area. These should reflect the flying-off of debris as the cores were worked, together with deliberate changes of position made by the artisans. Plotting the distribution of the small chips (fig. 10.2) had shown five areas of concentration and these coincided closely with the distribution of the components of eleven reassembled cores (fig. 10.3). The normal spread of discarded material seems to be about 1 m on either side of the center of distribution, often with a majority of flakes falling to one

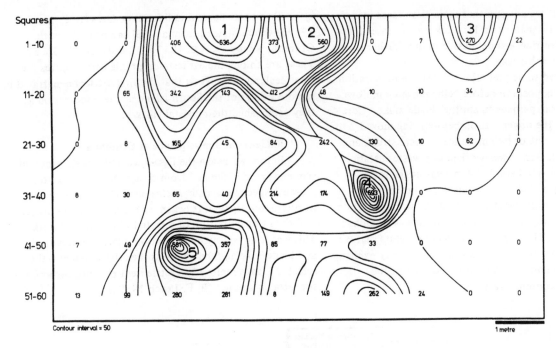

Fig. 10.2. Distribution of 7,713 small flakes in Area A, Oturehua.

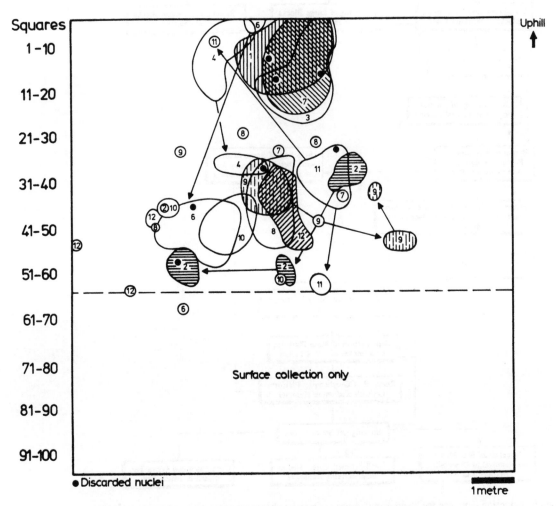

Fig. 10.3. Distribution of flakes/blades reassembled in eleven major cores/clusters at Oturehua.

side of the center. If we imagine that the artisan faces into the sun so as not to cast a shadow on his work, in five cases there is strong evidence for right-handedness, and in a further six no conclusive evidence either way.

Core 6 received some preliminary platform preparation in the upper working position before being moved 4 m downhill to a lower station, perhaps to another blade maker. Core 4 was also worked in the upper station before being moved 2 to 3 m downhill where one or two more blades were struck and the core abandoned. Core 2 was worked at a western station and then completed and discarded 4 m away at the lower station. On the way a blade was dropped and broke in two. A large corner blade which was struck off at the western station was discarded 3 m away uphill having been used as a hammer at the upper station. This type of movement suggests that we are dealing with a few blade makers who occasionally exchange raw materials and hammers. There is no doubt that the various concentrations are contemporary.

Two twig-charcoal radiocarbon dates (B. F. Leach 1969b) were obtained from a small campfire lit by the Oturehua knappers: A.D. 1053 ± 27 and A.D. 1023 ± 82. These are among the earliest acceptable carbon dates for New Zealand and suggest that the first settlers penetrated into remote valleys of the South Island at the same period as they established their coastal villages.

Blade-reduction sequence at Oturehua

Before we began the jigsaw we had a basic production-sequence model, derived from observations at the site, museum specimens, and articles on blade-making in the northern hemisphere. It began with quarrying and quartering and then transportation of selected blocks to the workshop. This was followed by decortication, platform preparation, and blade-making. The core was then discarded and the selected blades removed to settlement or multipurpose sites for retouch and use (B. F. Leach 1969a).

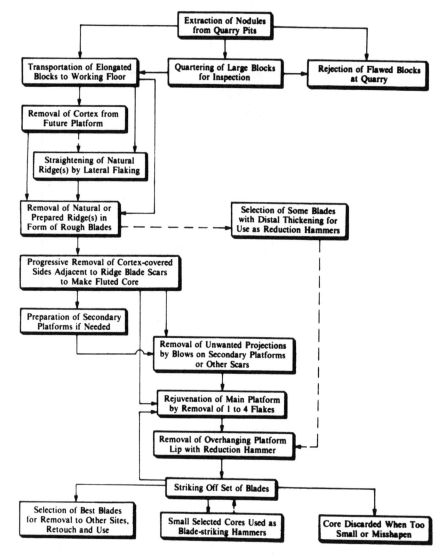

Fig. 10.4. Flow diagram of reduction sequence for blade manufacture at Oturehua based on cores with one main platform.

Fourteen major reconstructed cores have allowed us to refine the model and have revealed the range of variation caused by initial block irregularities. The new model (fig. 10.4) is based on an elongated block with a cortex-covered top and sides and a roughly fractured base. The sides have four to five natural corners. The top may or may not be prepared by flaking before the corner blades are removed, and the cortex-covered sides turned into a roughly fluted surface. The corners may be unprepared or laterally trimmed before being struck off. Commonly the corner blades exhibit marked distal thickening and were used as hammers. Adjoining blades may terminate halfway down the sides of the core leaving a thick mass as the base, and a minor platform may be prepared at the bottom of the core for striking blades or flakes to remove this mass. Alternatively a corner blade scar may be used as a platform for lateral reduction. The top platform is then rejuvenated by removal of one to four flakes and overhanging portions of the platform reduced by battering with the corner blade hammers. Another set of blades is removed before the platform is rejuvenated again. This process may be repeated two or three times more before the core is discarded.

The range of variation in procedure is considerable. Although most of the cores show concentration of effort on one main prepared and later rejuvenated platform, the larger cores may display up to seven different platform areas on three or more faces, some prepared, some retaining natural cortex. Previous blade scars may be used as platforms for blade-making on adjoining surfaces, as well. Corner blades are invariably used as 'starters' (cf. Crabtree 1968, 455–6). A few are laterally trimmed to ensure a straight ridge, while the majority are only slightly trimmed or untrimmed. The Oturehua approach can best be described as opportunistic – adapting a few basic techniques to particular shapes of core, and not wasting effort in preparing platforms and trimming corners if natural ones would do.

The profile of the blades and their irregularity suggest direct percussion. Apart from the corner blade hammers (fig. 10.5c) which have been worn partly concave by striking the edges (not the surface) of the striking platforms in order to reduce the overhanging lip (cf. Crabtree 1968, 457–8, 460, 465), only one other hammerstone was found in the workshop. This large elongated greywacke boulder of a shape amenable to hafting weighs 2.9 kg and appears to have been used as a quartering hammer. Two possible blade-making hammers have been found in a plowed field elsewhere in the Ida Valley. They are single-platform discarded blade cores with heavy battering on the ends opposite the platform (fig. 10.5a, b); they weigh 299.2 g and 335.8 g respectively. The absence of such blade-making hammers amongst the working-floor debris may suggest that they were carried away by the artisans as part of a valued personal tool kit.

Riverton adze quarry workshop

Although the jigsaw showed precisely how the Oturehua artisans made their blades, it did not answer the question of

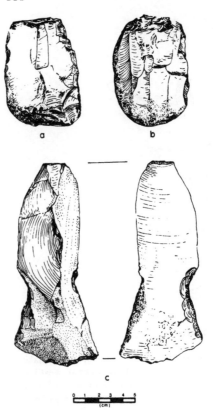

Fig. 10.5. Oturehua hammers. a, b: single-platform discarded blade cores with heavy battering on the ends opposite the platform. c: corner blade hammer, worn partly concave by striking the edges (not the surface) of the striking platforms.

where and how they acquired the knowledge and techniques. Material excavated in 1964 by L. M. Groube from another specialist quarry workshop at Riverton (Leach & Leach 1980) was available for comparison with that from Oturehua. At the Riverton site metamorphosed argillite was used and periodic occupations are dated two to four centuries later than Oturehua (a.d. 1254 ± 49, 1269 ± 36, 1402 ± 39, 1500 ± 54). Although later, there is no doubt that the prehistoric visitors to this quarry belonged to the same Archaic New Zealand East Polynesian culture as the blade users. Riverton was an Archaic adze manufactory which might display certain techniques transferable to blade production.

An area of just under 64 m^2 had been excavated, but the squares were not contiguous as at Oturehua, and balks had been left in place since reconstruction was not envisaged at that time. This made the task of reassembling cores from 9,523 pieces much more difficult. In addition, at Riverton there was evidence for the inclusion of large flakes and even broken adze preforms in fires, possibly for use as oven stones. As a result they were discolored, cracked, and further fragmented. A compensating factor was the greater variation in color, texture, and inclusions which sometimes allowed all the excavated portions of a particular block to be isolated. Only 143 matching pieces were found compared with 785 from Oturehua. Nevertheless the reconstructed clusters were

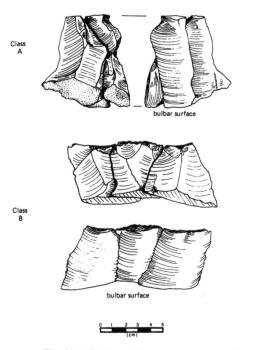

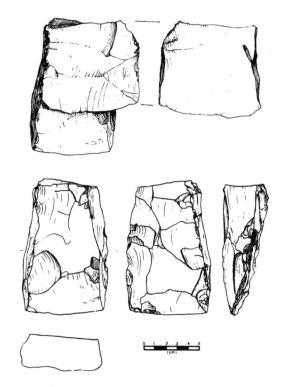

Fig. 10.7. Refitting flakes to adze preforms.

Fig. 10.6. Flakes at Riverton adze quarry. Top, Class A flakes with a high proportion of cortex (water-worn or air weathered) on their dorsal surfaces. Middle, Class B flakes, sets of joining flakes of characteristic recurring shapes, with tiny negative flake scars immediately below the outer lip of the platform on dorsal (nonbulbar) face.

extremely valuable because they fell into two distinct and technologically significant groups.

First, there were sets of contiguous flakes (Class A) with a high proportion of cortex (waterworn or air weathered) on their dorsal surfaces (fig. 10.6a). Sometimes they had been struck from a cortex-covered or natural fracture-plane platform, sometimes from the platform made by a single flake scar. They were highly variable in shape. The second group (Class B) consisted of sets of joining flakes of characteristic recurring shapes (fig. 10.6b), sometimes struck from platforms on opposite sides, sometimes joining to make two or three sides of a rectangle. In a few examples these flakes could be joined on to an adze preform (fig. 10.7). When this was accomplished it was obvious that this second group was composed of trimming flakes produced in the final shaping of the preform. The first group of irregular flakes with high proportion of cortex represented the primary stages of shaping the parent block.

One important difference was noted between Class A and B flakes: all Class B flakes possessed an area of tiny negative flake scars immediately below the outer lip of the platform on the dorsal (nonbulbar) face. This feature was seldom present on the primary flakes, but it was present in the same position on all blades recovered from Oturehua. There it was interpreted as the result of reduction of the overhanging lip of the platform between each sequence of blade removal. If it is not done the next blade may terminate in a hinge fracture a short distance from the platform. In adze-making by

direct percussion overhanging lips occur very commonly and it is therefore suggested that the operation which produced the multiple flake scars on Class B flakes was the deliberate reduction of the overhanging portions of edge by striking directly on the edge of the platform before the next set of flakes were detached. Hammers with concave battered edges comparable to the Oturehua corner blade hammers do occur at Riverton (fig. 10.8f, g), in addition to granite hammerstones presumed to have served as knapping hammers (fig. 10.8a, b, c). The latter range in weight from 92 to 313 g.

The ratios between Class B and Class A flakes are a useful guide to determining whether particular areas at Riverton were used more for primary or secondary flaking. For the whole site there were 11 Class B flakes for every 10 Class A. In two spots primary flakes become numerically dominant (5 Class B to every 10 Class A) while in a third area there are far more secondary flakes than primary ones (96 Class B to every 10 Class A). This supports the idea that movement of material from one location to another sometimes took place between stages of production, as at Oturehua.

Reduction procedures for adze production

Reconstruction of the manufacturing process was based on the analysis of preforms and waste flakes. Preforms alone can give a distorted picture of the objectives of the adze makers, since all the preforms have been rejected before completion as having one or more qualities that will prevent completion and/or efficient use. In every case the archaeologist needs to seek out the reasons for rejection before using the

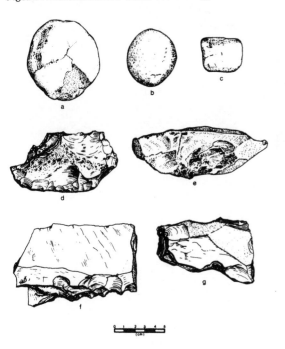

Fig. 10.8. Riverton hammers. a, b, c: granite hammerstones. d, e: broken hammers. f, g: hammers with concave battered edges comparable to Oturehua types.

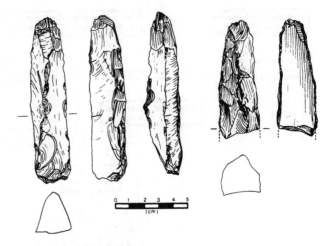

Fig. 10.9. Small triangular adzes made by trilateral flaking technique at Riverton.

preform as a guide to the appearance of a successful adze, 'frozen' at that particular stage of manufacture. If preforms are studied in conjunction with trimming flakes, any bias in proportions of adze types can be more readily recognized. At Riverton, thin Class B flakes with striking platform angles approaching 90° were detached during the final trimming of thick quadrangular-sectioned adzes (fig. 10.7), judging from core reconstruction and the appearance of the negative scars on the few quadrangular preforms that were recovered. On the basis of preforms alone it might be claimed that this adze was only rarely made (less than 7 per cent of the 269 preforms). However, the consistent appearance of these flakes in nearly all squares argues for the view that many more were manufactured, and at a high success rate. These, coupled with deliberate reworking of broken examples, has meant that they are underrepresented in the reject group.

The same argument seems to apply to large triangular adzes. No large triangular preforms were recovered but small triangular adzes made by the same trilateral flaking techniques (fig. 10.9) are represented by 20 preforms. The excavation also produced one highly diagnostic blade formed when the cutting edge of a large triangular adze is made. Struck from a narrow platform on the bevel side of the cutting edge, this blade effectively removes the beak formed by the front apex ridge in the vicinity of the cutting edge.

With these possible sources of distortion in mind, an attempt was made to formulate the reduction procedures used at this site (fig. 10.10). The manufacturing process began with the quarrying of the raw material from the headland close to the site (fig. 10.11) and the transportation of the parent

blocks to the workshop areas (Areas A, B, C). Inspection of Class A flakes showed that these blocks had possessed three sorts of surface: (1) waterworn, highly polished, and rounded, obviously obtained from the intertidal zone of the headland; (2) thick crusty cortex deeply weathered from exposure to the air, presumably obtained from higher up the headland; and (3) thin cortex showing discoloration, often planar. The latter surfaces often occurred on blocks which also displayed thick cortex or water-polished areas. They represent natural fracture planes running through all the *in situ* faces and eroded boulders. The quarrying process obviously took advantage of these planes to break open the boulders and obtain suitable sized blocks from the outcrops. Elongated beach cobbles were another source of material and ten cobble preforms were recovered (e.g. fig. 10.12), indicating opportunistic behavior by groups who normally obtained the bulk of their raw material as much larger pieces. Although the cobbles imposed size and shape restrictions on the adzes, they were undoubtedly easy to work.

Existing classifications of Polynesian adzes are based on finished cross-section (e.g. Duff 1977). When applied to preforms, these classifications cannot place more than a few of the items with certainty. Although quadrangular and steep triangular forms are usually recognizable, the rest fall into a continuum of cross-section shapes from trapezoidal to sub-triangular including variants with partially convex sides reminiscent of plano-convex and lenticular forms. Adzes undergo changes in cross-section throughout the manufacturing process and it is seldom possible to determine the final cross-section of a half-finished reject. The classification of preforms according to the number of lateral edges from which trimming blows were struck is far more appropriate and results in fewer ambiguous cases.

Three classes are distinguished (fig. 10.13): bilateral, trilateral, and quadrilateral. It must be stressed that these classes relate more closely to technological factors than to final cross-section. This classification has important impli-

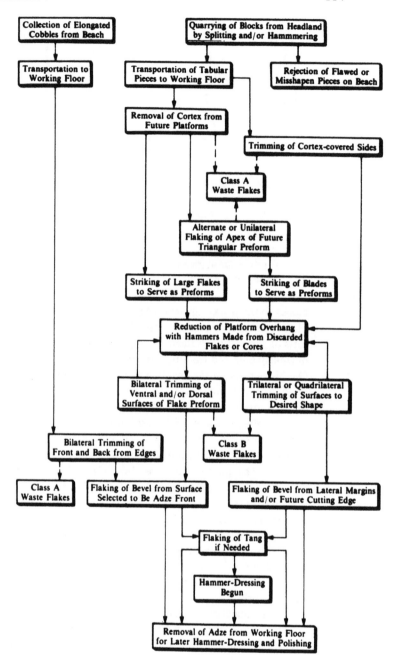

Fig. 10.10. Flow diagram of reduction sequence for adze manufacture at Riverton.

cations for Polynesian adze studies, for it adds even more variables on which similarities and differences may be evaluated. Fully polished adzes of similar morphology may conceal potentially diagnostic differences in manufacture. At Riverton, for example, it has been shown that the triangular-sectioned adze was made by both bilateral and trilateral trimming techniques.

Further opportunity for variation is evident in the stages between parent block and final trimming. Except in the manufacture of large quadrilateral and possibly large trilateral forms, many of the adze preforms are recognizably flakes. There is evidence both for the opportunistic selection of

suitably shaped flakes struck while a larger core adze was being made, and for deliberate preparation of the surfaces of the parent block so that a flake adze of a desired type can be detached. Core preparation of the latter type was of course the basis of successful blade-making at Oturehua. Making an adze from a flake is a far more economical operation than reducing a large parent block down to the desired size. In the first case the waste consists of the outer decortication flakes and the small trimming flakes, plus any misshapen flakes unsuitable as adze blanks. In the second case everything is discarded except for the preform (cf. Singer & Ericson 1977). The Riverton artisans seem to have blended both approaches for maximum

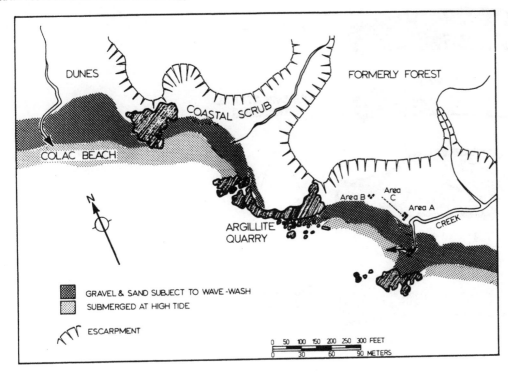

Fig. 10.11. Map of Riverton (Site S176/1) and excavation plan.

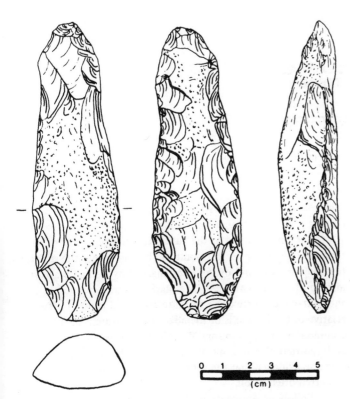

Fig. 10.12. Worked, elongated beach cobble from Riverton.

economy, an indication perhaps of the scarcity of good-quality material. They appear to have visualized large triangular and quadrangular adzes within the best parent blocks and to have reduced these with bold strokes that detached suitable flakes for smaller adzes at the same time. Less regular parent blocks may have been broken down for flake adzes alone.

The prepared-core technique represents an apparently contemporaneous refinement of flake adze manufacturing, since the artisan can predetermine to a far greater extent the shape of the flake blanks, and thus further reduce wastage of high-quality material. Assessing the degree to which flake adzes were preshaped before being struck from the parent block is very difficult because the diagnostic negative flake scars on the nonbulbar surfaces are usually obliterated by trimming scars which were struck from the direction of the bulbar face after the flake block was detached. In a few cases at Riverton, however, rejection of the blank occurred before this obliteration took place (fig. 10.14). These examples are all triangular preforms with either alternate sinuous flaking of the apex ridge or unilateral flaking. Ridge preparation on the core is a well-known procedure for initiating blade production (Crabtree 1968). The first blow following preparation detaches a triangular-sectioned blade in which the prepared ridge forms the apex. Making small triangular adzes from such ridged blades would have allowed the artisan to produce a

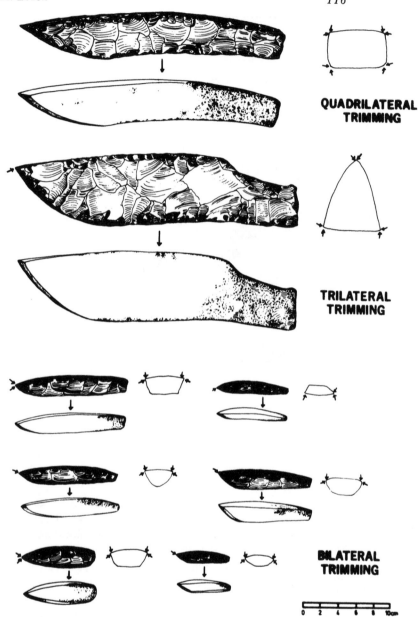

QUADRILATERAL
TRIMMING

TRILATERAL
TRIMMING

BILATERAL
TRIMMING

Fig. 10.13. Riverton preforms. Three classes of preforms classified according to number of trimming edges: quadrilateral, trilateral and bilateral.

highly symmetrical adze which needed only a little final trimming. There is now evidence for this technique from Riverton, the Nelson-D'Urville area, and from Pitcairn Island and the Marquesas (H. Leach 1981).

Following the trimming of the faces and (where present) the sides of the preform, the bevel was shaped by detaching flakes from one or two surfaces depending on the angle at which the two faces of the adze met. Flake adzes possessed several advantages in that the bulbar surface generally curves naturally to meet the nonbulbar surface. The bulbar surface provides a suitable platform both for trimming the opposite face and for shaping the bevel. This is not the case in large quadrangular adzes, in which the convergence of the faces is achieved by striking flakes from the sides, not from the cutting edge as in thinner flake adzes.

The final shaping of the adze butt took place after the bevel was made. Up to this point the butt is simply the slightly tapered narrower end of the adze, marked by a small platform instead of convergent faces. The platform quite frequently shows traces of cortex or a fracture plane and is often offset relative to the long axis of the adze. This feature is also common in Archaic Nelson-D'Urville preforms and it may be an important clue to a specific technique of core preparation. It is also evidence that the artisan held the blank with a preferred orientation.

Following preparation of the butt, hammer-dressing was

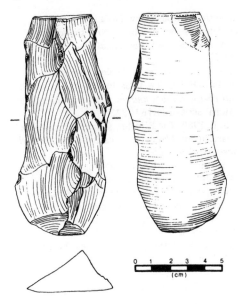

Fig. 10.14. Rejected adze blank at Riverton before obliteration of negative flake scars.

started to pulverize the high points in preparation for hafting, grinding and polishing. At Riverton there is sufficient evidence of hammer-dressing to argue that the process began at the site, but most of the flakes accidentally struck off during the process or deliberately removed in the reworking of a broken adze have the characteristic bruising only on their prominent ridges. It appears that hammer-dressing was completed away from this specialist workshop site. There is no doubt that polishing took place elsewhere since only three adze fragments showed traces of polish, there were no polished flakes, and only one possible grindstone was recovered.

Comparison of sites and technologies

The Riverton and Oturehua sites belong to a category rarely excavated by New Zealand archaeologists, that of the specialist camp primarily used as a base for extracting and preparing a raw material for export to multiactivity habitation sites. They may not have been occupied for more than a few days at a time and it is possible that the occupants were adult and adolescent males, who arrived by canoe or on foot unaccompanied by women and children. Since both sites are exposed to harsh winter conditions such as frost and driving rain or snow, it is reasonable to assume that the visits took place during periods of fine settled weather, in summer and autumn.

At Riverton the occupants' prime objective was the manufacture of a wide range of Archaic adzes from the local argillite. They displayed considerable skill in this activity as well as parsimonious and opportunistic attitudes to their raw material. A range of flaking techniques was employed including some which are also present at Oturehua: decortication, ridge preparation on a core, removal of triangular corner blades, and reduction of edge overhang. It is obvious from the recurring patterns of flake scars and the characteristic

shapes of most secondary trimming flakes that adze-making procedures were to some extent 'formalized', set by custom and thus transmitted between generations. At both Riverton and Oturehua the artisans understood the influence of dorsal surface features on flake morphology and manipulated this in prepared-core techniques. At the same time, shortcuts presented by natural attributes of the argillite or silcrete blocks were regularly followed.

Conclusions

There can be little doubt that the Riverton adze makers and the Oturehua blade makers shared the same knowledge about the behavior of conchoidally fracturing materials, and that this was at a level of basic principles regardless of the particular rock type used or the particular tool type being manufactured. Acquiring such knowledge must have taken many generations of stoneworkers including the ancestors of the New Zealanders in their island homes. It should no longer be seen as anomalous that these ancestral groups did not have a separate well-established blade industry, for the production-sequence analyses have shown that the prepared-core technique was included among adze-making procedures and in some cases gave rise to small triangular-blade preforms or waste blades. The extension of the technique to the manufacture of blade knives occurred in the southern area of New Zealand, presumably in response to economic pressures, as yet not fully documented. It amounts to a local return to the ancient art of making blade artifacts using adze-production methods.

These findings are largely due to the greater understanding of the actual manufacturing processes which followed analysis of the reassembled flakes, blades, and cores. Ideally, the jigsaw method requires material with a good range of color, grain size, and the presence of bands and inclusions. The waste material should represent a total assemblage from contiguous squares and details of location and layer should be marked on every piece before the jigsaw is begun. Although these preliminaries and the actual task of reassembly are time-consuming, reconstruction of even a low percentage of the total assemblage can supply evidence of procedures at all stages of the reduction sequence, though not necessarily within the one reassembled block. The Oturehua material, collected with the jigsaw method in mind, became fully comprehensible with the reassembly of nearly 800 pieces, and it was then possible to interpret other waste material of characteristic but previously unexplained shapes by reference to the components of the reassembled cores. In addition, actual transportation of materials and hammers by the artisans from one part of the working floor to another could be documented by plotting the final resting-place of each core component in relation to its position in the reduction sequence. The versatility of the jigsaw method, and its proven results even with a low reconstruction success rate (as at Riverton), make it a worthwhile procedure despite the prolonged processing time. In conclusion, it probably does not need to be said that, for some of us, time spent engrossed in a jigsaw puzzle can only be considered pleasure.

References

Best, S. B. 1977. The Maori adze: an explanation for change. *Journal of the Polynesian Society* 86 (3): 307–37.

Crabtree, D. E. 1968. Mesoamerican polyhedral cores and prismatic blades. *American Antiquity* 33 (4): 446–78.

Duff, R.S. 1977. *The moa-hunter period of Maori cutlure.* 3rd ed. Wellington: New Zealand Government Printer.

Gerard, B. 1976. Outillage sur éclat d'Eiao, Îles Marquises. *Journal de la Société des Océanistes* 32:98–102.

Jones, K. 1972. Prehistoric Polynesian stone technology. M.A. thesis, Anthropology, University of Otago, New Zealand.

Kirch, P. V. & Kelly, M. eds. 1975. *Prehistory and ecology in a windward Hawaiian valley : Halawa Valley, Molokai.* Pacific Anthropological Records 24.

Leach, B. F. 1969a. *The concept of similarity in prehistoric studies.* Studies in Prehistoric Anthropology, vol. 1, Anthropology Department, University of Otago, New Zealand.

1969b. Radiocarbon dates for the Oturehua quarry site, central Otago (S134/1). *New Zealand Archaeological Association Newsletter* 12 (1):52.

Leach, H. M. 1981. Technological changes in the development of Polynesian adzes. In B. F. Leach & J. Davidson, eds., *Archaeological studies of Pacific stone resources.* British Archaeological Reports International Series 104:167–82.

Leach, H. M. & Leach, B. F. 1980. The Riverton site: an archaic adze manufactory in eastern Southland, New Zealand. *New Zealand Journal of Archaeology* 2:99–140.

McCoy, P. C. 1976. A note on Easter Island obsidian cores and blades. *Journal of the Polynesian Society* 85 (3): 327–38.

Simmons, D. R. 1973. Suggested periods in South Island prehistory. *Records of the Auckland Institute and Museum* 10:1–58.

Singer, C. A. & Ericson, J. E. 1977. Quarry analysis at Bodie Hills, Mono County, California: a case study. In T. K. Earle & J. E. Ericson, eds., *Exchange systems in prehistory.* New York: Academic Press, 171–881.

Chapter 11

Quarry studies: technological and chronological significance
B. A. Purdy

Quarry sites contain thousands of years of debitage in quantities that can be studied statistically. Paradoxically, quarry sites, unlike other types of sites, have not been subjected to routine archaeological inquiry. In this paper I describe procedures we are using in Florida to resolve questions about lithic technology and the antiquity of chert quarries. The enduring consequence of the research is the realization that extraction methods utilized by prehistoric stoneworkers were applied eventually to other technologies and that the data resulting from the studies have implications extending beyond archaeological interests.

Introduction

As the papers in this volume confirm, studies of quarry sites contribute to the archaeological interpretation of a region and to an understanding of culture in general. In fact, a significant dimension of culture is missing if a people's stoneworking technology, including quarry-site behavior, is ignored.

Individuals who investigate quarry sites must be interested in technology, not merely finished products. The vast amounts of broken stone at quarries is uninteresting to most archaeologists and partially explains why procurement areas have not been studied thoroughly. Aboriginal chert quarries in Florida had not been investigated prior to my excavations at the Senator Edwards Site (Purdy 1975; 1981a, 105), the York Site (Purdy 1977), the Container Corporation of America Site (Purdy 1981b), and Hemmings and Kohler's work at the Lake Kanapaha Site (1974).

The antiquity of the use of quarries has received very

little attention, yet it is fascinating to envision the first visit of a small band thousands of years ago to a location that later became a traditional procurement area. The above statement has importance other than the appeal of human interest. I believe that over hundreds of thousands of years of cultural evolution, people had become good 'geologists'. They had learned where to look for suitable deposits of essential raw materials and, because of this accomplishment, the first human entry into an area can be documented at quarry sites. Exceptions to this assertion would be if people brought their total tool kit with them when planning to stay only a brief time with no intention of locating raw-material sources, or if their material culture did not include stoneworking technology. These exceptions are unlikely.

Of consequence also is that quarry debitage provides large amounts of material that can be examined; such quantities are not available at other sites. For example, a major criticism that inhibits the acceptance of a pre-Clovis habitation period in North America is that the information is scant at any one site. Since stone is the primary material recovered at early sites, I suggest that studies of quarries may provide the quantities of remains needed to demonstrate that humans were present in North America earlier than is now accepted.

Holmes's monumental volume (1919) is the only inclusive account of the quarrying and mining procedures of aboriginal Americans. Holmes does not include an analysis of quarry debitage nor does he discuss the ages when the quarries were utilized. Holmes did not consider these details because quarry-debitage analysis was an idea whose time had not yet come, and dating methods were not available to refute the belief by most 'reputable' prehistorians of the day that the peopling of the western hemisphere was a fairly recent event. More than 60 years later, the problems of dating stone and the antiquity of human occupation in North America have not been solved.

Students learn in introductory archaeology courses that prehistorians use stratigraphic position, typology, and dating methods to determine relative or absolute chronologies. Should archaeologists ignore sites (1) when there is little or no stratigraphy, (2) when few 'typed' implements are recovered, or (3) when conventional dating methods, such as radiocarbon analysis, cannot be applied? Chert quarry sites often contain all of these deficiencies. Is the investment in time and money to study quarry sites greater than the return in new information? The answer to that query lies in another question: what is meant by *new information* and who will benefit from it? Archaeological research is designed to provide knowledge about past human behavior but its value may extend beyond its original intent and furnish data applicable to the well-being of future generations.

The experiments that we have been conducting in Florida were undertaken after I realized that a dead end had been reached in my analysis of quarry sites unless new methods were utilized. I will discuss the difficulties associated with dating stone remains at quarries and suggest ways to overcome these difficulties. Those who are interested in scientific applications may find the methods described below useful in their own research. New equipment and approaches developed in the physical sciences continue to aid the archaeologist. It is, in fact, possible that in the opening phases of some investigations, archaeology as physical science is more necessary than archaeology as anthropology.

Materials and methods
The artifacts
Based on observations made of surface collections and posthole testing during a six-month survey at the Container Corporation of America (CCA) Site (8-Mr-154) in 1976, I suspected that there were vastly different stoneworking technologies at the site representing a long temporal break in human occupation. For example, there was extreme weathering on specimens displaying one kind of technology as compared to less-weathered specimens produced by another type of technology (Purdy & Clark 1979). When systematic excavations were carried out at the site, stone implements dating from 500 years ago to approximately 11,000 years ago were recovered from a sand horizon. The typologically distinct, weathered artifacts were recovered from a sandy clay horizon underlying the sand stratum. The implements from the sandy clay do not resemble any of the known stone-tool types in Florida that are recovered from the sand stratum (fig. 11.1).

The prime concern was to establish beyond question that the stone remains from the sandy clay zone of the CCA

Site were not eoliths. A second major problem was to verify that the artifacts from the sandy clay horizon are typologically distinct from the artifacts in the overlying sand stratum. In order to deal with both issues, attributes of identification, physical measurement, and other characteristics were recorded for all utilized pieces of chert (> 4,000) recovered at the CCA Site (fig. 11.2). Of significance to this study, the data (as determined by computer analysis), reveal the following information.

1. The specimens from the sand horizon are generally small, symmetrical, relatively unweathered thinning flakes possessing bulbs of force and carefully prepared or ground striking platforms. Projectile points and other formal implements are occasionally recovered from the sand. The specimens from the sandy clay horizon are larger overall than the specimens from the sand and are extremely weathered. Even the smaller specimens from the sandy clay lack symmetry, bulbs of force, or striking platforms.

2. Of all material recovered at the site, a larger percentage of utilized specimens was recovered from the sandy clay (15 per cent) than from the sand (12 per cent). There is a definite difference in angle of use on the specimens from the sandy clay (steep) overall than the specimens from the sand (more acute). A number of artifacts from the sandy clay have steep utilized edges similar to an end scraper or adze. Some similarities in utilization exist, however, between the specimens of both horizons; for example, 'shaft scraper' wear is quite common, and implements used as pounders are very uncommon. Only two implements from each horizon had surfaces indicating their use as battering tools or hammers. The functional reasons for this scarcity might differ between

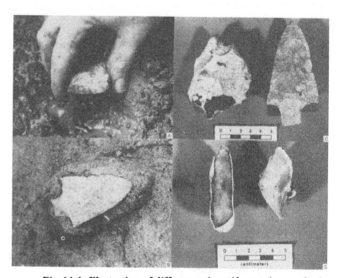

Fig. 11.1. Illustration of differences in artifact style, weathering and deposition: A, crude weathered scraper in sandy clay layer; B, Levy point (middle Preceramic Archaic, *c.* 6000 B.P.) in sandy level; C, (left), crude weathered implement from sandy clay layer; (right) Levy point from sand, 1 m above weathered implement; D (left), cross-section of A; (right) cross-section of unfinished biface associated with Levy point at C (right).

1-4	Artifact number (e.g., 0027)
5-6	Artifact category (e.g., 13=utilized flake)
7	Site (e.g., 2=CCA Site)
8	Area of find at site (e.g., 0=surface; 1=backhoe trench; 2=trench two; 3=3 meter square)
9-10	Square (e.g., 01=1; 02=2; 03=3; 04=4; 05=5; etc.)
11	Level (e.g., 0=not dug by levels; 1=level 1; 2=level 2; etc.)
12	Type of site (e.g., 1=workshop site; 2=quarry or outcrop; 3= habitation; 4=kill site; 5=mound; 6=quarry/workshop, etc.)
13	Area of site
14-16	Length in centimeters (e.g., 08.6)
18-20	Width in centimeters (e.g., 01.7)
22-23	Thickness in centimeters (e.g., 0.5)
25-27	Index (e.g., 0.23), length x width divided by thickness x 100
29-33	Weight in grams (e.g., 0024.6)
35	Heated, leave blank if question or do not know: (e.g., 0=no; 1=yes; 2=used with heat; 3=exposed to heat or heat damaged)
37	Pressure flaked (e.g., 0=no, 1=slight; 2=yes)
39	Symmetrical (e.g., 0=no; 1=not too symmetrical; 2=fairly; 3=very)
41	Does it show signs of use?, leave blank if cannot determine: (0=no; 1=yes, slight; 2=yes, heavy)
42-43	Type of use: (e.g., 00=abrader; 01=hammer; 02=scraper, etc.)
44	Patina (0=no; 1=slight; 2=moderate; 3=heavy; 4=chalky; 5=moderately patinated/reflaked; 6=heavily patinated/reflaked or shattered)
45	Solution weathering (0=no; 1=slight; 2=moderate), rate is based on visual or subjective determination
46	Angle of use or angle of edge (usually use): 0=<50°; 1=>50°; 2=>75°
49	Area of use: (0=single use area; 1=more than one area of use, single face; 2=more than one area of use, both faces)
52-54	Length of use (e.g., 01.1) applicable mostly to scraping or cutting
56	Cortex (0=no; 1=yes)
57	Flake type: (0=primary flake with cortex; 1=secondary flake, little or no cortex but also no multiple flake scars; 2=secondary flake with scars on dorsal surface; 3=flake with bifacial flaking)
58	Amateur (0=no; 1=yes), subjective; use only for projectiles
61	Striking platform (leave blank if missing); 0=big; 1=small; 2=prepared/ big; 3=prepared/small; 4=ground or roughed up/big; 5=ground or roughed up/small
63	Bulb of force: (1=salient; 2=diffuse)
65	Type of projectile point: (1=Paleo; 2=Bolen; 3=Archaic; 4=Early Ceramic; 5=Late Ceramic; 6=other or undeterminable)
66	Type of Archaic
68	Blades only: (1=triangular; 2=trapesoid; 3=triangular/nibbled; 4=trapesoid/nibbled; 5=nibbled)

Fig. 11.2. Information recorded on data coding sheets for attribute analysis.

horizons because it is likely that the fine chipping technique found on the artifacts from the sand horizon was produced with an antler billet which has not survived. The nonsymmetrical material lacking striking platforms and bulbs of force recovered from the sandy clay was probably produced by using a block-on-block technique, that is, hurling one rock against another or by careful application of the fire-setting method (Purdy 1982), and suitable pieces selected to perform tasks without further modification. If reports of stone-procurement practices are examined for areas such as Australia (Gould, Koster & Sontz 1971), where human technology is believed to be similar to the early lithic horizon in Florida, it is clear that one should not expect to find that all debitage is used or that it has the uniformity of blade and core or projectile-point assemblages. On the other hand, the people who lived in Florida remained hunters and gatherers until the very recent prehistoric past. Thus despite differences in stone-

extraction techniques and stone-tool production, stone-tool utilization remained fairly constant as the challenges of the environment were met in similar ways.

3. Despite the extreme differences in technology that produced the artifacts from each horizon, very few utilized specimens from either the sand or the sandy clay retain cortex. I believe this is an important observation because if the specimens in the sandy clay are not artifacts, then one should expect the specimens with cortex also to exhibit the 'fortuitous' use-wear. The flakes from both horizons were secondary flakes in that they did not have cortex, but the artifacts from the sand often had multiple flake scars on the dorsal surface while those from the sandy clay did not.

4. Of significance also is that chert specimens cannot be fitted together. It seems to me if the chert were fractured by natural processes, it would be possible to put nodules back together like a puzzle. There is no indication that the material

has been separated by down slope movement or by stream transportation, a statement supported by the observation that there is no rounding of the stone.

5. The majority of artifacts from both horizons had been used in more than one area and in more than one direction because use-wear is often evident in various locations and on both faces. The specimens from the sandy clay horizon were used more intensively on the whole than the specimens from the sand.

6. Throughout the Preceramic Archaic and more recent periods in Florida's prehistory, thermal alteration was practiced as one step in the process of manufacture of certain chipped-stone implements (Purdy & Brooks 1971; Purdy 1974, 1975, 1982). Many of the thinning flakes recovered from the sand in some squares at the CCA Site had been thermally altered but no intentionally heated artifacts were recovered from the sandy clay (Purdy 1981b), indicating to me that the technique of thermal alteration had not been introduced into Florida at the time the material in the sandy clay was deposited. Fire-exploded fragments occurred in both horizons but were very prevalent in the sandy clay horizon. In fact, many of the stone implements from the sandy clay had been partially destroyed by heat but use-wear was not always obliterated. The significance of the occurrence of chert that has been intentionally or accidentally exposed to temperatures high enough to induce some kind of alteration of the rock will be elaborated in the discussion of thermoluminescence.

Weathering studies

The following points have been assumed in gathering data for weathering experiments with Florida chert:

1. Stoneworkers will choose unweathered material for implement manufacture.

2. The stone artifacts recovered at a quarry site, including utilized chipping debris and nodules, will be from the local outcrop; in other words, why import the rock when it is at hand? (See Gramly, this volume, for an exception to the statement.)

3. Stone materials found in a single excavation unit (e.g., a 3 m square) at a quarry site will have been exposed to the same environmental conditions if they were discarded at the same time.

4. Because of nos. 1, 2, and 3, differences observed in weathering will reflect a difference in age.

Scientists have developed techniques and kinetic equations for predicting the extent of weathering during the expected lifetime of a material. Techniques include electron microprobe analysis (EMP), scanning electron microscopy-energy dispersive X-ray analysis (SEM-EDXA), infrared reflection spectroscopy (IRRS), and auger electron spectroscopy (AES) coupled with Ar-ion milling (IM). D. E. Clark of the Materials Science and Engineering Department at the University of Florida is using similar analyses to estimate the age of heavily patinated artifacts recovered from the sandy clay horizon at the CCA site by measuring the thickness of

the weathered layer. This thickness depends upon time of exposure, material composition, and environment (fig. 11.1c, d).

The techniques and equations used in weathering studies have been described in detail elsewhere (Purdy & Clark 1979; Clark & Purdy 1979a, 1979b). The reactions of interest are those that occur between alkali-alkaline earth-silica materials (composition of Florida cherts) and aqueous environments (Clark, Pantono & Hench 1978). Patina formation is a dynamic weathering process occurring when the pH of the environment is maintained relatively neutral or slightly acidic. The pH of both the sand and the sandy clay horizons is 4.0 but, of course, we have no way of knowing whether the pH was the same in the past.

The primary objective of the weathering study is to develop a technique to date Florida chert artifacts based on surface chemical and structural changes that accompany weathering. This will be accomplished by (1) evaluating the surface alterations that have occurred on field specimens subjected to the natural environment, (2) evaluating surface changes that occur on fresh specimens of similar material during artificially controlled laboratory weathering using several 'burial' conditions, and (3) experimentally correlating exposure time and surface properties to calculate reaction-rate constants. Once these constants have been determined, the physical properties (patina thickness) may be used to determine the age of artifacts. Certain assumptions will have to be made such as an average environmental temperature and soil pH. The error in dating associated with these assumptions will also be calculated based on the sensitivity of the reaction-rate constants.

Preliminary and tentative results are consistent with thermoluminescent data (Clark & Purdy 1979a) and with research findings of an experiment to be reported in the future (Clark 1980, personal communication). The experiment involved a comparison of patina thickness on an 8,500-year-old Kirk-Serrated projectile point with patina thickness on a heavily weathered chert artifact recovered from the same square and 1 m below the Kirk-Serrated point during systematic excavations.

The techniques developed to measure the extent of weathering can be used to determine variations in weathering that are not as visually apparent as those between the artifacts from the sand and the sandy clay horizons at the CCA Site. It is possible that differences, nearly imperceptible to the naked eye, can be shown to represent an amazing length of time. Our experiments indicate that Florida cherts possess excellent chemical resistance, that is, patina formation is very slow to develop and is not linear. If man-made materials could be produced that possessed the chemical resistance of Florida chert, they could be used for chemical and nuclear waste encapsulation.

Thermoluminescent dating

Thermoluminescence is a technique that is used to date

certain inorganic materials in the time range of zero to 1 million years. Thermoluminescence has become an acceptable dating method and can be used in Florida to solve various problems of antiquity. It is an excellent dating method because it can (1) date inorganic remains, (2) verify the reliability of radiocarbon dates, (3) date inorganic remains when organic materials are not preserved, (4) date specimens older than 50,000 years, the present limit of radiocarbon analysis, and (5) reduce the dependence on typological comparison for chronological placement of archaeological remains.

Since 1973, I have been interested in establishing a thermoluminescent (TL) dating laboratory at the University of Florida (Purdy & Roessler 1975). I was prompted to pursue this objective with increased effort after the untimely death of D. W. Zimmerman who, with S. R. Sutton at Washington University, had been attempting to date heat-altered Florida chert. I was able to purchase equipment to conduct thermoluminescent research with funds received from the Division of Sponsored Research at the University of Florida. The Laboratory is now functioning thanks to F. N. Blanchard, Department of Geology and C. Maurer, Department of Materials Science and Engineering, University of Florida. These individuals possess the necessary technical skills to install and operate the equipment.

It is not my intent to describe here in any depth the principle upon which TL dating depends (for an excellent review article, see Zimmerman 1978), but to discuss how the thermoluminescent technique can be used to help solve problems of dating in Florida when organic materials do not survive for radiocarbon analysis.

Thermoluminescence is a property of certain crystalline minerals which emit energy in the form of light radiation when heated. These materials have 'excess' energy trapped within their structure that is released when heat is applied. Because the amount of this stored energy is proportional to the length of time between the material's last heat treatment and the current reheating, measurement of the emitted radiation can provide a clue to the age of the sample. In other words, the dating clock is reset to zero when an object is heated and the thermoluminescent data gives the time since that event occurred (Zimmerman 1978).

Chert has luminescent properties and it is, therefore, possible that the intentionally thermally altered artifacts from the sand horizon and the fire-exploded chert from the sandy clay horizon at the CCA Site can be dated using the thermoluminescent technique. The thermoluminescent-dating study using heat-altered Florida chert has first priority for the laboratory at the University of Florida.

Pedological study

I am indebted to C. T. Hallmark, a soils characterization specialist, formerly at the University of Florida and now at Texas A & M, for conducting the study described below.

The stratigraphic position of the stone implements in the sandy clay horizon presents an interesting pedologic, geologic, and archaeologic problem. It is generally accepted by geologists in Florida that the red and reddish-brown sandy clay layer is the Alachua Formation which formed during the Pliocene while the overlying sands are of Pleistocene age (Teleki 1966). The problem exists since the stone implements are not at the contact of the sand and sandy clay but are recovered 15 to 20 cm below the contact. Evidence was needed to show that the sandy clay horizon at the CCA Site is not of Pliocene age but is either pedogenic or geologic in origin and is genetically resultant from processes occurring during or after Pleistocene time. Also a break in time (disconformity) would be required between the deposits containing the artifacts of known time periods and the stone implements found in the sandy clay.

During soil formation, the movement of clay from overlying horizons into zones of clay accumulation (illuviation) is recognized (Buol, Hole & McCracken 1973). If indeed the upper portion of the sandy clay horizon is pedogenic with the clay illuviating from the overlying sands, then the condition should be reflected as a lithologic discontinuity.

Lithologic discontinuity is a term applied by pedologists to describe a condition existing in a horizon sequence where one of the horizons is overlain by a distinctly different horizon and the difference in the two horizons is geologic rather than pedologic in origin (Buol, Hole & McCracken 1973). A lithologic discontinuity indicates that the soil horizons developed from two distinctly different geologic deposits. Therefore, a lithologic discontinuity is the manifestation of a change in the depositional environment which may coincide with a long exposure of the lower material at the surface before burial by younger materials and indicates either different sediment sources or different depositional modes.

Particle-size distribution analysis was used by C. T. Hallmark to substantiate the field observation that a lithologic discontinuity exists at the CCA Site. Particle-size distribution was determined by the hydrometer method (Bouyoucos 1937) with five subfactionations of the sand (Kilmer & Alexander 1949). Four subsamples from each 10 cm depth increment were taken through the soil horizons. Subsamples from the same depth increment permit the calculation of variability within the increment and serve as a basis for statistically establishing the position of the discontinuity. Each increment was considered as a group and tested by analysis of variance and multiple-range tests of the means. Since clay is a mobile constituent — it may move from upper horizons to lower horizons as colloids suspended in water—the data were calculated on a clay-free basis to remove the effects of dilution of larger particles by clay. The data clearly show a lithological discontinuity in three sand subfractionations at 27 cm below surface in a square at the CCA Site where a nicely made unifacial humped-back scraper was recovered at this depth and marked the boundary between the sand and sandy clay horizons. One can speculate that a second discontinuity exists in the soil in this square. Conditions, specifically a high water table, at the time of soil sampling of this square prevented sampling below 65 cm. Results from another square at the CCA Site show two lithologic breaks in four sand subfractionations, one at 72 cm and the other at 94 cm below surface which correlate almost perfectly with the archaeological findings. Levels 8, 9, and part of 10 (70−95 cm below surface) of this square contained primarily fire-exploded rock, while in Levels 10 and below, there was a marked increase in size and sophistication of the chert artifacts. It should be noted that the discontinuity analyses were performed independent of knowledge of the position and type of artifacts that were recovered. It is also noteworthy that the presence or absence of crude chert implements is not apparently related to clay content of the soil horizons. Clearly, discontinuities show that changes occurred in the depositional process and augment the data of the archaeological phase of the study (tables 11.1 and 11.2, fig. 11.3).

Two independent methods for determination of lithologic discontinuities are desirable because single methods may sometimes be misleading (Brewer 1964). In the future elemental analysis of Zr and Ti in the sand (0.05−2.0 mm) fraction will be performed by X-ray emission spectroscopy.

Discussion

Holmes (1919) and others who investigated quarry sites during the nineteenth and early twentieth centuries commented upon (1) geographic locations of known sites, (2) quantities of waste material, (3) manufacture of implements, specifically points, and (4) use of fire in quarrying. Little work has been done since these initial contributions. Because Holmes was a thorough and reputable scholar, I believe most archaeologists consider his work definitive and finite; that is, it represents the totality of what can be learned by studying aboriginal exploitation of quarries. Holmes, however, did not include analyses of debitage nor a discussion of the time periods that quarry sites were utilized.

Most archaeological sites are now being excavated with new questions in mind and recently developed equipment can solve problems that were formerly impossible to tackle. New questions and techniques can be applied also to quarry-site studies but often the techniques applicable to other kinds of sites cannot be used at quarries. Quarries have no settlement patterns, no burial mounds or temple-mound complexes, no skeletal remains, and no ceramics. In addition, quarry sites are

Table 11.1. *Means (3 replicates) of particle size distribution with depth for squares 2 and 5 of area 3, CCA Site.*

Horizon	Depth	VCS	CS	MS	FS	VFS	Si	C
Square 2								
A1	0−10	0.1	5.1	38.9	36.8	7.1	7.4	4.6
A2	10−27	0.5	6.1	36.7	38.7	7.9	6.0	4.0
B1t	27−36	0.4	3.8	26.7	35.9	9.2	13.0	11.0
B21t	36−58	0.4	3.5	24.7	30.5	7.9	9.2	23.8
B22t	58−95	0.3	3.7	21.1	32.7	8.3	9.2	20.7
Square 5								
A1	0−8	0.2	3.6	35.8	43.1	9.6	6.0	1.7
A2	8−21	0.1	3.5	33.4	45.4	10.7	5.4	1.5
B11t	21−42	0.2	3.5	31.4	44.1	9.8	5.4	5.6
B12t	42−54	0.2	3.2	31.0	43.3	9.6	4.7	8.0
B13t	54−72	0.3	3.3	29.8	40.0	8.1	5.4	13.1
B21t	72−94	1.5	4.1	20.1	23.9	5.3	12.5	32.6
B22t	94−117	3.1	5.3	13.9	15.2	4.1	18.7	39.7

*VCS − very coarse sand (2−1 mm)
CS − coarse sand (1−0.5 mm)
MS − medium sand (0.5−0.25 mm)
FS − fine sand (0.25−0.10 mm)
VFS − very fine sand (0.10−0.05 mm)
Si − silt (0.05−0.002 mm)
C − clay (< 0.002 mm)

Table 11.2. *Means (3 replicates) of medium sand (MS), fine sand (FS), very fine sand (VFS), and silt (Si) expressed on a clay-free basis with depth for squares 2 and 5, area 3, CCA Site.*

Horizon	Depth	Particle Size * (%)			
		MS	FS	VFS	Si
Square 2					
A1	0–10	40.7 a*	38.6 a	7.4 a	7.8 ac
A2	10–27	38.3 a	40.4 a	8.1 a	6.2 a
B1t	27–36	30.0 b	40.3 a	10.3 b	14.6 b
B21t	36–58	32.5 b	40.0 a	10.4 b	12.1 abc
B22t	58–95	31.7 b	41.2 a	10.5 b	11.6 abc
Square 5					
A1	0–8	36.4 a	43.9 a	9.7 a	6.1 a
A2	8–21	33.9 ab	46.1 a	10.8 a	5.5 a
B11t	21–42	33.3 ab	46.7 a	10.4 a	5.7 a
B12t	42–54	33.7 ab	47.0 a	10.4 a	5.2 a
B13t	54–72	34.2 a	46.0 a	9.4 ab	6.3 a
B21t	72–94	29.9 b	35.5 b	7.8 bc	18.6 b
B22t	94–117	22.9c	24.9 c	6.7 c	31.2 c

*Means of particle sizes are significantly different (95% level) if followed by different letters. Tested by Duncan's multiple-range test.

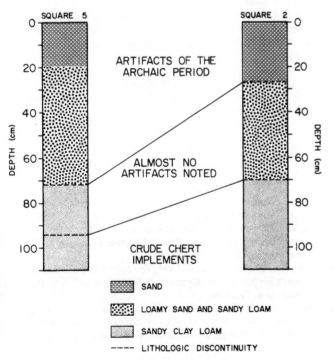

Fig. 11.3. Relationship between artifacts and the soils at squares 2 and 5, area 3, CCA Site.

not deeply stratified and organic materials have not been preserved that would make radiocarbon dating possible and furnish insights into the kinds of plants and animals eaten or used for various purposes. Archaeologists who wish to study human behavior at quarry sites must supplement or even replace conventional methods with techniques specifically adapted and applicable to examining artifactual remains at quarries. New approaches are even more essential when greater antiquity is suspected and stone becomes increasingly important because it represents nearly 100 per cent of the evidence.

In this chapter I have described a prehistoric stone-procurement site in central Florida where weathered stone implements were recovered below and separated by a lithologic discontinuity from less-weathered implements produced by a different technology. The discovery at the Container Corporation of America Site of implements in a sandy clay horizon below more formal stone implements from a sand horizon was a bonus that permitted better control of the hypotheses being tested. Using data from the CCA Site I have addressed the following general questions:

1. Is it possible to determine the time periods that quarries were utilized when no organic materials are preserved for radiocarbon analysis, little or no stratigraphy exists, and very few diagnostic implements are recovered?

2. How long does it take chert material to weather and can weathering studies provide a clue to age?

3. Can the thermoluminescent method be used to date intentionally heat-altered flakes and fire-exploded debris?

4. Are there variations in lithic techniques at quarry sites that can be shown statistically to correspond with differences in weathering, TL dating, and provenience (when present)?

5. Are there notable inferences about technological evolution that are supported by data available from quarry sites?

6. Do the results of quarry-site research have any far-reaching implications?

The answers to the first question are dependent upon affirmative responses to questions 2, 3, and 4. We have compiled extensive attribute data about the stone remains, established a thermoluminescent laboratory to date heat-altered and fire-exploded chert, and initiated experiments to date weathered chert artifacts by determining the rate of patina formation. The preliminary findings are reported in the text and the investigations are continuing at the University of Florida. These studies are possible because of the large quantities of stone that are preserved through time at quarries: *only stone and only at quarry sites.* It is apparent that people in the past as people today wasted surplus resources and it is fortunate that metal tools replaced stone implements before stone resource areas were exhausted necessitating the reworking and reuse of long-discarded stone tools and debitage.

The answer to question 5 is affirmative. Stoneworkers probably were the first chemists when they observed, perhaps accidentally, that changes occur in rocks when they are exposed to heat. Thermal alteration can be beneficial or detrimental depending upon how heat is applied. I believe that the huge nodules and tabular chert from the sandy clay horizon at the CCA Site were fractured by the fire-setting technique. The fragments which resulted were more manageable and could be used on the spot without modification or could be removed to other areas for further reduction. I recently completed an extensive study (Purdy 1982) of the fire-setting technique. My conclusion from that study is that fire setting would have to have been very carefully controlled if the material was going to be used for stone-tool production and utilization. Since direct fire is destructive to rock, the fire-setting technique, before explosives, was used beneficially in mining and quarrying operations to destroy rock matrices containing metal ores. I conducted a fire-setting experiment from which I calculated that 7 to 8 feet of rock overburden can be easily removed in one day using this technique. Some of the fine chipping debris from the sand horizon, on the other hand, was intentionally thermally altered (Purdy & Brooks 1971). The precise and controlled application of heat to induce beneficial changes in chert may have been a vital step before ceramic, plaster, glass, and metallurgical techniques could be developed and added to the cultural inventory. It is, of course, because heat was applied to materials with luminescent properties that the thermoluminescent technique can be used to provide absolute dates for the time of first heating. The importance of attaining and controlling high temperatures can be appreciated best by considering that even today mankind has still not achieved the thermal technology necessary to produce nuclear fusion.

Question 6 will be answered some time in the future. Understanding the weathering phenomena of artifacts that have been buried for thousands of years may benefit future generations. One plan for disposing of chemical and nuclear wastes is to encapsulate them in a borosilicate matrix and bury them below the surface of the ground. We have buried man-made glasses with compositions similar to chert at the Container Corporation of America Site. Samples will be retrieved periodically and subjected to laboratory analysis to determine rate of weathering.

In summary, the quantities of debitage that accumulate at outcrop sites are more than adequate for statistical analysis. Since flint will eventually weather, flake scars and use-wear can be reduced or obliterated if subject to weathering and erosion processes. Differential weathering, therefore, when accompanied with technological and other evidence, may be an indication of age (Goodwin 1960). There is more than one way to approach the problem of fracturing rock — fire setting, block-on-block, or by careful percussion and pressure methods. Since extraction technologies changed through time, variations in procurement techniques can serve as time markers in much the same way that stone-tool typologies are used as index fossils.

References

Bouyoucos, G. J. 1937. A sensitive hydrometer for determining small amounts of clay or colloids in soils, *Soil Science* 44:245–6.

Brewer, R. 1964. *Fabric and mineral analysis of soils.* New York: Wiley.

Buol, S. W., Hole, F. D. & McCracken, R. J. 1973. *Soil genesis and classification.* Ames: Iowa State University Press.

Clark, D. E., Pantano, C. G., Jr. & Hench, L. L. 1978. *Glass corrosion.* New York: Glass Industry.

Clark, D. E. & Purdy, B. A. 1979a. Electron microprobe analysis of weathered Florida chert. *American Antiquity* 44 (3): 517–24.

1979b. Surface characterization of weathered Florida chert. *Proceedings of the Symposium on Archaeometry and Archaeological Prospection,* Bonn, Germany, March 1978: 428–39.

Goodwin, A. J. H. 1960. Chemical alteration (patination) of stone. In R. F. Heizer & S. F. Cook, eds., *The application of quantitative methods in archaeology.* Chicago: Quadrangle Books, 300–24.

Gould, R. A., Koster, D. A. & Sontz, A. H. L. 1971. The lithic assemblage of the western desert aborigines of Australia. *American Antiquity.* 36:146–69.

Hemmings, E. T. & Kohler, T. A. 1974. *The Lake Kanapaha site in north central Florida,* Bureau of Historic Sites and Properties, Bulletin 4, Tallahassee.

Holmes, W. H. 1919. *Handbook of aboriginal American antiquities, part 1:Introductory — the lithic industries.* Bureau of American Ethnology, Bulletin 60, Smithsonian Institution, Washington, D. C.

Kilmer, V. J. & Alexander, L. T. 1949. Methods of making mechanical analysis of soils. *Soil Science* 68:15–24.

Purdy, B. A. 1974. Investigations concerning the thermal alteration of silica minerals: an archaeological approach, *Tebiwa* 17:1. Pocatello, Idaho.

1975. The Senator Edwards chipped stone workshop site (8-MR-122), Marion County, Florida: a preliminary report of investigations. *Florida Anthropologist* 28:178–89.

1977. The York site (8-AL-480), Alachua County, Florida: observations on aboriginal use of chert. *Florida Anthropologist* 30: 3–8.

1981a. *Florida's prehistoric stone technology*. Gainesville: University Presses of Florida.

1981b. An investigation into the use of chert outcrops by prehistoric Floridians. *Florida Anthropologist* 34 (2): 90–108.

1982. Pyrotechnology: prehistoric applications to chert materials in North America. In *Early Pyrotechnology,* Smithsonian Institution Press, Washington, D. C.

Purdy, B. A. & Brooks, K. 1971. Thermal alteration of silica minerals: an archaeological approach, *Science* 173:322–5.

Purdy, B. A. & Clark, D. E. 1979. Weathering studies of chert: a potential solution to the chronology problem in Florida, *Proceedings of the Symposium on Archaeometry and Archaeological Prospection,* Bonn, West Germany, March 1978:440–50.

Purdy, B. A. & Roessler, G. S. 1975. Thermoluminescent dating of heat-altered Florida chert. Paper presented at the 40th Annual Meeting of the Society for American Archaeology, Dallas.

Teleki, P. G. 1966. Differentiation of materials formally assigned to the 'Alachua Formation'. M. S. thesis, University of Florida, Gainesville.

Zimmerman, D. W. 1978. Thermoluminescence: a dating and authenticating method for art objects, *Technology and Conservation* 3 (1): 32–7.

Chapter 12

Characterization of selected soapstone sources in southern New England
W. A. Turnbaugh, S. P. Turnbaugh and
T. H. Keifer

Color, texture, mineralogy, thin-section petrography, and atomic-absorption spectrophotometry are used to characterize soapstone samples from several prehistoric quarry sites in Connecticut, Rhode Island, and Massachusetts. Using the petrographic profiles generated by these analyses, the authors attempt to attribute a number of soapstone artifacts from archaeological contexts to their respective quarry source. The encouraging results suggest that a combination of major-element analyses and observable characteristics may serve, in at least some cases, to differentiate adequately soapstone sources and their derivative artifacts.

Archaeologists recently have come to recognize geo-archaeology as an area of productive endeavor (Butzer 1971; Shackley 1975; Davidson & Shackley 1975; Gladfelter 1977; Vita-Finzi 1978). Straddling the flexible boundaries between geology and archaeology, this new research has contributed to at least three major concerns. One, geoarchaeological dating, includes the application of archaeologically derived chronologies to recent geological strata and features (Haynes 1968; Butzer 1974); dating of archaeological sites by geological means also has been attempted with some success (Zeuner 1958; Giddings 1966). A second concern has been archaeologists' explicit recognition of the applicability of geomorphological principles in the formation of archaeological landscapes (Bryan 1926; Butzer 1971; Hassan 1978; Turnbaugh 1977, 1978; Vita-Finzi 1978). This focus has highlighted new aspects of ancient humans' interrelationship with the environment, including their impact upon it. Third, geochemistry has

proven to be a fruitful technique for research in archaeological contexts, particularly with regard to discussions about prehistoric lithic exploitation, trade, and technology. Familiar studies of this nature have focused on the obsidian trade in the Aegean, in Mesoamerica, and in eastern North America's Hopewell manifestation (Cann, Dixon & Renfrew 1970; Sidrys, Andresen & Marcucci 1976; Griffin, Gordus & Wright 1969). The use of native copper from the Great Lakes area also has been examined by using such methods (Bastian 1961; Olsen 1962; Friedman *et al.* 1966).

The present inquiry follows this third, geochemical approach in addressing a problem of archaeological interest in the northeastern United States. Rock specimens from six selected soapstone quarries in southern New England are examined in order to determine whether each of these outcrops might be characterized by a distinctive geochemical profile. The analysis, which is an extension of Turnbaugh and Keifer's initial work (1979), will focus on a consideration of major elements as revealed through color, texture, mineralogy of specimens, thin-section petrographic analysis, and atomic-absorption spectrophotometry. Analysis and discussion of several soapstone artifacts and their possible relations to these quarries then follows. The results should demonstrate that major elements profiling often can provide a useful method for 'fingerprinting' soapstone quarries and for artifact materials source identification. When such proves to be the case, and when an adequate data bank of these profiles can be compiled, it ultimately should be possible to trace the origin of archaeological soapstone back to known sources of the raw material.

Soapstone

In general, soapstone, talc, and steatite are closely related forms of hydrous magnesium silicate; they may vary from each other only slightly in mineral percentages. Talc $-H_2 Mg_3 (SiO_3)_4-$ is the primary form; soapstone and steatite are massive varieties of talc that often contain associated minerals such as chlorite, tremolite, and calcite. Talc or soapstone may originate in regionally metamorphosed zones where igneous rocks are intrusive in chemically basic sedimentary strata (Brown 1973). All of these metamorphosed materials share a distinctive greasy or soapy feel. Depending upon exact mineral compositions, soapstones may vary in color from white to green to brown, and may range in hardness from 1 to 2.5 on the Moh scale.

Primarily due to its easy carvability and probably also because of its heat-retention properties, soapstone of various types was utilized prehistorically throughout the United States wherever the raw material could be quarried, and even in some areas far removed from any outcrops (Turnbaugh 1977, 142−55; Witthoft 1953, 13−14).

Northeastern soapstone sources pertain to a talc belt or zone that stretches through the western area of southern New England and continues as far south as the Carolinas. This belt is related and generally runs parallel to the Appalachian Mountains (fig. 12.1) (Chidester, Engel & Wright 1964, plate 1; fig. 1). Several of the quarry sites under consideration here lie within the boundaries indicated in figure 12.1. Others, which are located beyond the limits set on this map, may be associated with the fringe or contact zone, where isolated talc or soapstone outcrops may be expected. The belt depicted in figure 12.1 represents a concentration of contemporary commercial quarry activity, not the prehistoric quarrying that is of concern here.

Ancient soapstone workshop activities were fairly specialized in southern New England, as suggested by the duplication of many characteristic tool types from quarry to quarry. Artifacts that have been interpreted as scrapers, reamers, chisels, picks, shavers, and gouges pertained to the local soapstone industry (Fowler 1945, 1961, 1972, 1975). In this region, soapstone artifacts generally have been assigned a Late Archaic affiliation or occasionally an association with the earlier Archaic stages (Fowler 1956; Ritchie 1969, 230). Radiocarbon dates on charcoal found within the tailing of New England soapstone quarries have a temporal range of some 3,000 years (Fowler 1972, 1975).

The Quarries

Specimens from six southern New England soapstone quarry sites (fig. 12.2) will be discussed subsequently, but a brief consideration of the six quarries themselves seems warranted. All six have been known to artifact collectors for

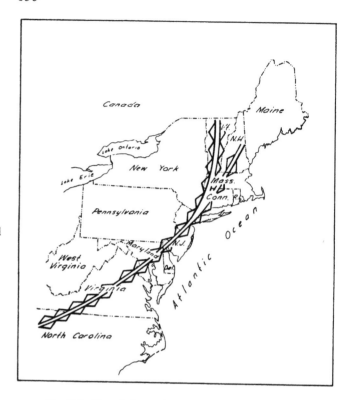

Fig. 12.1. Map of the northeastern United States, showing the 'talc belt' that transects the region.

many years and several have been nearly obliterated either by relic hunters or by modern construction, or both. The two major Rhode Island quarries are threatened especially by urban sprawl.

The Oaklawn quarry site in Oaklawn, Rhode Island, appears to have been the most extensive of the six aboriginal quarries. It is currently endangered by a housing development in the immediate area; the site has been granted National Register status. Soapstone bowls and fragments and pipe blanks numbering into the hundreds have been excavated at Oaklawn for at least six decades. More recently, Fowler revealed a section of the quarry that was associated almost exclusively with pipe-making (Fowler 1978). He considers this pipe workshop to be much later than the stone-bowl-making activity that is most evident elsewhere throughout the quarry area, and his opinion is supported by a radiocarbon date of A.D. 731, which he obtained from associated charcoal (Fowler 1967, 1978, 4).

The concentration on pipe-making in this period may possibly indicate a specialization for the purpose of trading the stone smoking devices, as was the case in historic times (Wood 1898, 65; Turnbaugh 1976). As will be discussed below, a platform pipe, apparently manufactured from Oaklawn soapstone, was recently recovered from an Indian burial mound that has been estimated to date between A.D. 800 and 1100 (M. F. Seeman, 1979, personal communication), a span which is within close range of Fowler's radiocarbon date for the Oaklawn pipe workshop. Moreover, very similar

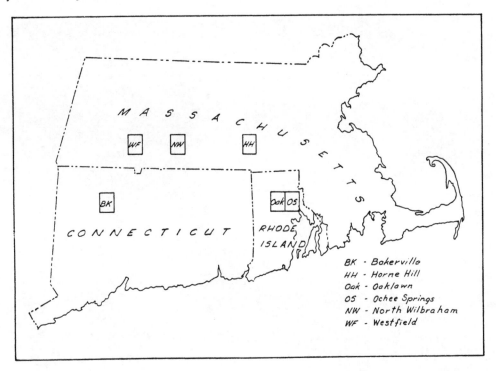

Fig. 12.2. General index map of selected soapstone quarry locations in southern New England.

pipe specimens and uncompleted preforms from other Rhode Island sites are included in the Congdon and Sherman artifact collections at the University of Rhode Island. The linkage between soapstone pipes and sources of the raw material will be further explored below.

The Ochee Springs site in Johnston, Rhode Island (fig. 12.3), has recently been added to the National Register, but only after a century of damage had reduced it dramatically. In 1878, workmen on the Horatio Angell farm exposed the earth-covered ledge and evidence of its ancient use as a quarry and workshop. Three hundred cartloads of chipping debris, along with slate and quartzite picks, abraders, and hammerstones, were hauled from the site as private collectors and representatives from area museums and universities congregated at the Ochee Springs quarry (Saville 1919). Frederick Ward Putnam, then director of the Peabody Museum at Harvard, described the numerous complete and unfinished bowls, fragments, and other soapstone artifacts that were removed during subsequent excavation (Putnam 1878). Aboriginal bowl-manufacturing methods have been further reconstructed from physical evidence at this quarry (fig. 12.4) (Chapin 1924, 15; Turnbaugh & Keifer 1979, 37). After the initial brief flurry of interest, the site continued to remain exposed to vandalism and deterioration as a result of nearby construction until very recent times.

Three years of amateur excavation followed the discovery of the Bakerville, Connecticut, quarry. From the debris came a wide variety of specialized stone tools used in quarrying and manufacturing processes (Neshko 1970). The Westfield quarry near Little River in Westfield, Massachusetts, was excavated during the years 1937–1940 by William Fowler (1943, 1945, 1968). The familiar evidence for stone-bowl production was abundant, as well as a few indications of pipe-making. Adjacent to this quarry, Fowler found a workshop and three caches of tools made from an exposed quartz vein. The Wilbraham quarry was located in North Wilbraham, Massachusetts. Of the original nine soapstone boulders that were quarried, the last one remaining has been removed to the Springfield Museum of Science, where it is currently on display. Excavations at the quarry site produced two soapstone pipe blanks, many bowl products, and a number of the same tool types found at the other quarry sites (Fowler 1969). The Horne Hill quarry at Bramanville, Massachusetts, has in recent years become the site of a new home and driveway. Little evidence of ancient activity survives except for soapstone fragments that are scattered around a rockshelter that is located near the quarry site. Fowler's excavation here some years ago produced quarry tools similar to those found at the other quarries (Fowler 1966).

Analysis and interpretation

In the autumn of 1977 and the spring of 1978, field reconnaissance was conducted at four of the six quarries. At the time, at least six hand samples each were collected from the Bakerville, Horne Hill, and Oaklawn quarries. Those samples were selected which seemed most typical of the approximate major mineral compositions that could be observed in the individual quarry areas. One sample each from the Westfield and Wilbraham quarries in Massachusetts were courteously provided by the Springfield Museum of Science

Fig. 12.3. Main soapstone quarry pit at Ochee Springs site, Johnston, Rhode Island, showing extensive evidence of aboriginal bowl cutting.

in Springfield, Massachusetts. The number of samples analyzed from the two Rhode Island quarries now amounts to more than thirty from each.

Several types of analyses have proven to be particularly useful for profiling major elements of soapstone specimens from each of these quarries. The color and texture of the samples have been analyzed by using both the Rock-Color

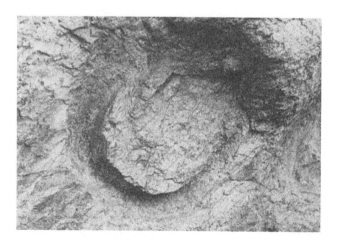

Fig. 12.4. Pedestal base of 26 cm bowl cut out of soapstone outcrop, Ochee Springs site.

Chart and the Munsell color system and by measuring grain size in millimeters. Petrographic analysis of thin sections ground from quarry samples has resulted in estimated bulk mineral compositions for each rock specimen. And atomic absorption analysis has been used to determine percentages of the major elements present in pulverized quarry samples. Along with the rock powder, standards JB-1 and mica magnesium of known chemical components were dissolved in solution, using a technique known as the lithium metaborate fusion method. Powdered rock samples were analyzed for the major elements – aluminium (Al), calcium (Ca), iron (Fe), potassium (K), magnesium (Mg), sodium (Na), and silicon (Si) – using salt solutions of these elements as standards, along with unknowns (the quarry samples) and knowns (JB-1 and mica magnesium), on a Perkin-Elmer Model 303 Atomic Absorption Spectrophotometer at the University of Rhode Island.

Distinctive variation among hand samples from the six quarry sites occurred in such characteristics as color, texture, and mineralogy. Color is by no means always a foolproof distinguishing characteristic for soapstone since an overlapping degree of color variation between sites is often present and observable. Munsell designations (National Research Council, Rock-Color Chart 1948; Munsell Color Company, Soil Color Chart 1954), however, provide a method for precisely defining

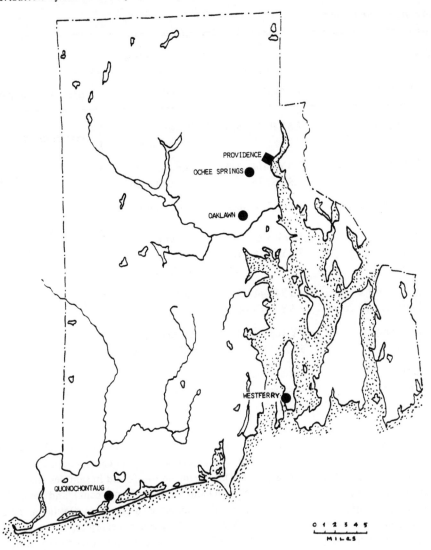

Fig. 12.5. Rhode Island, showing quarry sites and artifact recovery locations mentioned in the text.

the color of rock specimens in terms of a color's hue, value, and chroma. These color descriptions, combined with the patterning of the color, are satisfactorily individual for each soapstone quarry. It should be noted that table 12.1 gives the results of analyzing the color of dry samples; wetting the specimens merely darkened them, thus decreasing their value ratings, though hue and chroma remained virtually the same.

Oaklawn, Ochee Springs, and Westfield materials are characterized by light grays and olive grays that fall in the same Munsell range (5Y7/1–5/1). But each quarry has a distinctive pattern for its soapstone's brownish inclusions of iron oxide. All of the Oaklawn samples had light yellowish-brown to brownish-yellow oxidation (10YR7/4–5/6). This oxidation was primarily on the surface, with few isolated deep inclusions. Ochee Springs samples, on the other hand, had a stronger brown oxidation (7.5YR3/4–5/6). Most of this oxidation consisted of isolated inclusions that create a speckly pattern. No oxidation coloring or patterning could be observed in the Westfield quarry material.

The remaining three quarries – North Wilbraham, Horne Hill, and Bakerville – had a light gray to gray color that was described by a separate Munsell color range (2.5Y7/0–5/0). Again, each had a distinctive iron-oxide coloration or pattern. Both North Wilbraham and Horne Hill samples had speckly iron-oxide inclusions similar in pattern to those of Ochee Springs. However, the North Wilbraham coloration is reddish brown (5YR6/3–4/3), while Horne Hill's is a stronger brown with a more yellow hue (7.5YR5/6, 4/4–3/4). Bakerville samples had a strong brown oxide coloration, like those from Horne Hill (7.5YR5/4–5/6). But oxidation of Bakerville samples is on the surface with virtually no isolated inclusions. As will be shown subsequently, these colors and coloration patterns may be very useful for matching artifact materials with quarry sources, since the patterns are often preserved in typical soapstone artifacts such as bowls and pipe preforms that are usually fairly large.

Texture of the samples was another key consideration and proved to be useful for preliminary quarry identification

Table 12.1. *Color characterization of soapstone hand samples.*

| Quarry | Grays | | Browns | | |
	Munsell	Description	Munsell	Description	Brown oxide patterning
Bakerville	2.5Y7/0–6/0	light gray	7.5YR5/4–5/5	brown to strong brown	few isolated inclusions
Horne Hill	2.5Y7/0–5/0	light gray to gray	7.5YR4/4–3/4 7.5YR5/6	dark brown strong brown	speckly inclusions
Oaklawn	5Y7/1–5/1	light gray to gray	10YR7/4–6/4	light yellowish-brown	few isolated inclusions; some surface staining
	5Y6/2–5/2 2.5Y6/2	olive-gray light brownish-gray	10YR6/6–5/6 7.5YR6/6–4/6	brownish-yellow reddish-yellow to strong brown	
Ochee Springs	5Y5/1–5/2 2.5Y7/0–5/0	gray to olive-gray light gray to gray	7.5YR4/4–3/4 7.5YR5/6–4/6	dark brown strong brown	deep speckly inclusions
North Wilbraham	2.5Y7/0–6/0	light gray	5YR6/3–4/3 5YR5/4	reddish-brown reddish-brown	deep speckly inclusions
Westfield	5Y6/1–5/1	gray	none observed		none observed

purposes, particularly when assessed in combination with other characteristics discussed here. Average grain size, measured in millimeters, was fairly uniform among samples from a specific quarry (table 12.2). Oaklawn samples had the finest average grain size; both talc and chlorite fell between 0.2 and 0.5 mm. Ochee Springs' average grain size was medium to coarse; talc fell between 0.5 and 0.7 mm. Westfield was coarse, with chlorite averaging 1.0 mm. Bakerville had the greatest range of grain size, from coarse to very coarse, with chlorite at 0.7 to 1.0 mm and talc at 0.5 to 1.3 mm. Wilbraham grain size was also very coarse with talc averaging 1.0 mm and chloride 1.0 to 1.3 mm.

The mineralogies, and more precisely the minerals themselves, often permit further distinctions between materials from different quarries. Some of this difference is apparent in hand samples, but petrological analysis of thin sections reveals more important variation. The key minerals for distinguishing these six quarries from one another are anthophyllite, biotite, calcite, magnetite, serpentine, and tremolite. They were present in samples of only one, two, or three of these six quarries (table 12.3). Coarse-grained fibrous anthophyllite comprised an average 25 per cent of the composition of Bakerville samples. Only North Wilbraham samples (2 per cent) also contained a small amount of anthophyllite. The Westfield material was 20 per cent biotite; no other quarries' samples contained this mineral. Ochee Springs samples contained an average of 30 per cent calcite. Only Horne Hill also had small quantities (3.5 per cent) of this

mineral present. Magnetite was present in samples from Horne Hill (7 per cent), Oaklawn (15 per cent), and Ochee Springs (18 per cent). Serpentine was found in samples from Horne Hill (4 per cent) and Oaklawn (5 per cent), and tremolite was present in North Wilbraham (8 per cent), Oaklawn (12 per cent), and Westfield (25 per cent) samples.

Atomic-absorption analysis reinforced these mineralogical distinctions. Percentages of seven oxides – Al_2O_3, CaO, FeO, K_2O, MgO, Na_2O, and SiO_2 – present in quarry samples were determined (table 12.4). The Westfield quarry material contained the only potassium oxide (K_2O). By using a t-test of means, statistically significant differences between means for iron oxide (FeO) could be detected for Bakerville and Horne Hill samples and for Bakerville and Oaklawn samples at the 95 per cent confidence level (table 12.5). Similarly, significant differences between means for sodium oxide (Na_2O) existed for all of the four quarries—Bakerville, Horne Hill, Oaklawn, and Ochee Springs — for which more than one sample underwent atomic-absorption analysis.

Rho correlations of the atomic-absorption-analysis data for these four quarries were all very strong. When atomic-absorption data for hand samples from each individual quarry were correlated, Bakerville, Horne Hill, and Oaklawn each had positive R values greater than 0.98 (Bakerville was 0.998, Horne Hill was 0.994, and Oaklawn was 0.985). Ochee Springs's R value was greater than 0.900. When compared with each other, the R value for all six southern New England quarries was greater than 0.91. Thus, these R values demon-

Table 12.2. *Texture and mineralogy of soapstone hand samples.*

Quarry		Average grain size (mm)	%	Texture	Fabric
Bakerville	chlorite	0.7–1.0	28.5	coarse–very coarse	nonfoliated[1]
	talc	0.5–1.3	33.5		
Horne Hill	chlorite	0.5	35.0	medium coarse	both foliated
	talc	0.5–0.7	47.0		and nonfoliated
Oaklawn	chlorite	0.2–0.5	21.5	fine	nonfoliated
	talc	0.2–0.5	40.0		
Ochee Springs	chlorite	(minimal)	5.0	medium coarse	nonfoliated
	talc	0.5–0.7	43.0		
North Wilbraham	chlorite	1.0–1.3	35.0	very coarse	nonfoliated
	talc	1.0	30.0		
Westfield	chlorite	1.0	22.0	coarse[2]	nonfoliated
	talc	1.0	28.0		

[1] Tends to look somewhat foliated
[2] Chlorite from this quarry exhibits more elongated crystalline structure

Table 12.3. *Mean mineral percentages in thin sections of soapstone hand samples.*

Mineral	Bakerville (n = 3)	Horne Hill (n = 3)	Oaklawn (n = 3)	Ochee Springs (n = 3)	North Wilbraham (n = 1)	Westfield (n = 1)
Anthophyllite	25.0 ± 15.0	—	—	—	2.0	—
Biotite	—	—	—	—	—	20.0
Calcite	—	3.33*	—	30.0 ± 13.23	—	—
Chlorite	28.33 ± 7.64	31.67 ± 17.56	21.67 ± 3.54**	4.67 ± 7.07**	35.0	22.0
Magnetite	—	6.67 ± 4.16	15.0 ± 13.23	18.33 ± 7.64	—	—
Opaque	4.33 ± 3.21	(magnetite)	(magnetite)	(magnetite)	22.0	1.0
Quartz	9.0 ± 2.65	3.33*	6.67 ± 7.07**	3.33 ± 4.24**	2.0	4.0
Serpentine	—	4.0*	5.0*	—	—	—
Talc	33.33 ± 7.64	47.33 ± 13.28	40.0 ± 16.07	43.33 ± 5.77	30.0	28.0
Tremolite	—	—	11.67*	—	8.0	25.0

*Mineral apparent in only one of the three samples
**Mineral apparent in only two of the three samples

strate that greater variation generally exists between these quarries than within an individual outcrop in southern New England.

Archaeological applications

Finally, using the profiles generated by specific distinctions in color, texture, and mineralogy for each quarry's samples, a number of soapstone artifacts have been tentatively identified with their probable soapstone sources. To date, soapstone bowls, kettles, and pipe preforms have been examined. These items usually are large enough that they retain patterns of color and texture, and mineralogy typical of a particular quarry, especially when the artifacts lack a polished surface. We will briefly discuss six Rhode Island specimens here (table 12.6). The first, a pipe blank found on a surface site in the Pawcatuck River drainage at Westerly,

Table 12.4. *Mean oxide percentages in atomic-absorption analysis of soapstone samples.*

Oxide	Bakerville (n = 3)	Horne Hill (n = 3)	Oaklawn (n = 3)	Ochee Springs (n = 3)	North Wilbraham (n = 1)	Westfield (n = 1)
Al_2O_3	4.19 ± 0.71	4.10 ± 1.75	3.62 ± 3.33	3.47 ± 2.75	6.14	3.31
CaO	0.26 ± 0.11	1.28 ± 1.62	0.83 ± 0.80	4.36 ± 6.17	1.05	6.16
FeO & Fe_2O_3	7.59 ± 1.91	4.67 ± 0.63	4.76 ± 0.46	7.46 ± 2.27	7.72	3.47
K_2O	0	0	0	0	0	0.90
MgO	20.25 ± 0.86	21.11 ± 1.50	20.94 ± 0.85	21.11 ± 1.54	29.84	16.91
Na_2O	0.12 ± 0.0	0.25 ± 0.17	0.10 ± 0.06	0.08 ± 0.07	0.01	0.23
SiO_2	58.07 ± 1.62	48.73 ± 5.19	56.01 ± 6.96	42.95 ± 8.56	40.88	49.23

Rhode Island, is of soapstone that has a typical mottled olive gray coloration and fine texture of material from Oaklawn quarry. A partially finished elbow pipe from a surface site about 1.6 km from Oaklawn also has been matched with the Oaklawn source on the basis of color, oxide color, and surface patterning, as well as grain size.

One soapstone kettle and three bowls excavated by William Simmons at the West Ferry site, Jamestown, Rhode Island (Simmons 1970, 1971), may also be tentatively matched with quarry sources on the basis of major element distinctions. All four vessels were excavated from aboriginal graves, one of which, Burial G1, has two radiocarbon dates that place it between 3190 and 3335 B.P. Two of these vessels — large and small kettles with lugs — almost certainly are of Ochee Springs material. The vessels' light gray coloration,

their iron oxide staining and speckly patterning, and their grain size (greater than 0.5 mm) closely match the quarry samples' characterizations, as does their method of manufacture, when compared with unfinished bowls from the several quarries. Two smaller somewhat irregularly shaped bowls were fashioned from an olive-gray material that is more similar to Oaklawn quarry specimens with regard to the overall coloration, distinctive surface staining of iron oxide, and fine grain size. All of these bowls were fashioned from soapstone that necessarily was transported over water by canoe from the two quarries to the island location of the site on Jamestown, more than 40 km away.

There are also indications that Rhode Island soapstone may have been another of the commodities that entered extraregional exchange systems in prehistoric times. Earlier

Table 12.5. *t-Test of means using atomic-absorption-analysis data for soapstone samples (two-tailed test, $\alpha = 0.05$).*

Oxide	Comparisons*	t-value	Confidence level (lower/upper)
Al_2O_3 CaO MgO	no significant differences among quarries		
FeO & Fe_2O_3	Bakerville/Horne Hill	+ 2.515	(− 6.14/+ 0.30)
	Bakerville/Oaklawn	+ 2.501	(− 5.98/+ 0.31)
Na_2O	Bakerville/Horne Hill	+ 1.289	(− 0.15/+ 0.40)
	Bakerville/Oaklawn	+ 0.711	(− 0.11/+ 0.07)
	Bakerville/Ochee Springs	+ 1.127	(− 0.15/+ 0.06)
	Horne Hill/Oaklawn	+ 1.449	(− 0.44/+ 0.14)
	Horne Hill/Ochee Springs	+ 1.612	(− 0.46/+ 0.12)
	Oaklawn/Ochee Springs	+ 0.396	(− 0.14/+ 0.10)
SiO_2	Bakerville/Horne Hill	+ 2.979	(− 18.06/− 0.64)

*Only the quarries from which three or more samples were examined are represented in this analysis: Bakerville, Horne Hill, Oaklawn, Ochee Springs

Table 12.6. *Characteristics of soapstone artifacts.*

Artifact	Provenience	Texture (gain size in mm)	Color Grays (Munsell)	Browns (Munsell)	Oxide Patterning	Probable source
large kettle	West Ferry, R.I. (burial G1, *c.* 3300 B.P.)	0.5	2.5Y7/0–6/0	7.5YR5/6	speckly inclusions	Ochee Springs
bowl with handles	West Ferry	0.5	2.5Y7/0–5/0	7/5YR3/4	speckly inclusions	Ochee Springs
Irregularly shaped small bowl	West Ferry	≤ 0.5	5Y6/1	10YR6/4–6/6	surface stain	Oaklawn (?)
Irregularly shaped small bowl	West Ferry	≤ 0.5	5Y6/1	10YR6/4–6/6	surface stain	Oaklawn (?)
pipe blank	Quonachontaug, R.I. (Congdon, Site 70)	< 0.5	5Y6/2–5/2	10YR7/4	very slight surface stain	Oaklawn
elbow pipe bowl	Oaklawn, R.I. (Congdon, Site 31)	0.2–0.5	5Y6/2–5/2, 5/1	10YR7/4–6/4	slight surface stain	Oaklawn

mention has been made of a stone platform pipe from Indiana, which was found recently in the central burial feature of a low mound at the Catlin site, Vermillion County. According to M. F. Seeman of Kent State University, the pipe's association with Albee cord-marked pottery places it between *c.* A.D. 800 and 1100. Results of neutron-activation analysis carried out at the University of Virginia suggest that the artifact is probably made from New England soapstone, and that the material represented is most likely from Oaklawn quarry in Rhode Island (M. F. Seeman 1979, personal communication). Moreover, the estimated date for this pipe corresponds fairly well with the A.D. 731 radiocarbon date obtained from the pipe workshop area at Oaklawn, as already noted. Obviously, what is needed is the recovery and attribution of other pipes of this material in distinct areas, which could support a hypothesis relating to a Middle Woodland or early Late Woodland trade in smoking apparatus, similar to that which was recorded in the northeast during historic times.

Discussion

Though some of this preliminary research has had promising results, it is still too early to declare that major-element profiling alone will permit the confident assignment of individual soapstone artifacts to their respective southern New England sources. Major-element profiling will not always be precise enough to be used independently. However, even at this relatively gross level of analysis, highly significant compositional variation appears to exist among soapstones from southern New England and those from, for instance, New York or Montana (cf. Chidester, Engel & Wright 1964, table 5). And, as the present inquiry has demonstrated statistically, somewhat greater geochemical variation exists between most southern New England soapstone quarries than within the individual outcrops of this region. Finer analyses using neutron activation have demonstrated a similar trend for Virginia and Labrador soapstones (Luckenbach, Allen & Holland 1974; Allen, Luckenbach & Holland 1975; Luckenbach, Holland & Allen 1975; Nagel *et al.* 1980). Since such is the case, it should now be possible to trace a number of eastern United States soapstones and soapstone artifacts to their known sources with a higher degree of certainty.

To conclude, these results suggest that major-element profiling will permit the tentative assignment of a number of individual soapstone artifacts to their respective southern New England sources. Color and its patterning, texture, and mineralogy can provide a 'fingerprint' of the major-element composition of a specific quarry's material. It is likely that more extensive neutron-activation analysis of southern New England soapstones could prove to be of similar diagnostic value. In the interim, the combination of quantitative and qualitative analytical techniques used here to describe the geochemical compositions and observable traits of selected New England soapstones has allowed for the tentative assignment of *some* unknown artifacts to *some* known sources.

References

Allen, R. O., Luckenbach, A. H. & Holland, C. G. 1975. Application of instrumental neutron activation analysis to a study of prehistoric steatite artifacts and source materials. *Archaeometry* 17 (1): 69–83.

Bastian, T. 1961. Trace element and metallographic studies of prehistoric copper artifacts in North America: a review. *Anthropological Papers of the Museum of Anthropology, University of Michigan* 17:151–75.

Brown, C. E. 1973. Talc. *United States Geological Survey Professional Paper* 820:619–26.

Bryan, K. 1926. Recent deposits of Chaco Canyon in relation to life of the prehistoric peoples of Pueblo Bonito. *Journal of the Washington Academy of Sciences* 16:75–6.

Butzer, K. W. 1971. *Environment and archaeology*. Chicago: Aldine.
   1974. Geological and ecological perspectives of the Middle Pleistocene. *Quarternary Research* 4 (2): 136–48.

Cann, J. R., Dixon, J. E. & Renfrew, C. 1970. Obsidian analysis and the obsidian trade. In D. Brothwell & E. Higgs, eds., *Science in Archaeology*, 2nd ed. New York: Praeger, 578–91.

Chapin, H. M. 1924. *Indian implements found in Rhode Island*. Rhode Island Historical Society, Providence.

Chidester, A. H., Engel, A. E. J. & Wright, L. A. 1964. Talc resources of the United States. *United States Geological Survey Bulletin* 1167.

Davidson, D. A. & Shackley, M. L. eds. 1975. *Geoarchaeology : earth science and the past*. London: Duckworth.

Fowler, W. S. 1943. Soapstone bowl making as practiced at the Westfield quarry. *Massachusetts Archaeological Society Bulletin* 4:42–4.
   1945. Tool-making at the Westfield steatite quarry. *American Antiquity* 11 (1): 95–101.
   1956. The stone bowl industry, its importance as a culture diagnostic. *Massachusetts Archaeological Society Bulletin* 17:74–7.
   1961. Domestic evidence at steatite quarries. *Massachusetts Archaeological Society Bulletin* 22:49–55.
   1966. The Horne Hill soapstone quarry. *Massachusetts Archaeological Society Bulletin* 27 (2): 17–28.
   1967. Oaklawn quarry: stone bowl and pipemaking. *Massachusetts Archaeological Society Bulletin* 29 (1): 1–17.
   1968. Stone bowl making at the Westfield quarry. *Massachusetts Archaeological Society Bulletin* 30 (1): 6–16.
   1969. The Wilbraham stone bowl quarry. *Massachusetts Archaeological Society Bulletin* 30 (3–4): 9–21.
   1972. Some aboriginal stone works in New England. *Massachusetts Archaeological Society Bulletin* 33 (3–4): 18–27.
   1975. The diagnostic stone bowl industry. *Massachusetts Archaeological Society Bulletin* 36 (3–4): 1–9.
   1978. Stone pipe making. *Report of the Narragansett Archaeological Society* : 1–10.

Friedman, A. M., Conway, M., Kastner, M., Milsted, J., Metta, D., Fields, P. R. & Olsen, E., 1966. Copper artifacts: correlation with source types of source ores. *Science* 152:1504–6.

Giddings, J. L. 1966. Cross-dating the archaeology of northwestern Alaska. *Science* 153:127–35.

Gladfelter, B. G. 1977. Geoarchaeology: the geomorphologist and archaeology. *American Antiquity* 42 (4): 519–38.

Griffin, J. B., Gordus, A. A. & Wright, G. A. 1969. Identification of the sources of Hopewellian obsidian in the Middle West. *American Antiquity* 34 (1): 1–14.

Hassan, F. 1978. Sediments in archaeology: methods and implications for paleoenvironmental and cultural analysis. *Journal of Field Archaeology* 5:197–213.

Haynes, C. V. 1968. Geochronology of late quarternary alluvium. In R. B. Morrison & H. E. Wright, Jr., eds., *Means of correlation of quarternary successions*. University of Utah, Salt Lake City, 591–631.

Luckenbach, A. H., Allen, R. O. & Holland, C. G. 1974. The use of rare earth element concentrations in neutron activation analysis of soapstone. *Newsletter of Lithic Technology* 3 (3).

Luckenbach, A. H., Holland, C. G. & Allen, R. O. 1975. Soapstone artifacts: tracing prehistoric trade patterns in Virginia. *Science* 187:57–8.

Munsell Color Company. 1954. *Munsell soil color charts*. Baltimore: Munsell Color Co.

Nagel, C., Fitzhugh, W., Allen, R. & Storey, M. 1980. Neutron activation analysis characterization of soapstone sources, and Dorset archaeology in Labrador. Paper presented at the Society for American Archaeology annual meetings, Philadelphia.

National Research Council. 1948. *Rock-Color chart*. Washington, D.C.: United States Government Printing Office.

Neshko, J., Jr. 1970. Bakerville stone bowl quarry. *Massachusetts Archaeological Society Bulletin* 31 (1–2): 1–10.

Olsen, E. 1962. Copper artifact analysis with the X-ray spectrometer. *American Antiquity* 28 (2): 234–8.

Putnam, F. W. 1878. The manufacture of soapstone pots by the Indians of New England. *Report of the Peabody Museum of Archaeology and Ethnology* 11:273–6.

Ritchie, W. A. 1969. *Archaeology of Martha's Vineyard*. Garden City, N. Y.: Natural History Press.

Saville, F. H. 1919. Steatite quarry at Johnston, Rhode Island. *Rhode Island Historical Society Collections* 12:103–5.

Shackley, M. L. 1975. *Archaeological sediments : a survey of analytical methods*. New York: Wiley.

Sidrys, R., Andresen, J. & Marcucci, D. 1976. Obsidian sources in the Maya area. *Journal of New World Archaeology* 1 (5): 1–14.

Simmons, W. S. 1970. *Cautantowwit's house : an Indian burial ground on the island of Conanicut in Narragansett Bay*. Providence: Brown University Press.
   1971. *Guide to exhibits in the Sydney L. Wright Museum*. Wright Museum, Jamestown, R.I.

Turnbaugh, W. A. 1976. The survival of a native craft in colonial Rhode Island. *Man in the Northeast* 11:74–9.
   1977. *Man, land, and time : cultural prehistory and demographic patterns of north-central Pennsylvania*, rev. ed. Evansville, Ind.: Unigraphic Press.
   1978. Floods and archaeology. *American Antiquity* 43 (4): 593–607.

Turnbaugh, W. A. & Keifer, T. H. 1979. Chemical variation in selected soapstone quarries of southern New England. *Man in the Northeast* 18:32–47.

Vita-Finzi, C. 1978. *Archaeological sites in their setting*. London: Thames & Hudson.

Witthoft, J. 1953. Broad spearpoints and the Transitional period cultures in Pennsylvania. *Pennsylvania Archaeologist* 23 (1): 4–31.

Wood, W. 1898. *New England's prospect*. Boston: E. M. Boynton.

Zeuner, F. E. 1958. *Dating the past : an introduction to geochronology*, 4th ed. London: Methuen.

Chapter 13

**Reconstructing Corbiac: the context of
manufacturing at an Upper Paleolithic quarry**
E. C. Gibson

Quantitative analysis of lithic technological attributes enables
the reconstruction of stone-tool-making behavior at the Upper
Paleolithic quarry of Corbiac. These attributes display a consistent
and uniform appearance characterized by low variability. This
observation is used as the basis for suggesting that the Evolved
Perigordian component of Corbaic may have been produced by a
group of socially related, part-time, flintknapping specialists. The
ramifications of such a possibility for lithic studies in general and
models of Upper Paleolithic social systems in particular are considered.

Introduction

The Upper Perigordian quarry of Corbiac is in the
Central Perigord region of southwestern France near the town
of Bergerac (LaVille, Rigaud & Sackett 1980, fig. 6.2).
Excavations at the site were directed by François Bordes from
1962 to 1967 (Bordes 1968). The upper stratum (Level 1)
yielded an estimated 100,000 blades, over 1,000 cores in
various stages of reduction, and approximately 10,000 finished
tools (Bordes & Crabtree 1969, 1). Based on the abundance of
microgravettes, Gravettian points, and dihedral burins, Bordes
judged the Level 1 assemblage to be transitional between
Perigordian VI and proto-Magdalenian, and suggested a relative
date of *c.* 20,000 B.C. for it. He called the assemblage Evolved
Perigordian, because it exhibited Upper Perigordian and
proto-Magdalenian traits. This assemblage had an important
role in the argument that was advanced that the latter industry
was the terminal phase of Perigordian development (Bordes &
De Sonneville-Bordes 1966; LaVille, Rigaud & Sackett 1980).

In this study Level 1 is examined with the following
objectives: (1) to systematically extract new data on lithic
technology from attributes of lithic debitage; (2) to reconstruct
the Level 1 technology; (3) to examine the reconstructed
stone-tool-making behavior in order to assess the nature and
degree of variability present in this one industry; and (4) to
consider the extent to which this variability may reflect the
social context of manufacturing.

The Upper Paleolithic cultures of southwestern France
have had a long tenure of archaeological research and are
known for their complex succession. A great deal of debate
has been generated in the literature over the nature and
measurement of style and the significance of stylistic variability
in these industries (Bordes & De Sonneville-Bordes 1970;
Binford 1973; Sackett 1982). Recently, the importance of
identifying those lithic attributes that reflect the range of
choices made by prehistoric artisans in the design and manufacture of their craft products has been emphasized by Sackett
(1982). In suggesting this perspective Sackett has redefined
and enlarged Binford's (1965) long-maintained axiom that
studies of stylistic variability should emphasize those formal
attributes that vary within the social context of manufacturing.
This study focuses on this issue.

Archaeological and environmental context

Corbiac is in a dry valley that merges with the south
terrace of the Caudau River approximately 4 km southwest of

its confluence with the Louyre River. The Caudau is a tributary of the Dordogne and joins it 8 km southwest of its confluence with the Louyre. Areal topography is complex and is characterized by large river valleys and alluvial floodplains, joined by narrow tributary streams that have cut a mosaic of elevated plateaus from massive limestone ridges and slopes. Corbiac is located in a transitional zone, on the edge of one such plateau (Gibson 1980, 1982).

Two Upper Cretaceous limestone beds, the Maestrichtian and Campanian, form the slopes of the region. At Corbiac, however, only the hard, yellowish, Maestrichtian beds are present. These have been subdivided as follows:
1. The Upper Subdivision: a yellow, glauconitic limestone which only outcrops in the immediate vicinity of Bergerac.
2. The Middle Subdivision: a yellow to whitish yellow, sometimes sandy sometimes dolomitic limestone.
3. The Lower Subdivision: a limestone with zones of glauconitic sand (Cartes Géologique 1920, Bricker 1975).

The Upper Subdivision is the only source of cryptocrystalline silicate (CCS) at Corbiac. Valenski (1960), conducted the first investigation of CCS sources for artifacts and debitage found at Abri Pataud in the Vézère Valley. He identified 'Series B' as occurring only in the Corbiac region, based on microscopic characteristics, invertebrate fossils, and crystalline structure. Bricker (1975, 195) has further defined this series of the Upper Subdivision: 'Series B: These flints are of Maestrichtian age. The most distinctive variety is a banded flint (silex rubané) usually having a buff background with red, white, purple, or brown bands. The basic background color may however be dark grey or black.'

Series B is a high-quality raw material commonly called 'Bergerac flint', which occurs in long nodules often exceeding 50 cm in length and containing few impurities. The presence of artifacts made from Bergerac flint at Abri Pataud, located 25 km from Corbiac, suggests that this raw material was valued by prehistoric flintknappers. At the Corbiac quarry, the CCS nodules lie exposed on the surface. They are remnant deposits produced by solution and mechanical weathering of the limestone beds and talus. As Bricker affirmed (1975), the Corbiac quarry was 'one very prolific source' of raw material. One can readily understand why 99 per cent of the artifacts at Corbiac were made from this locally available stone (Gibson 1980).

Reconstructing prehistoric lithic technological systems requires two inferences: 'first, product groups must be inferred from shared technological attributes among artifacts. Then, reductive stages and the particular technology by which each was accomplished, are inferred from the characteristics of and relationships between product groups' (Boisvert *et al.* 1979, 61). Interpretations and conclusions can be drawn through logical inferences based on interrelationships of artifacts and attributes. Such an interpretive process is not simple.

In the initial task of acquiring raw material, for example, usually the stone best suited to the flintknappers' needs is selected from whatever sources are accessible. Archaeologists frequently do not know all of the prehistoric conditions that were present, such as the various environmental and social conditions affecting availability of known raw material. Given the archaeologist's partial understanding of the prehistoric context and cultural system, interpretations of the artisan's needs and objectives are somewhat problematic.

Thus, the crucial problem in most archaeological analyses is, as Binford stated, 'what significance can we as prehistorians justifiably attach to our contemporary observations on the archaeological record? All our observations are contemporary, only by attaching significance to certain observations can we succeed in referring these observations reliably to the past' (1973, 252). The reconstruction of prehistoric stone-tool-making is an analytical process that has many elements of uncertainty. The formulation of hypotheses may be strongly influenced by experiments, intuition, experience, the archaeological literature, and ethnographic data. Deductive and inductive reasoning is used to identify attributes which reflect technological behavior. The descriptive and analytical framework for this study of Corbiac is to isolate and to test specific attributes which are technological characteristics of artifacts. *States* are the various forms in which the attributes are manifested. Attribute analysis of blades and flakes in this study follows Clay (1976, 304):

> It is a method whereby multiple dimensions of variability in tool classes and all stone tools are described, measured, and used singly and in combination in diverse analytical operations. It is no more than that, for what has been done with attributes once recorded in the excavated sample has been dependent upon the interests of particular archaeologists. The approach has merely provided a body of standardized observations.

The following discussion provides a background for understanding how the technological interpretations were derived. The most important interpretive constraint is the lack of comparable research in lithic analysis. Some archaeologists (Collins 1975; Boisvert *et al.* 1979) have conducted similar research with different objectives and analytical units (for example, description of all of the manufacturing steps represented in a sequence of assemblages at a particular site and how they change through time). At present it is not clear to what extent, if any, technical imperatives conceal individual flintknapping styles or vice versa (Johnson 1977). For example, does indirect percussion as a technique cause blades to have consistently similar forms? Or can an individual using direct percussion produce blades identical in form to those produced by indirect percussion? To the latter question Newcomer (1975) would probably answer yes, but other researchers (Bordes & Crabtree 1969; Gibson 1981) would disagree. This is an important unknown factor. In the specific case of Corbiac, it is also possible that uniform raw material and indirect percussion could cause consistent blade forms and mask individual flintknapping styles. On the other hand, perhaps these factors would not conceal technological norms or the social context of manufacturing.

Though the uniform raw material which characterizes Corbiac's Evolved Perigordian assemblage to some extent enhances interpretation, it also provides limits. It would be interesting to examine to what extent the use of different CCS sources influences blade forms and attribute frequencies.

Another limitation is the absence of absolute dating of the component and temporal placement of it. The duration of the occupation is not known. This assemblage may represent one episode of use or many. Since the sample is small, perhaps it is not representative of the site. Bordes thought the entire excavated portion of the Evolved Perigordian component represented only 1 per cent of the whole site (personal communication). Thus the nature and the context of the excavated portion is not well understood.

The data and analytical procedure

Marks and Volkman (n.d.) have recently shown that the final form of a lithic artifact may contain less information concerning its 'cultural' and typochronological placement than has been traditionally assumed in archaeology. They have conclusively demonstrated the need for quantitative analysis of lithic technological attributes in order to enhance our understanding of such assemblages. The following study is directed toward extracting such data from lithic artifacts and their attributes.

The analytical framework for this study of Corbiac is a model derived from lithic technological attributes described below, provided by ethnographic and experimental data (Bordes & Crabtree 1969; Crabtree 1972; Tixier 1972, 1974; Collins 1974; Newcomer 1975; Gibson 1980). Although archaeologists have shown that blades may be produced through diverse methods (Bordes & Crabtree 1969; Tixier 1972; Newcomer 1975; Marks & Volkman n.d.), I have recently demonstrated that the probable technique of blade detachment in the Corbiac Evolved Perigordian component was indirect percussion using a 'punch' (Gibson 1980, 1981).

A final map of the excavations is not available although a preliminary map has been completed (Bordes 1968). The Corbiac sample and the fieldwork can be summarized. Bordes supervised the excavation of $120 \, m^2$ of Corbiac (i.e., the sample universe). The horizontal extent of Level 1 was never defined. De Vallat, under Bordes's direction, supervised the excavation of $30 \, m^2$, or 25 per cent of the total Level 1 area. De Vallat's excavation was selected as the study sample population. A random sample of four 1 by 1 m excavation units was taken from this sample population. These were the units designated by Bordes as R13, R14, S15, and S19 (cf. Bordes 1968); they comprise 7.5 per cent of De Vallat's excavation. The average thickness of Level 1 was 15 cm and the total number of codable objects (blades and flakes) was 3,070. Additionally, 741 complete blades were arbitrarily selected from all of De Vallat's units.

Essential measurements were thickness, length, and width (as measured at the observed midpoint) of the objects. Measurements of the platform consisted of width and depth.

The angle of the object's platform to the core surface was also recorded. The final measurement was the axis of flaking (these attributes are described in detail in Gibson 1980). Blades and flakes were also described by recording such nominal attribute shapes as platform, bulb, bulb-platform intersect, platform exterior, body, and longitudinal cross-section. It was thought that these procedures provided efficient data recovery for inferring the prehistoric technology of Corbiac. Due to time constraints the Corbiac analysis was confined to 'debitage' only (flakes and blades, utilized and unutilized).

In the following presentation, flake-attribute-frequency data precede the blade data. The differences in the total sample size which vary among attribute categories reflect problems in measurement. If the recorder could not ascertain a particular attribute, the sheet was left blank for that value. Approximately 2,500 flakes and 1,200 blades were codable for most of these attributes. In this study, the emphasis is on discerning patterns; thus attributes occurring in frequencies lower than 5 per cent are usually not listed (cf. Gibson 1980, appendix).

Table 13.1 shows the nine most important flake attributes for this assemblage. As expected, flakes without cortex occur in a much higher percentage than cortex flakes. The low percentage of primary cortex flakes possibly indicates that decortication and initial core preforming occurred more frequently outside of the study area.

Faceting, part of the process of platform preparation, is accomplished by detaching small flakes along the platform. Single-faceted flakes are relatively common, and could indicate that the nodules had rounded surfaces and required the preparation of a tabular platform surface before initial reduction occurred.

Another attribute that indicates platform preparation is the exterior platform surface. Over 65 per cent of all flakes in the Corbiac study assemblage reflect some degree of trimming. Trimming enhances control of removal, strengthens platforms, and removes overhangs left from previous flake removals. Thus it is not particularly surprising that the majority of flakes show some degree of platform trimming.

Outline as an attribute indicates that the largest percentage of flakes are parallel sided and slightly expanding, almost 'bladelike' in form.

The bulb of percussion is a pronounced swelling on the ventral side at the proximal end of a flake. This attribute's states were cross tabulated with all other attribute states and the correlations were extremely low or not significant, thus supporting the interpretation that the factors that determine bulb shape are primarily amount and kind of applied force. Therefore, the different bulb states may be directly related to the mass or density of the tool used in the application of force and to the amount of applied force (Gibson 1980, 1982).

The bulb-platform intersection is located on the interior surface immediately adjacent to the platform and takes the

Table 13.1. *The frequency of flake attributes and states.*

Attribute	States	%
Cortex	Primary	5.7
Total 2,483	Secondary	16.2
	Noncortex	78.1
Facet	Cortex	6.8
Total 2,483	Single	59.6
	Double	12.6
	Multiple	16.5
Exterior platform	Untrimmed	34.1
Total 2,368	Slightly trimmed	26.9
	Moderately trimmed	26.0
	Heavily trimmed	12.6
Bulb	Normal	51.6
Total 2,272	Exuberant	51.6
	Flat	33.0
Bulb-platform intersect	Lipped	77.7
Total 2,234	Not lipped	22.3
Body	Thin	39.5
Total 2,384	Medium	48.7
	Thick	7.9
Outline	Parallel	30.3
Total 2,364	Slightly expanding	29.2
	Strongly expanding	11.0
	Irregular	22.9
Longitudinal cross-section	Straight	87.5
	Concave	12.5
Platform angle	110°	8.0
Total 2,309	100°	19.5
	90°	70.5

form of a ridge or 'lip.' A continuum existed from distinct, clearly observable lipping through small lips that could not be seen but only felt, to the absence of lips. The significance of this high number of lips is difficult to assess, but most likely it is produced by the kind and amount of applied force.

Body as an attribute shows that there is a high frequency of thin and medium flakes. Bordes and Crabtree (1969, 3) described the process of preforming the core and noted that the initial detachment of the first thick cortex flake was accomplished through direct hard hammer percussion. One would expect very few of these flakes in an assemblage because after completion of the initial core preforming, much smaller, thin to medium, flakes would be detached to guide blade removal, which is observable in this sample.

The longitudinal cross-section attribute shows a high frequency of straight flakes perhaps reflecting the consistency of Corbiac technology, which occurs at the early stage of initial reduction and preparation for blade removal. This aspect is paralleled in the corresponding blade-attribute states described in table 13.2.

Platform angle is the angle of the flake platform to the bulbar face. The high frequency of platform angles in the 90-degree range demonstrates the consistency of the Corbiac artisans in flake detachment. The regularity of this angle may represent how the core was supported or held while flakes were removed. Unfortunately comparable data are lacking for resolving this case.

In table 13.2, very few blades have any trace of cortex; comparing this attribute with flakes indicates that most flakes and cortex surfaces were removed earlier in the reductive sequence.

The high frequency of single facets indicates the consistency of the manufacturers. The increase of 10 per cent for single-facet platforms on blades compared to flakes may reflect the decreasing need for platform preparation and the overall skill of the Corbiac artisans in detaching blades, and/or sampling error.

It is clear that platform trimming was quite common in this blade technology. Three reasons are proposed for exterior platform trimming on blades: the removal of overhangs produced by exuberant bulbs; the straightening of dorsal ridges prior to blade removal; and the removal of excess platform prior to the seating of the punch (Gibson 1980, 1982).

The blade bulbs are flatter in contrast to the flake bulbs. The less pronounced the bulb of percussion, the easier are subsequent blade removals, since exterior platform trimming is less necessary. The normal and flat bulbs account for 85 per cent of the codable blades. I think this reflects consistency in flintknapping as accomplished through indirect percussion.

The data on blade-body attributes are quite significant. Ridged blades appear to have been produced more often than thin blades. Alternatively, thin blades may have been used, worked, recycled, and carried away from Corbiac more often than ridged blades. Bordes (personal communication in Gibson 1980) observed in replicative experiments that the range of how many blades a given Bergerac flint core yielded was 30 to 50 blades. A blade in an aret or 'crested' form occurred once in 50 times (or 2 per cent) according to Bordes and Crabtree (1969). Arets occur in lower frequencies in the study sample. As expected, demi-arets occur much more frequently. They may be produced in any of at least three ways: the technical equivalent of an aret when one side of the core is composed of the interior surface and flat; the second blade removal when the intended aret blade splits in half and forms two demi-arets; and the detachment of a demi-aret blade in order to straighten a curved ridge (Gibson 1980, 1982).

The comparison of bulb-attribute states is interesting. Parallel-sided blades occur in the same frequencies as blades with flat bulbs. These data attest to the consistency of the blade technology represented in Level 1. Irregular blades should have been discarded more often. Yet we see a tremendous regularity in the debitage. These flintknappers apparently

Table 13.2. *The frequency of blade attributes and states.*

Attribute	States	%
Blade cortex	Primary	4.1
Total 1,150	Secondary	4.1
	Noncortex	91.8
Facet	Single	70.7
Total 1,152	Double	12.9
	Multiple	13.4
Exterior platform	Untrimmed	24.5
Total 1,152	Slightly trimmed	40.2
	Moderately trimmed	6.0
	Heavily trimmed	27.4
Bulb	Normal	44.5
Total 1,078	Exuberant	4.5
	Flat	51.0
Bulb/platform intersect	Lipped	75.6
Total 1,131	Not lipped	24.4
Body	Thin	34.0
Total 1,150	Thick	23.8
	Ridged	37.7
	Demi-aret	4.3
	Aret	0.3
Outline	Biconvex	4.2
Total 1,059	Parallel-sided	51.7
	Irregular	31.4
	Expanding	7.1
	Contracting	5.6
Longitudinal cross-section	Straight	84.7
Total 1,083	Concave	14.6
Platform angle	110°	9.1
Total 1,210	100°	18.0
	90°	72.0

were quite expert in their craft. It should be stressed that this uniformity in the assemblage is characteristic of the Corbiac debitage. Perhaps the actual formal tools from the site were highly standardized.

The high frequency of straight blades is very important and has ramifications on observations made by Bordes and Crabtree (1969) and Tixier (1972). Bordes and Crabtree (1969, 7) suggested that concave interior longitudinal cross-sections were produced when the core was not well supported. Their observation was enhanced by a hand-held experiment which produced pronounced blade curvatures (Newcomer 1975). They provided descriptive information on ways in which the cores were supported – under the feet, or knees, or wrapped in hides. All of these supportive techniques produced blades with straight or nearly straight interior longi-

tudinal cross-sections. In the Corbiac sample the frequency of blades with straight interior longitudinal cross-sections is 84.7 per cent of the 1,083 codable specimens. This prevalence reflects a consistent technique of core support (Gibson 1980, 1982).

The high frequency of 90-degree platform angles with a tolerance of 5 degrees for blades is similar to flakes. Possibly this reproducibility in the platform angle is another demonstration of the consistency of the Evolved Perigordian technology. The statistical tests for interrelationships between these attributes demonstrated very low correlations (Gibson 1980).

As described above, the replicative work of Bordes and Crabtree (1969, 5–6), suggested that there might be a relationship between the form of the platform and other attributes such as bulb shape, platform shape, body, and outline. To establish whether a dependent relationship existed, cross tabulations of frequencies of all of these attributes were conducted for flakes and blades. These cores tabulations showed very low correlations. Kendal's tau b was the statistical measure selected, with a theoretical maximum value ranging from $+1.0$ to -1.0. The correlations for blade attributes ranged from -0.131 (for bulb/platform intersection with interior longitudinal cross-section) to 0.207 (for outline with interior longitudinal cross-section). Correlations for flake attributes ranged from -0.143 (for bulb/platform intersection with body form) to 0.141 (for platform angle with body form). Chi-square correlations, for example between platform shape and interior longitudinal cross-section, showed similar patterns (correlations were independent as Chi-square value was 0.66 which was less than Chi-square tabulated value with two degrees of freedom at a level of significance of 2.71). This implies that there is no covariance between these attributes and all others (Gibson 1980). Thus, these statistical tests suggest that the coded attributes are independent variables. One objective of Collins (1974) in constructing the coding procedure was to select independent variables. This is an important result because if all of these attributes are independent variables, it might mean that technical imperatives do not mask individual styles to any significant degree. Since 99 per cent of the raw material was Bergerac flint, source material can be excluded as a distorting factor in this question of technical imperatives and their relationship with final product form.

In the excavated Evolved Perigordian assemblage approximately 100,000 blades and blade fragments were recovered. Additionally 10,000 formal tools and 1,000 cores were found (Bordes & Crabtree 1969, 1). Most of the tools were made from blades and a ratio of 10 blades for every formal tool exceeds similar frequencies at possibly contemporaneous sites (for example, the proto-Magdalenian level at Abri Pataud; Movius 1977, 11). The Evolved Perigordian assemblage at Corbiac represents primarily manufacturing rejects and expeditious tool discards. Undoubtedly, thousands of other blades and blade tools were removed from the site by the regional inhabitants. The amount of potential blade production represented in the site is thus considerable.

Discussion

The above data indicate that the assemblage is relatively uniform. Its overall consistency is particularly striking when one considers that both utilized tools and unutilized debitage are included in the sample. At Corbiac where high-quality raw material was abundant, most likely the prehistoric inhabitants were extremely selective in choosing blade and flake forms for use. We would expect the discard behavior at Corbiac to be different from that at a cave or rockshelter lacking immediately available quality raw material. The consistency observed in this study assemblage containing both utilized and nonutilized artifacts suggests the existence of strong 'technological norms' in the society of the prehistoric artisans of Corbiac. Arguments about the merits or demerits of the 'normative' approach aside, I submit that traditional modes of manufacturing craft products contain technological elements that are learned or conditioned through social interaction and that such elements reflect to some extent the social context of manufacturing. These manufacturing behavioral modes can be viewed as technological norms.

Sackett (n.d.) has suggested that the size of the local community may have considerably influenced technology and style. He argues that at least a few specialists had to work alongside one another for group norms to emerge and attain enough coherence and sanction to control the preference of individual artisans. Recently Sackett (1982, 75) has contended that 'ethnicity in the archaeological record is represented by the patterning of formal variation over time and space; that this patterning is the product of socially conditioned choices made by artisans.' Sackett emphasizes the importance of identifying those attributes that reflect 'the degree of similarity in choices observable in the design and manufacture of craft products' (*ibid.*, 74). Thus a prehistoric group's technological choice to a large extent 'constitutes a reasonably direct measure of the social interaction' (*ibid.*), within the context of the group which made the choice and the artifacts (or put another way, within the social context of manufacturing). It is within this context that the individual's 'mental template' (Deetz 1967) is formed and the initial stylistic elements of a tool are produced. As Clay observed (1968, 46), any lithic assemblage either wholly or in part can be viewed as: '(1) the product of a traditional technology, and (2) a response to the biological needs of the social group within the context of a specific settlement.'

Sackett's model of a few specialists working together as the social unit wherein group norms emerged may be reflected by the Corbiac sample's highly uniform technological appearance. I suggest that Corbiac's organization was at least as complex as that of the Nunamiut Eskimo (Binford 1978, 1980).

One segment of Corbiac's Evolved Perigordian society may have produced the entire assemblage: a group of socially connected, part-time, flintknapping specialists. Such a mode of production (part-time specialists in task performance) is not unknown in the ethnographic literature. For example, among such diverse groups as the Yir Yiront (Sharp 1934–1935), the Wintu (Dubois 1935), the Kwakiutl (Boas 1921), and the Patwin (McKern 1922), various forms of part-time task specialization have been documented.

A few flintknapping specialists most likely produced the Corbiac sample, as it only includes 1,200 blades. Bordes could produce approximately 50 blades from one core in two hours (Gibson 1980, 105). Prehistoric flintknapping specialists of an equivalent productivity could have manufactured the entire Evolved Perigordian component of Corbiac, not just the study sample, in a period of one to three seasons, depending on the number of flintknappers involved (cf. Gibson 1982).

Thus, Corbiac in Late Perigordian times may have been the location of specialized activities conducted within a seasonal subsistence pattern or a 'logically organized extractive locality' (Binford 1980, 10). At Corbiac the critical resource was probably the copious amounts of high-quality Bergerac flint.

Perhaps specialists at Corbiac were making blades for a larger population. This proposal is very tentative because it is not known whether the consistency and precision that was interpreted in the study sample characterizes the entire Evolved Perigordian assemblage. If this were the case, then apparently the hypothetical group of specialists produced many more blades than needed for their own use. Most likely they were producing these blades for the needs of a larger local population (cf. White 1982, 176). Mellars has suggested that 'while estimates of the actual group sizes involved are difficult, estimates in the region of 100–500 people do not seem unreasonable for some of the larger paleolithic settlements (e.g., Laugerie Haute, La Madeline, Solvieux)' (1973, 271).

Possibly in the Upper Paleolithic we are witnessing the origins of a significant cultural development: part-time flintworking task groups which continue for many millennia. Torrence (1981, 186–93) has examined the problem of commercial craft specialization in a study of the Neolithic and Bronze Age obsidian industry on the island of Mylos in the Cylades, and presents a list of archaeological expectations for craft specialization within a commercial economy: (1) very high degree of skills utilized; (2) low incidence of errors; (3) small quantities of industrial waste per unit of manufacture; (4) end product composed of a minimum amount of raw material; (5) technology which minimizes the inputs of time, effort, and raw material; (6) use of standardized techniques of manufacture; and consequently (7) standardization in the types of errors made in methods for recovery from errors; and (8) a high degree of consistency in the size and shape of both the products and the waste materials. With the exceptions of categories 3, 4, and 7, the Corbiac sample appears to parallel most of the criteria presented by Torrence (1981). I am not suggesting that the Evolved Perigordian flintknappers were commercial craft specialists. Instead, I am suggesting that the rudimentary cultural process, part-time task specialization, that later led to commercial craft specialization, can be recognized in the Upper Paleolithic. Gilman (n.d.) has suggested that the Upper Paleolithic was characterized by a critical change in the balance of social security, a change brought about by the development and refinement of the forces of production, which differed significantly from that of the Middle Paleolithic. Gilman also maintains that as Upper Paleolithic technology improved, population densities increased and local groups gradually became more self-sufficient. An end result of such a gradual development, according to Gilman, would be an overall increase in production security and a decrease in the scope of social alliances. I agree with Gilman's reconstruction: 'production security' is represented in the Evolved Perigordian component at Corbiac.

A very narrow range of choices seems to have been selected by the flintknappers at Corbiac, both in the design and in the manufacture of their blades. Sackett has suggested that the standardization the technological system 'brings about in craft products creates a structured environment which may promote coherence in the social fabric itself' (1982, 107). Corbiac in Late Perigordian times may represent the remains of a human group characterized by significant social coherence and productive security.

Conclusions

Year by year, evidence of complex societal relationships and settlement systems in the Upper Paleolithic continues to accumulate (Mellars 1973; White 1980, 1982). It is possible that in the Corbiac region different social groups existed side by side with quite different technological norms. However, the technological regularity of the study sample supports a model of a single group of socially conditioned, part-time flintknapping specialists possibly producing the assemblage over a span of several generations, or production by very similar socially related groups. In either case, these groups may have constituted a distinct social unit and possibly a distinct ethnic unit. The name selected by Bordes for this group, 'Evolved Perigordian', is an appropriate appelation in light of the presented evidence.

This study has demonstrated the need for quantitative analysis of replicative lithic technological attributes. Until we have these comparable data, we are restricted to making inconclusive statements like 'technique x was probably used prehistorically but it could also have been technique y.' At the present time, it is not clear if the low variability of the Corbiac data is characteristic of a few or of most technologies. More controlled, similar replicative data are needed. Crabtree (1975) pointed out how important such research on lithic production systems is: '99.5 per cent of the history of mankind is represented by the Stone Age, and if we correctly approach an analysis of both his stone tools and the associated manufacturing debitage, we can attempt an interpretation of his behavior patterns and effects at survival.'

References

Binford, L. R. 1965. Archaeological systematics and the study of culture process. *American Antiquity* 31:203–10.

1973. Interassemblage variability – the Mousterian and the 'functional' argument. In C. Renfrew ed., *The explanation of culture change*. London: Duckworth, 227–54.

1978. *Nunamiut ethnoarchaeology*. New York: Academic Press.

1980. Willow smoke and dog's tails: hunter-gatherer settlement systems and archaeological site formation. *American Antiquity* 43:4–20.

Boas, F. 1921. *Ethnology of the Kwakiutl*. 35th Annual Report, Bureau of American Ethnology.

Boisvert, R. A., Driskell, B. N., Robinson, K. W., Smith, S. D. & Duffield, L. F. 1979. Materials recovered. In M. B. Collins, ed., *Excavations at four Archaic sites in the Lower Ohio Valley, Jefferson County, Kentucky,* University of Kentucky Occasional Papers in Anthropology 1: 60–418.

Bordes, F. 1968. Emplacements de tentes du Périgordien Supérieur Évolué a Corbiac (près Bergerac, Dordogne). *Quärtar* 19: 251–62.

Bordes, F. & Crabtree, D. 1969. The Corbiac blade technique and other experiments. *Tebiwa* 12:1–22.

Bordes, F. & De Sonneville-Bordes, D. 1966. Protomagdalenian ou Périgordian VII? *L'Anthropologie* 70:113–22.

1970. The significance of variability in Paleolithic assemblages. *World Anthropology* 2:61–73.

Bricker, H. 1975. Provenience of flint used for the manufacture of tools at the Abri Pataud, Les Eyzies (Dordogne). *American School of Prehistoric Research Bulletin* 30, 194–7.

Cartes Géologique. 1920. Détailée de France, Map 182, Bergerac.

Clay, R. B. 1968. *The Proto-Magdalenian culture*. Ph.D. dissertation. Department of Anthropology, Southern Illinois University.

1976. Typological classification, attribute analysis, and lithic variability. *Journal of Field Archaeology* 3:303–11.

Collins, M. B. 1974. A functional analysis of lithic technology among hunter-gatherers of southwestern France and Western Texas. Ph.D. dissertation, Department of Anthropology, University of Arizona.

1975. Lithic technology as a means of processual inference. In E. Swanson, ed., *Lithic technology*. Chicago: Aldine Press, 15–33.

Crabtree, D. 1972. An introduction to flintworking. Occasional Papers, Idaho State University Museum 28.

1975. Comments on lithic technology and experimental archaeology. In E. Swanson, ed., *Lithic technology*. Chicago: Aldine Press. 103–14.

Deetz, J. 1967. *Invitation to archaeology*. Garden City, N.Y.: Natural History Press.

DuBois, C. 1935. *Wintu ethnography*. University of California Publications in American Archaeology and Ethnology 36:1–248.

Gibson, E. C. 1980. Quantitative analysis of artifact attributes: the upper Paleolithic blade technology of Corbiac (Bergerac) France. M.A. thesis, Department of Anthropology, University of Kentucky.

1981. An analysis of the Upper Paleolithic blade technology of Corbiac, France. Paper presented at the 46th Annual Society for American Archaeology Meetings, San Diego, California.

1982. Upper Paleolithic flintknapping specialists? The evidence from Corbiac, France. *Lithic technology*. 3:41–9.

Gilman, A. n.d. Rethinking the Upper Paleolithic revolution. Unpublished Ms.

Johnson, L. L. 1977. A technological analysis of an Aguas Verdez quarry workshop. In Hill, J. & Gunn, J. eds., *The individual in prehistory : studies of variability in prehistoric technologies*. New York: Academic Press. 205–30.

LaVille, H., Rigaud, J.-P. & Sackett, J. 1980. *Rockshelters of the Perigord.* New York: Academic Press.

Marks, A. E. & Volkman, P. W. n.d. Changing core reduction strategies: a technological shift from the Middle to the Upper Paleolithic in the Southern Negev. In E. Trinkhaus, ed., *The Mousterian legacy: human bioculture change in the Upper Pleistocene,* British Archaeological Reports International Series.

McKern, W. C. 1922. *Functional families of the Patwin.* University of California Publications in American Archaeology and ethnology 13:235–58.

Mellars, P. A. 1973. The character of the Middle-Upper Paleolithic transition in southwest France. In C. Renfrew, ed., *The Explanation of culture change.* Liverpool: Duckworth 258–77.

Movius, H. L., Jr. 1977. Excavation of the Abri Pataud, Les Eyzies (Dordogne): stratigraphy. *American School of Prehistoric Research Bulletin* 31, Peabody Museum, Harvard University.

Newcomer, M. H. 1975. 'Punch technique' and Upper Paleolithic blades. In E. Swanson, ed., *Lithic technology.* Chicago: Aldine Press. 97–102.

Sackett, J. R. n.d. A prologue to style in lithic archaeology. Unpublished Ms.

1982. Approaches to style in lithic archaeology. *Journal of Anthropological Archaeology* 1:59–112.

Sharp, L. 1934–1935. Ritual life and economies of the Yir Yiront of Cape York Peninsula. *Oceania* 5:19–42.

Tixier, J. 1972. Obtention de lames par debitage 'sous le pied'. *Bulletin de la Société Préhistorique Française* 69:34–39.

1974. Glossary for the description of stone tools, with special reference to the Epipaleolithic of the Maghreb. *Newsletter of Lithic Technology Special Publication* 1.

Torrence, R. 1981. Obsidian in the Aegean: towards a methodology for the study of prehistoric exchange. Ph.D. dissertation, department of Anthropology, University of New Mexico.

Valenski, L. 1960. De l'origine des silex Protomagdaleniens de l'Abri Pataud, Les Eyzies (Dordogne), *Bulletin de la Société Préhistorique Française* 57:80–4.

White, R. K. 1980. The Upper Paleolithic occupation of the Perigord: a topographic approach to subsistence and settlement. Ph.D. dissertation, Department of Anthropology, University of Toronto.

1982. Rethinking the Middle/Upper Paleolithic transition. *Current Anthropology* 23:169–82.

INDEX

For EU product safety concerns, contact us at Calle de José Abascal, 56–1°, 28003 Madrid, Spain or eugpsr@cambridge.org.

www.ingramcontent.com/pod-product-compliance
Ingram Content Group UK Ltd.
Pitfield, Milton Keynes, MK11 3LW, UK
UKHW030905150625
459647UK00025B/2879